Circle
of Lions

Circle of Lions

Nicholas Ray, Gloria Grahame and Me: A Love Story

Anthony Ray

Sticking Place Books
New York

Special thanks to Steve Wilson,
Robert De Niro Curator of Film
at the Harry Ransom Center,
for giving this book a home.

© Kelsey J. Ray and Eve J. Ray
Introduction © Patrick McGilligan
© Sticking Place Books 2025

www.stickingplacebooks.com

Cover design by Ryan Bojanovic

ISBN 979-8-89976-005-1

Contents

Tony and Kelsey Ray.

Foreword by Kelsey Ray

My dad Tony Ray titled this memoir *Circle of Lions* to honor and acknowledge the impacts of generational trauma that goes untended. One vicious lion begets another vicious lion, on and on, until someone is brave enough and capable enough to break the cycle.

As his youngest child, and only daughter, I have significant insight into the ways that his personal trauma trickled into every aspect of his later life and affected those closest to him. What I did not know—or understand—until recently, was that my dad's greatest hope in life was to have a family and to be the father that he had always longed for. Despite his valiant efforts, he was ultimately unable to break free from his deep-seated trauma, learned behaviors and destructive coping mechanisms. While he relentlessly attempted to have me read his writing, undoubtedly to better understand him, I was, admittedly uninterested.

About two years ago I was approached by a gentleman named Patrick, who lives in the town I grew up in and, unbeknownst to me, knew my father. Pat was involved with a local theater that was preparing to celebrate its one hundredth birthday. When asked for ideas, he suggested that they showcase the work of my father, my grandfather Nicholas Ray, and Gloria Grahame, who was at one time married to both my father and grandfather.

Initially, it felt foreign that anyone would reach out about highlighting my family in a celebratory way, but Pat and I met anyway. We sifted through my personal archive of photographs and documents, exchanged stories, and daydreamed about what could potentially come to fruition for this local film festival. Somewhere in the midst of our conversation, I asked if he had read my dad's manuscript. He perked up with excitement, not knowing that this existed. I gave him a copy to take home.

Soon after, Pat explained: "A few pages in I realized that these were Tony's trapped words that he wanted to be heard. Tony had a story to tell and his book was a step toward healing." With Pat's encouragement and genuine belief that my dad's story has a place in the world, I made it my mission to get his book published. To honor my father. To honor his healing.

My dad was 53 when I was born. He and my mom, Eve, had moved from New York City to a small town in southern Maine in hopes of giving me a "shot at a normal life," away from the madness of Hollywood. Coincidentally, this was also after his career had ultimately fizzled for the same reasons that my grandfather's had. My dad always referred to this as the "triple threat"—the unmanageable task of dealing with three addictions: drugs, alcohol and gambling.

In addition to grappling with these vicious threats, my dad was introduced to another later in life. Constantly swinging from one end of the pendulum to the other: euphoric and grandiose mania to deeply destructive catatonic, depressive episodes.

The truth is that I learned the language of suffering at a very young age. While I wasn't able to understand the depths of despair he was experiencing, it is clear as an adult, that my dad spent much of his life burying his trauma, shame and guilt. Regrettably, I resented him for the majority of my life and never cared to truly know him. Until now.

As a young person, I never realized how deeply I resembled him or how much I yearned for his presence, love, attention, care and protection. These longings echo throughout this book. The story will likely make you uncomfortable at times, and appropriately so. On the other hand, I suspect that my dad's story will resonate with many readers in some way.

Something I will forever remain grateful for was the commitment to having art, of all kinds, at the core of our relationship. My dad's mother was the daughter of Russian Jewish immigrants and a wildly talented writer, storyteller and photographer. She instilled in him the importance of art, theater and music, emphasizing that you needed these outlets to get through life. Art of any kind is a form of expression, a channel into the messiness, chaos, depth and beauty of the human experience.

Though the curiosity about my family always lingered, it was never something I celebrated or identified with. It wasn't until recently that I felt a strong pull to learn about where I came from; to learn about who my family were as people. Surely there is more to

Tony and his mother Jean (née Abrahams).

this side of my family than the headlines of *Vanity Fair* or the *Hollywood Reporter*.

My dad dropped hints about his childhood which only now I'm beginning to understand. After reading *Circle of Lions* for the first time, I couldn't help but remember that the first novel he insisted I read was J. D. Salinger's *The Catcher in the Rye*. I must have been seven or eight years old, able to muddle my way through the words but not developed enough to understand the themes. Reflecting back, I can see so much of my dad in Holden Caulfield. The turmoil, the teenage fury, the boredom and fear of living a mundane life. Interestingly enough, *The Catcher in the Rye* was published only a few weeks after my dad made the trip from New York City to Los Angeles. Whether or not he read Salinger back then, in Nick and Gloria's Malibu beach house, or in his boarding school room, I don't know. But he was clearly living his own Holden-esque existence.

I wish I could talk to my dad, that I had had more compassion and understanding of who he was as a human being. To learn and tend to the grief and guilt he carried each day. He was so much more than the man and father I knew, or had believed him to be.

One of the most profoundly powerful moments I have ever witnessed occurred just a few hours before my dad passed away in 2018 from a devastating battle with Alzheimer's. We were at Gosnell Hospice House, in Scarborough, Maine. My mom chose to put on a DVD of the movie *Oklahoma!* as a way to comfort him. She wanted to make sure he wasn't afraid and that he knew he would soon be reunited with so many loved ones. The moment my dad heard Gloria's voice, he briefly but abruptly lifted his head, and with a soft smile gently laid back down.

What I can tell you with certainty is that my dad loved Gloria until the day he died. Perhaps equally, or of more importance, is that my mom, Eve, not only embraced this part of him, she honored and celebrated the love he had for Gloria until my dad took his final breath.

It wasn't until he was gone that I decided to open a series of letters my dad had sent me years prior. They include stories, advice, apologies and pleas for us to have a relationship. I will never forget reading them, curled up and drowning in tears. It was as if the hate and rage toward him left my body and I filled with forgiveness. I'm unable to explain why, but the longer my dad is gone, the closer I feel to him.

The last letter that my dad sent me, dated 2013, included the following excerpt:

> *I had dreamed of them [Tony Jr. and Jimmy]*
> *growing up with a father, as I had had none, but I*
> *failed them—and they have paid the price. And then*
> *I dreamed again, when you, Kels, were born—and*
> *again I failed. I literally slept through more than one*
> *block of ten years of your childhood… And now, here*
> *we are. I have an almost 24-year-old daughter;*
> *I have a 50-year-old son. I feel responsible for*
> *Jimmy's death (I will never get over his suicide).*

I'm taking a breather—to have a cig and pull myself together... Do you think you can forgive me?

I love you deeply, Kels.
You will make it and we will be proud.

This one's for you, Dad.
I forgive you.
I love you.
And I hope to God that I've made you proud.

Introduction by Patrick McGilligan

For movie-lovers who grew up on the auteurism of the 1950s and 1960s, Jean-Luc Godard's early proclamation—"The cinema is Nicholas Ray"—was taken as gospel. It remains an article of faith for that aging demographic, and for younger conscripts among film fans and scholars.

Besides being the father of Anthony (Tony) Ray, the author of this remarkable memoir, Nicholas Ray was the movie director best known nowadays for *They Live By Night*, his debut noir released in 1948, followed by *In a Lonely Place*, *On Dangerous Ground*, *Johnny Guitar*, *Rebel Without a Cause* and *Bigger Than Life*, although true cinephiles will insist there is also greatness in the lesser or overlooked Ray titles *Knock on Any Door*, *The Lusty Men*, *Bitter Victory*, *Wind Across the Everglades*, *Party Girl* and *The Savage Innocents*. Basically, there are riches in any Nicholas Ray film.

Twenty Hollywood films between 1948 and 1961, when Ray petered out or self-destructed—your choice—linked by iconic stars in signature performances (foremost, Bogart and James Dean, but let's not forget Gloria Grahame or Joan Crawford), visual elegance and complexity, wounded protagonists, stories that autopsied familial and societal dysfunction. Searching dramas or melodramas—no comedies.

As the author of one authoritative biography (*Nicholas Ray: The Glorious Failure of an American Director*, HarperCollins, 2011) and the devoted reader of another, Bernard Eisenschitz's *Nicholas Ray: An American Journey* (Faber & Faber, 1993), I can attest that Ray's life boasts a rich backstory (Thornton Wilder, Frank Lloyd Wright, Alan Lomax, Losey and Kazan, etc.) and a surprising list of accomplishments in radio and theater even before Hollywood. But it was also a life, from Wisconsin birth to death in New York City as a legend at age 67, filled (especially from his point of view) with missteps, betrayals, compromises, drink and drugs that didn't stop the pain.

Much of that is reflected in his work, but this is not a book about the films of Nicholas Ray. We meet him in this memoir on the very precise date of June 10, 1950, when he was between directing jobs—the low period between *Born to be Bad* and *Flying Leathernecks*—and we leave him six months later.

It was a difficult time also because Ray's relationship with Gloria Grahame, today as beloved by cinephiles as is her then-husband, was falling apart. The couple had been married for three years. Ray had directed his wife with Bogart in the seminal *In a Lonely Place* and, never a fun couple, he and Grahame had separated and reconciled several times and recently moved into a Malibu beach house. They had a toddler, Tim, who in this narrative is mostly off-stage with a nanny.

Into their world arrives 12-year-old Tony, the director's only progeny from his first marriage to journalist Jean Evans, who worked and resided in New York City. Evans thought Tony, a kid who got into minor troubles in school, might benefit from living in Los Angeles, learning about the film industry from his famous father, and spending quality time with Dad.

This book tells the story—from the point of view of Tony, who wrote it when he was 21—of the six months he spent in Hollywood trying to connect with his distant, demanding father while falling in puppy love with the more caring and libidinous Grahame. His visit spelled the end to the marriage between the director and actress, and presaged Tony's own marriage, nine years later, to the woman who was once his stepmother. A lost grail, Tony's memoir recalls with agonizing honesty the messy three-way entanglement whose repercussions undoubtedly contributed not only to Ray's, but also Tony's and Grahame's, lifetime of hurt.

Again and again, Nicholas Ray disappointed his son, who stepped off the TWA flight hoping to be wrapped in a warm embrace from his father. Of course, Ray was not there; he was too busy that day, in this account, as he was too busy for most of the six months Tony was in Los Angeles. His father dodges Tony's pleas to go fishing, swimming, give him tennis tips, go horse-riding, teach him how to drive a car, even play a single game of cards with him. Usually, Ray was off at the studio, or meeting with agents

Gloria and Nick at their wedding in 1948.

or bookies—at the racetrack, poker playing—or socializing at industry events. Just as often he was drunk, or mysteriously absent from the house, or had stormed out after arguing with Gloria and then slept over at a bungalow the studio provided on the lot.

Grahame met Tony at the airport; this was his first encounter with his father's wife and an actress he realized was a movie star. He captures her vividly here and elsewhere in his book. Wreathed in perfume, she wraps her arms around him and gives him a kiss.

She has shiny blonde hair, squinting blue eyes, and is dressed in a V-neck cashmere sweater "cut very low."

Ray is approaching the age of 39 and the milestone of middle age. Grahame is 26 going on 27. Tony is about to enter ninth grade in the fall at a school that must be okayed by his father. It amuses Grahame that the difference between her age and her husband's was only a few years more than that of her and Tony, who with his sturdy build and dark hair looked handsome and older than his young years.

Ray seldom took his son on outings. One was to RKO, where the filmmaker wanted to show off his parking space, office and secretary, but rather than give Tony any grand tour, Ray sends him off on his own to gawk at celebrities crossing his path. Howard Hughes, in one of those automobile rides in which the studio boss offers Ray half of his lunch sandwich, has ordered the director to helm *Flying Leathernecks* starring John Wayne and Robert Ryan. Ray is chafing at the assignment, even though his impressively competent secretary assures him it would be a box-office hit. "He likes to think of himself as an artist," Grahame explains the enigmatic father to his puzzled son, "but he won't pay the price of risking not making much money for a while."

This is not a tell-all about filmmaking. The only inside-Hollywood flashes are of Ray playing tennis with old friend Elia Kazan, canasta at the Bloomingdales, and Joan Crawford striding towards her close-up but not in *Johnny Guitar*. Grahame has the best dialogue because Ray is murky when he talks. (Nick's a Nordic type, Grahame tells Tony, withdrawn and detached.) Gloomy, angry at himself and the world, Ray lectures Tony about smoking and drinking, and vetoes public high school in favor of a military boarding school, replete with olive drab uniform and dawn Reveille, that will keep him away from home except on a few weekends. Grahame is sympathetic towards Tony but explains that Ray needs to buy an expensive education for his son so he can brag about it. "You are a small man," Ray tells Tony, overruling one discussion. "I am a big man. I hold the cards in this game, okay?"

The boarding school is run by a stern Episcopalian priest. Ray forces his son to play the manly sport of football, which he himself did in high school (he was also, later, a sportswriter for the LaCrosse, Wisconsin college newspaper), then gets miffed when Tony doesn't make varsity. A council of seniors corners the newbie for an

Tony and Gloria at the premiere of *Shadows* (1959).

infraction and group-thrashes Tony. Ray seems more concerned about the hazing of the son of one of his cameramen, a boy who was Tony's roommate and chief instigator of his punishment.

The author meticulously reconstructs the ugly domestic scenes (birthday and Christmas eruptions) that build to a grim climax: a road trip with the uneasy trio, which winds from Malibu to Lake Tahoe, where the mecca for Ray is, of course, a casino. Louis Prima and Keeley Smith make a cameo appearance. Ray is a killjoy and hangs out losing big at the craps table.

To be fair, all three principals had poor role models. Ray's mother was a cold cod and his father died of alcoholism above a speakeasy when Nick was 15. Grahame abhors her stage mother and tells Tony she never wants to see her father again even if he is handing out the Academy Awards. She too suffered a bad first marriage and thought she was being rescued by Ray. Tony's single mother struggled financially. She had good reasons to be estranged from Nick (among other things, in order to get himself off the hook he named her as a Communist to HUAC investigators), but seems the most equable personality.

Despite it all, throughout his Hollywood stay, Tony pines for his father's love and adores him. He never loses hopes and basks in Ray's rare smiles, which are "wonderful promises" never kept. He writes feelingly in this memoir, never more so than when closely observing him: "Dad's face was chiseled out of dark red quartz and his skin was rough. He clasped his long manicured fingers under his skin and looked at Gloria without saying anything, just raising his eyebrows. His hair curled in black and grey specks like ocean spray hitting the rocks at the end of the cove."

A few short years after the events of this book, Ray would make *Rebel Without a Cause*, the quintessential film about clueless parents and adolescent angst. The director said in interviews that there were elements of his relationships with his sons in the story.

Again and again, Tony and Grahame are abandoned to their own pleasurable devices.

Tony wonders, in hindsight, if his father left them alone together as a devious means of ruining his marriage. Also in the mix was Sumner Williams, the oldest son of Ray's favorite sister, who had become his general dogsbody behind the camera and acted bits in his uncle's pictures. (Sumner is noticeable in *Knock on Any Door* and *On Dangerous Ground*.) He was nine years older than Tony and thought of himself as a blonde Adonis. When Ray goes on location for *Flying Leathernecks* (Camp Pendleton, down south), Williams keeps an eye on Grahame. Tony thought Ray's nephew was also trying to bed her. Unclear if he did or didn't.

Tony's searching portrait of Grahame is the real joy of this memoir. It's hard not to like her, as well as not to scratch your head over her dubious behavior. She indulges Tony's furtive smoking, encourages his learning to drive (she herself gets ticketed speeding

Tony and Nick.

in her new black Cadillac convertible), brings him squeezed orange juice in bed—and then when he complains that he likes the pulp she left behind, eturns to the kitchen and brings him another glass with pulp.

Her aphorisms, freshly remembered by Tony, are priceless. "Simple things," she consoles Tony at one point, "aren't always easy to get." He overhears Grahame talking to a girlfriend. "You can't talk to men," she says. "I found that out years ago. It's always an act."

Both lonely, they find solace in each other. He accompanies her to the bank, to her day in court for speeding (a secret kept from his father), and to her sessions with a psychiatrist (Ray will later insist his son also see a psychiatrist because, as Grahame explains, Ray thinks everyone should see psychiatrists). She takes Tony along shopping and to the hairdresser, picks out his clothes, explains the differences in perfumes—floral for innocent girls, animal scents for tigerish women. Her favorite: Joy, from Paris. Grahame is mulling plastic surgery and asks his advice about a possible cleft in her chin. She teaches him how to dance. They start every day with him brushing her hair.

She is months away from *The Greatest Show on Earth* and spends an amazing amount of time reading a variety of intelligent books: Stanislavski, Shakespeare, novels, poetry. Feeling blue, she listens to jazz and Edith Piaf, or suggests going for a drive, which ends in necking with Tony.

The actress was just as hard-shelled and vulnerable as on screen in *It's a Wonderful Life*, her Oscar-nominated role in *Crossfire*, or the neighbor enamored of Bogart in *In a Lonely Place*—three career highlights thus far. The book takes place before her great triumphs of the 1950s, including the Best Supporting Actress Oscar for *The Bad and the Beautiful*. "Gloria was a beautiful wild animal defying man to capture her, tormenting the hunter with insanely exciting invitations, then changing in the blink of an eye to an image of purity, a little girl," Tony writes.

He is homesick for New York, and misses his mother. Whenever he is with Grahame, they "explode in conversation." She wants to cuddle for comfort at night. She walks around in diaphanous nightgowns and asks him to dry her back when she steps out of the shower. She *relates* to him. His emotions stir; his body tightens. "The way Gloria made me feel inside wasn't right, like a butter churner in motion." She complains—and she is not much of a complainer—that after marrying Nick her sex life "went from occasional to nonexistent." Then she gives Tony his first hand job, the most explicit scene in a narrative otherwise tender and discreet. The two are constantly drinking overmuch and misbehaving, and at one point Ray acts on his suspicions, files for divorce, and forces Tony to make a tape recording attesting to their misdeeds. Whether or not they ever actually slept together is not disclosed and is still disputed.

Grahame countered in divorce court with several instances of Ray's physical abuse. Something not on that list was Ray whipping Tony with his big black belt, because Grahame, always sticking up for the boy, stopped him.

Tony takes the reader on colorful side trips without his father or Grahame, exploring Santa Anita Racetrack and Hollywood Boulevard. His authorial voice, his sensitivity and honesty, ring true 65 years after the writing. The antiquated language at times ("wetbacks," "queers"), while regrettable from today's perspective, reinforces his authenticity. Grahame takes her ward to a Hollywood party where Tony is worried about the "faggots" as well as the "black guy" who seems to be putting the make on the actress. Grahame invites the young black actor into their conversation. "George Freeman," she introduces him, "George will be a star someday." (Gloria can startle but rarely disappoints.) "Who ever heard of a Negro movie star?" scoffs teenaged Tony. "You're right," says Freeman graciously, "there aren't any black movie stars."

It would be nice but wrong to say everyone lived happily ever after. George Freeman (perhaps Tony created a pseudonym) did not become a movie star. Grahame died miserably of cancer two years after Ray, in 1981, her last days ably documented by ex-lover Peter Turner in *Film Stars Don't Die in Liverpool* (Chatto, 1986), credibly filmed with Annette Bening as the ill-fated actress.

Tony was married to Grahame from 1960 until 1974. It was not a blissful marriage, as documented in Nicca Ray's heartfelt book *Ray by Ray* (Three Rooms Press, 2020), which contains an illuminating interview with an older, wiser Anthony Ray. There were infidelities and substance abuse on both sides. Perhaps Grahame fared worse, with her stardom sliding and mounting neuroses about looks and aging. She did not get out of bed to feed their two children, dress them, or take them to school. When they divorced, Tony was awarded custody of the kids.

Yet there are no saints in this narrative. All things considered, Tony carved out a good career. After acting small parts on Broadway and TV and in films (including a role in John Cassavetes' *Shadows*), in time he became an assistant director for television and movies, forming a kinship with Paul Mazursky on *Bob & Carol & Ted & Alice* and serving as Mazursky's regular assistant for numerous films, a partnership that climaxed with Tony's Oscar-nomination as co-producer of Mazursky's feminist *An Unmarried Woman* in 1975. Mazursky helped Tony kick his addictions and straighten out his life. Tony met and married Eve Jorjorian, a modern dancer who later worked in special education, retired to Maine, taught for a time at Emerson College in Boston, and lived to a ripe age. He died at 80 in 2018. It was Kelsey, Tony and Eve's daughter—who recalls learning to play the family piano upon which sat the Oscar, won in 1953 by Grahame for *The Bad and the Beautiful*—who unearthed this manuscript and wrote the foreword.

It will be tempting for people nowadays to slap the label of "child molestation" on this book, but one of the great things about Tony's writing is how unjudgmental it is, how unsparing he is of himself. During the mid-1980s, Tony was treated for manic depression, and when he related the story of his 1950 Malibu intimacies with Grahame—let's call it a folie à deux—his therapist told him flatly, "You were molested." Tony had promised his mother he would not publish his youthful memoir until all the people in the story were dead. Jean Evans died at age 87 in 1997. Tony waited another decade before he dusted off the manuscript and re-read his book. Even then, doubts nagged him: Was the 1950 episode in his life an experience that traumatized him forever, or was it a youthful romance? The question haunts this book still.

Anthony Ray in John Cassavetes' *Shadows* (1959).

This manuscript was written when I was the ripe old age of 21, in 1958. It is my recollection of experiences I had as a 12- and 13-year-old. I promised my mother I would not publish it until the people in the story had left us. In re-reading it, I have come to realize that the events contained in this work led to my being traumatized for over fifty years. The relationships have still not been resolved, and may never be.

Anthony Ray

Circle of Lions

1
Arrival

"Dear Son," it began. I imagined Dad on the telephone with Western Union.

> I will meet you at Los Angeles International Airport. You have reservations on TWA flight 91 leaving La Guardia Airport, New York, at 11:05 AM your time on June 10. You arrive in Los Angeles at 6 P.M. our time. Best regards to your mother. Good travelling. Love, Dad

He didn't say where I was to meet him at the airport. Whenever I had come home by train from boarding school, Mom always told me she would meet me at the information booth at Grand Central. Dad would be there, though, and that was all that mattered. I put away his telegram and watched the patches of flat farmland move slowly below. I kept my knees straight so I wouldn't wrinkle the new blue suit Mom had bought me at Barney's Basement. New York City was far behind us now.

I thought about Mom's and my apartment, a third-floor walk-up on West Houston Street. We had a hot water heater and two big washbasin sinks in the kitchen. Nothing was very modern, but it was cheerful, and it was home. Mom was a feature writer for a newspaper and didn't make a lot of money. I wondered what Hollywood would be like. Dad was a movie director. Did he live in a house or in an apartment? I leaned my head against the window and pulled my legs up under me. The engines droned dully, hypnotically. The plane seemed to be drifting. I was drifting. It was cold outside. A pot of thick fudge was making slow bubbles on the stove at home. My thoughts were bubbling too, slower and slower, until I fell asleep.

"Fasten your seat belt, please." The stewardess was shaking my shoulder. "Wake up. We're landing in Los Angeles."

"Here we go," I whispered as the plane dipped into the clouds. "Here I come, Dad."

Should I rush into his arms and hug him, or was I supposed to shake hands like a man? I wanted to hug him, but decided to wait and see what he did first. I hadn't seen him for a couple of years, since I was ten, though there had been some letters and a few phone calls on birthdays.

The plane grazed the field and vibrated as though the ground had stripped it of its wings. The pilot braked the craft down to the speed of a fast-moving car and we taxied to our parking spot. Everybody got up the moment the plane stopped. I felt sick to my stomach with nerves. I pulled the white laundry bag full of clothes Mom and I couldn't stuff into the trunk down from the rack over my seat. The stairs were wheeled up and we all got off the plane. At the edge of the field, fifty or sixty people were milling around greeting each other. They hadn't seen their families in a long time either, I thought, as I worked my way through the crowd looking for Dad. He wasn't in the group, or at least I didn't see him, and he didn't see me. I decided to try the terminal. Maybe they had an information booth. I felt heavy in the middle, as though I were carrying a brick in my chest. It was the same feeling I got when Dad was supposed to meet me on a street corner to visit and didn't show up. I stopped to comb my hair in the mirror of a gum machine, and did the best I could with the help of some spit. My eyes are the same blue gray as Dad's. Girls thought I looked alright. Mom says all kids my age worry about how they look.

"Ray. Passenger Ray. Tony Ray, please report to the Trans World Airline ticket counter."

I spotted the counter and made a beeline for it. There were two lines of people waiting to have their bags weighed in. A girl was standing apart with her back to me, but there was no sign of Dad. I pushed my way over all the luggage and through the lines of people to the counter.

"Mister, were you calling me?" I asked the ticket man. Without looking up from his work he said, "Over there," and pointed. I glanced at the people around me but saw no one I knew. "Excuse me," I said, because as I pushed through to the counter again,

I brushed the girl with my laundry bag. "Sir, were you calling me?" I tried again. "My name is Ray. Tony Ray."

"Tony!" I heard behind me. I started to turn to the voice. The next thing I knew I was wrapped up in arms and lips and a whole roomful of perfume. I didn't have time to think.

I hugged and kissed back without knowing who it was. She could have been cut right out of a movie magazine, she was so beautiful. For a moment I just gaped, then I stuck out my hand. "How do you do," I said, "I'm Tony." Her long, tanned fingers squeezed mine and she smiled at me with squinting blue eyes. I was staring again.

"Stop it, silly," she giggled, "I'm Gloria, Nick's wife."

"Oh, hi," I said. God! Her shiny blonde hair shone right through a light blue bandana. She wore white toreador pants and a navy-blue cashmere sweater with a V-neck cut very low.

"I would have met you at the plane but I didn't know what you looked like. The only picture I could find was years old. You're cute."

"Where's Dad?"

"Working." Then she smiled that way again and said, "He's always working or playing poker."

I was disappointed, sure. But he did have to earn a living.

"My trunk is at the baggage claim."

"Over there," pointed Gloria.

"Are you tough?" she asked while we were walking. She said it as though I wasn't at all the kind of boy she had pictured.

"I don't like to fight, if that's what you mean."

We reached a long three-sided counter with a bunch of other people. Men stood in the middle, sorting luggage. "Why?" I asked.

"I don't know. You're dark. And you're from New York." She shrugged her shoulders. "I met a lot of boys when I was working on Broadway. They were sharper than the boys out here. And you look old for your age."

"Age," I muttered. "I hate my age."

The man behind the counter asked if I saw my things. I spotted the black trunk and he went to get it for me. How much should I tip, I wondered. I dug some change out of my pocket. I had never been in a spot like this before. I chose a quarter.

"Thank you, sir," the man said when I handed him the coin. That was nice. *Thank you, sir.* I glanced up at Gloria to see if she had noticed what he'd said.

"Help you to your car?" asked another porter with a cart. I said no thanks, and Gloria took the laundry bag from me. I struggled with the trunk. It was heavy as hell to tell the truth, but I tried to make it look easy. I didn't want to spend money for someone to carry my stuff. We stepped out of the terminal into the hot, dry sun.

"Wait here," Gloria said, "I'll get the car." The drive around the terminal was lined with geraniums and palm trees. I thought of my mother, how every spring she would buy a potted geranium and put it on the kitchen windowsill. She would care for it until it became a stick in the fall. Gloria pulled up in a sleek black Cadillac convertible.

"Wow," I said, "Dad sure has a nice car."

"It's mine," Gloria said. "A brand new 1950." She tossed the laundry bag in the back seat and we put the trunk next to it. We got in and Gloria put on a pair of sunglasses. She was quiet for the first time since I met her. The sky was clear and the air smelled of flowers and fresh cut grass. Once we were out of the airport, and a neighboring town, we passed over a sun-parched hill covered in oil towers. The pumps that stroked with a methodical whooshing sound and the grease-coated telephone poles rushing past us made the day seem even hotter. We stopped for a red light at an empty intersection at the crest of the hill. I slapped at a fly that landed on my cheek.

"Nick wanted to meet you," said Gloria. "He really did." The clicking of the traffic signal going through its change cycle put butterflies in my stomach. The instant change from red to green made me queasy. There was no turning back.

As we drove toward the beach, Gloria asked questions about my mother, how long the flight took, what kind of schools I had been going to. She was just making conversation, I thought. I was thinking about what it was going to be like moving in with a strange family. It was hitting me that I didn't really know my father at all. I had only seen him four or five times since he left, when I was only two. But the visits were short and often there were other people around from his work. He had worked on Broadway, too. And after he moved to California to become a movie director, he never came to New York just to see me.

"Light me a cigarette, will you?" Gloria handed me a pack of Pall Malls. I didn't know what to do. I was sure Dad would flip if he thought I even touched a cigarette, but I didn't want Gloria to think I was a baby, either. I hesitated long enough to take a good look at her. She smiled. I took a cigarette from the pack and pushed in the lighter.

"How old are you?" I asked.

"Twenty-three. Why?"

"I don't know. I just wondered."

"What month were you born?" she asked.

"November."

"I was born in November, too. And Tim was born on the twelfth. That's your half-brother. And my father was born on the fifteenth. We have a Scorpio-Sagittarius family. Except your father. He's a Leo."

I handed her the cigarette. She placed it between her lips and let it hang there. Her upper lip came to a sharp point in the middle.

She was sure young to be married to Dad, I thought. I tipped my head back and let the smoke out of my lungs. I wanted the smoke to be carried straight up and off by the wind.

"I imagine that's part of the reason I'm so glad you're here," she said. "My father never came back or sent for me. At least yours did. But your father is a Leo." She seemed puzzled. "That doesn't figure either. Oh well. Nick doesn't figure any way you look at him."

"When's the last time you saw your dad?"

"Fifteen. I don't really believe in all that astrology stuff. I wouldn't see my father even if he were handing out Academy Awards. Did you know I was nominated two years ago?"

"No, that's great. But why wouldn't you see your dad?"

"And give him the pleasure?" Gloria stuck her nose in the air. "Ha!"

We were quiet for a few seconds. Then Gloria laughed to herself.

"What's so funny?" I asked.

"Nothing. I was thinking about life, and all of a sudden it made me laugh for no reason. Does that ever happen to you? It does to me all the time."

She put her hand on the back of my neck as if searching for the answer to her question by touching.

"Sometimes," I told her.

"Do you see it, Tony?" She pointed. "We're nearly home."

A patch of blue-green ocean sparkled through the trees a mile or so away as we wound around the curves that led steadily down. "This is the end of Sunset Boulevard," she said as we reached the bottom of the hill. A man was standing on the corner wearing a red visor cap. He was holding a bunch of pamphlets, and strapped over his shoulders was a sign that read "Movie Stars Homes." Gloria turned the corner onto the beach highway.

"Are those maps any good? Or are they fake?"

"They don't have my name on them, so they must be fake, right?"

We drove along the beach, which was sure different from those beer can-strewn areas at the end of the subway line in New York. The road had been carved between white sand and brown rocky cliffs that rose straight up. We passed a road sign that said "Slide Area." Sunlight bounced off a million whitecaps.

"Turn on the radio, Tony. I always need music before I get home at night. It calms my nerves."

"What kind do you want to hear?" I asked, but she didn't answer. Her attention had left me and wandered back somewhere into a part of her world I didn't know. Figuring it would take an older kid to choose classical music, I picked a symphony. It was sad.

"There's a good disc jockey on 1400," Gloria said.

Several miles north, the cliffs flattened out into rolling hills. Tree-lined dirt roads wound by small horse ranches, farms and tracts of beautiful flowers, then disappeared mysteriously into canyons. A huge Spanish mission sat proudly on a high plateau overlooking the ocean. We turned off the highway onto an unlined asphalt street. Homes were built close to each other, hugging the narrow strip between the street and the water.

Gloria slowed the car. Damp salt air filled my nose and chest. It was the smell of high adventure. Waves cracked loudly against the hard-packed sand on the other side of the houses. We turned left and stopped before a heavy wooden gate. All that was missing from the castle entrance was a moat. "Open it," said Gloria. I got out of the car, lifted the wrought iron latch, and pulled back the two heavy sides. Gloria drove past me into the empty garage. "Nick isn't home yet." She stopped smiling for the first time since I had met her. In fact, she seemed angry. I was disappointed, too.

I followed Gloria through a low picket gate. "We have to keep this closed all the time," she instructed, "so Mingo, my dog, and Tim can't get out on the road."

My new home was a white, weathered beach house with green shutters. A flagstone path led across the lawn to the door. On one side was a small white cabin. "Tim and Constance, our nanny, live there," said Gloria, pointing. Running behind the garage, the cabin, and all along one side of the house, was a row of trees, behind which was a wire fence about fifteen feet high. "That's the tennis court. The curse words really fly when balls get stuck in the trees. Nick plays with Kazan on the weekends. I don't think Nick has ever won." We kept walking slowly to the house, stopping every few steps. Gloria was giving me a good chance to look around. The house was raised three or feet off the ground on pilings. The front door wasn't like a front door at all but a screen door with another one of plain white wood behind it up six creaky steps. We went inside, into the kitchen.

"Constance," Gloria called out. Constance came into the kitchen through a swinging door with a small window in it.

"Yes, Mrs. Ray." Constance had graying black hair that was tied behind her head in a bun and a beaked nose. "And Tony, we're all so glad you're here."

"Thank you, ma'am," I said.

"Show Tony his room," Gloria said, "so he can bring in his things from the car. I want to see Tim."

"He's sound asleep, Mrs. Ray. He plain tuckered himself out playing on the beach today."

Gloria tousled my hair. "See you in a little while."

Constance stirred something in a pot on the stove. I went through the service door and found myself in the combination living room and dining room. It was white, too, all white. On one entire wall next to the dining table was a bay window that looked out on the ocean behind it. There was a door next to the window that led to a small fenced-in yard and the ocean. I crossed a gray string rug to the dining table. A whole massive bed of seaweed rose and fell beyond the surf with the swell of each new wave. It was like looking at a postcard of some faraway place you dreamed of visiting.

I felt very alone. I picked up one of the heavy silver knives. There was an "R" engraved on the handle.

"Tony," Constance called out. I pushed through the service door to the kitchen. "Why don't you bring in your things and I'll show you to your room.

At the bottom of the stairs I peered through the entrance to the tennis court. I would have to learn the game so I could play with Dad. Gee, I wished he would get home. On the way to the garage I met Mingo, Gloria's toy poodle. He was standing in the middle of one of the flagstones. When I got to his flagstone he defended it playfully, nipping at the cuffs of my pants. A tinny sounding phonograph played a children's song in the little house. I wondered what Tim looked like. What was it going to be like having a brother, even a half brother? I guessed it wouldn't be so bad. After all, Tim was just a baby.

Why couldn't Dad have gotten off from work to meet me? Mom always had, no matter what.

The record player was still going.

> Ha, ha, this a-way
> Ha, ha, that a-way
> Ha, ha, this a-way
> then, oh, then.

It was a folk song I had heard a million times. I had even learned how to play it on the guitar that Burl Ives gave Mom a long time ago. I waited for the beginning of a verse and joined in softly:

> When I was a little boy, little boy, little boy,
> When I was a little boy three years old.
> Daddy came and got me, got me, got me,
> Daddy came and got me, I was told.

I sang the chorus louder so Gloria could hear:

> Ha, ha, this a-way
> Ha, ha, that a-way

"Tony," Gloria said from the door.

"Yes, ma'am."

"For God's sake stop calling me ma'am. I'm Gloria. You're Tony. That's it."

The bandana was off her head and her tan glowed against her shoulder-length blonde hair. "Aren't you going to get cleaned up?" She sounded like she wanted me to go. We stood there looking into each other's eyes for a long time. It was as though we were figuring out how we were going to get along. I had already decided we were going to like each other. "Come in and meet your brother."

I followed her into the tiny two-room house. Constance's room had a single chair, a bed against one wall and a bureau next to the door. A small writing desk was wedged between the bed and the other wall. There was a foyer, just long enough for the bathroom door, and my brother's room on the other side of it. Tim was sitting in his crib with his legs spread out, one behind him, one in front, in what would have been an impossible position for an adult. He seemed to know exactly what he was building with his alphabet blocks.

"Did Dad give you a lot of folk songs to play for Tim?" I asked. "We always had plenty, and sometimes the people on the records would come to the house, especially at Christmas. Lead Belly, Josh White, Burl Ives, Pete Seeger, and sometimes Woody Guthrie, and Sonny Terry and Brownie McGhee. I spent a lot of time at Lead Belly's apartment. He looked after me a lot. They didn't stop seeing my mother just because my father was gone. Dad collected music for the Library of Congress during the Depression and had a radio show called *Back Where I Come From*."

The phonograph was on a small bureau that was made for a baby. It fit under the window that faced the lawn. The bureau was white and had pictures of chickens, dogs, and horses painted on it.

"What a great room for a baby," I said. There was even a picture of the cow that jumped over the moon on one wall, and another of the dishes that ran away with the spoon on the wall over the crib.

"Nick never told me too much about his life in New York. I don't know why," said Gloria.

"How old is Tim?" I asked.

"A year and a half." It was hard to see how this could be Dad's son, too. And Gloria his mother. I mean, Gloria was so young. She held Tim on her shoulder. He gazed blankly at me.

"Go outside while I try to put him down," Gloria said. "I'll be out in a minute."

I waited outside the door and could hear from the sounds of muffled crying, then soft singing and no crying, that Gloria was calming him down. "They're all cranky when you wake them up," she said when she joined me. "He went back to sleep."

I lugged the trunk and Gloria took the laundry bag. We passed through the kitchen, through the living room, past the bar and hi-fi set, through a door and down a hallway. "What time does Dad usually get home?" I asked.

"About this time. But you can never tell. His hours are different every day. Sometimes he doesn't come home until the middle of the night. Let's not talk about that."

She opened a door at the head of the hallway. "This is our room." It was a large, pale blue room with white antique furniture, another bay window, deep blue drapes, and a king-size bed. The old house was furnished like a million bucks. "C'mon," she said, "I'll show you your room."

It was a dream come true. Mom used to kid me by saying that if I kept growing, my head would be on the bed and my feet somewhere between the fire escape and the clothesline. My room was at the back of the house with my windows facing the lawn. I had bunk beds, a closet, a dresser, even my own bathroom. The sheets were turned down on the upper. "Can I use the bottom?" I asked.

"Sure," Gloria said, "I just thought it would be fun to sleep on top."

"I've had the upper bunk plenty of times in boarding schools. The top is much harder to make."

"And I went out and got bunk beds." Gloria was disappointed. "I'm a terrible shopper."

"You're going to be a movie star, aren't you?"

"I'm a good actress. We'll see what that brings. So far, so good."

"Do you and Dad own this house? Mom and I could never own anything. We always had to find a place to rent where they would let us stay a long time."

"No, we don't own it. I want to find a place to buy but Nick is against it. There's something in him that doesn't want to be tied down. I'll tell Constance to change the linens."

"I'll do it."

We were standing at the door, just looking at each other again. Somehow, I felt I had known Gloria for a very long time. It was as if I was looking at myself in the mirror. She looked so alone, so lonely. I tried to break the silence. "Have you ever been cross country in a plane?"

"We lived in New York and Boston until Mother brought me here."

"Your Dad still lives back east?"

"Yes." Gloria picked at one of her fingernails, then dropped her hands self-consciously and searched the room with her eyes, going from object to object, looking for another subject.

"It's great, isn't it? I mean, to go from one end of the country to the other in less than a day. Three thousand miles! And then it's three hours earlier when you get here."

"I hate planes," Gloria said. "And they take the three hours away when you go back. It's no bargain."

"Well, they'll never get those three hours back from me," I said.

"I hope they don't," she said. Her eyes weren't laughing anymore. "See you in a little while." I watched her slender back and long legs go down the hall and disappear into the big bedroom.

I hung my windbreaker and leather jacket in the closet, then put my other clothes in the dresser. I worked fast. This was the first time I had been somewhere I really wanted to be, and I was going to unpack for real. With Dad there was always an open suitcase piled high with clean and dirty shirts, scripts, papers and notes in the corner of some hotel room. I took off my jacket and hung it over a chair, then went into the bathroom and turned on the water. Gloria must have been cleaning up, too, because I could hear her water running. It was a thin wall. Their bathroom and mine were back-to-back.

Then I heard: "Son? Son, where are you?"

"In here!"

With my toothbrush in hand, I stopped in the bathroom door to see what he was going to do. Dad held out his arms and took a step toward me. I ran to him. That was just what I had wanted him to do, hold out his arms. I didn't want to just shake hands. We hugged each other.

"Let me look at you," Dad said. He held me at arm's length. "How was your flight?"

"Fine."

"Have you seen the beach? Do you want to take a swim before dinner?"

"Sure."

"I'll get you a bathing suit." He started for the door, then stopped and turned around. "I'm sorry I couldn't get to the airport.

I was busy. Work. You know." Dad started to say something else but decided not to.

I went back to the bathroom to turn off the water I had left running.

"I need a bathing suit," I heard Dad say.

"Why?"

"Tony and I are going to take a quick swim. He looks good, doesn't he?"

"He's a very attractive boy. Dinner's ready, Nick."

"We'll have dinner twenty minutes later."

"Keep going and we won't be eating at all."

"What do you mean by that?"

"Are you sober, Nick? Or are you making a career of these story conferences?"

Her angry voice faded as she left the bathroom. A few moments later Dad came to my room and handed me a bathing suit.

"Meet you outside when you're ready," Dad said.

I remembered something Mom had said to me at the airport. I was having a hot dog at the snack bar and she was trying to tell me things that would be helpful. She was concerned about my going to California. She never said it in so many words, but I could tell. "All people have problems," she said. "Nobody's perfect, including your father." She told me he would try to do his best for me, but that I should try very hard not to be impressed by people on face value, or by the value I would like them to have. It was better to draw back and take a good look before you leaped with all your faith and love. I told Mom I already knew that, but that I also knew once I was out there, in California, with Dad, that everything would be fine. It worried her that I was so sure. Well, I thought, it worried me that she was so sure it *wouldn't* work. Mom acted like there was something wrong with Dad.

The tighter I tied the bathing suit strings, the more it billowed. I didn't care. All I knew was that I was happy to be there. If Dad and Gloria wanted to argue, it was their business. I wasn't going to let it bother me.

Gloria was sitting on the black sectional couch in front of the fireplace reading a fat brown book. Constance was putting a dish upside down on a bowl of vegetables on the dining table. She wanted to keep them warm.

"Nick's outside," she said without taking her eyes off her book.

"Thanks."

I crossed the shaggy rug to the door next to the dining table. Dad was on the other side of the picket fence that bordered the yard facing the late afternoon sun. It bathed the sand, the water, the houses. The cove was quiet in its final hour of warmth. Dad stood still, looking out on the ocean. I wondered what he was searching for. The sun glowed on his skin. His legs and chest were hairy. The towel he was holding moved more from the breeze than any part of his body. I could almost feel the weight of his concentration. I closed the door gently, noiselessly, behind me, and walked across the grass yard. The ground was cool under my feet. The only sounds were the gentle tide, an occasional burst of laughter from one of the other houses, and the screams of seagulls as they swooped up and down from the water trying to find food. I passed through the gate and stood next to Dad. He was much taller than me. He didn't move to greet me, and I said nothing because I felt I wasn't supposed to.

A boat was churning toward the pier a mile or so down the beach with its haul of fish and fisherman. I wouldn't be disappointed in Dad, I thought. I wondered what it was going to be like going from having so little to having so much.

"We'll have to call your mother right after dinner," Dad said. His voice was little more than a whisper.

"Yes, sir."

"Let's get our feet wet, son." Dad draped his towel over the weathered gray fence. I put mine next to his. Then he was off running to the surf. He didn't hesitate a moment, and before I had even taken my first step into the water, he was on the other side of the breakers, swimming along on his back. "C'mon in!" he yelled. I tried to run and get in as fast as Dad had. I dove under a wave, came up on the other side, and swam to him.

"It's much cleaner and warmer than the Atlantic," I said. We swam side by side.

"During the summers when I was in college," he said, "I worked as a lifeguard. When my father died, I was sixteen. He left me in a house full of women—two older sisters and my mother."

I could see the whole cove now. It looked like a town you might see on a postcard of the French Riviera. There were no stores, movie houses or boardwalks—just white, yellow and green houses. There was even a pink one. The cove came to a sandy point at one end and a rocky cliff with waves breaking against it at the other.

"It's beautiful, isn't it!" I shouted, to be heard. "I'm so glad to be here."

"I'm happy to have you," Dad said. Then, suddenly, he caught a wave and rode it to shore. I got the next one in.

"That was great fun," I said. We stopped at the fence for our towels and dried off.

"Let's take a walk," he said. We threw the towels over our shoulders and headed toward the rocky end of the cove. For three or four minutes, neither of us uttered a single word. That's a long time. I just didn't know what to talk about. The last house was little more than a brown wooden shack raised thirty feet on pilings. It leaned precariously forward and I was sure it would tumble into the ocean if one large wave ever hit it. We walked almost underneath it on slippery, slime covered rocks, then climbed halfway up the cliff. Dad sat down behind me on a dry rock.

"How important would our lives and thoughts on Earth be if we could see them and the whole universe in relationship to each other from some remote point of view?"

"Do you believe in God?" I asked.

"I believe in man's pursuit of God, but I don't yet know if there is a God."

"I don't either."

"I have a sailing invitation with Humphrey Bogart next weekend. Would you like to go?"

"Would I!" Humphrey Bogart was a star. "Is he a good friend of yours?"

Dad nodded his head and gritted his teeth. He seemed annoyed I was so impressed.

"I just directed Bogart and Gloria in a film called *In a Lonely Place.* A year and a half ago I directed him in *Knock on Any Door.*"

"I want to see them."

"We better get back," Dad said. On the way to the house, I asked where I would be going to school in the fall. Dad didn't know yet but said I should find out what schools were nearby. He said I should ask other kids as I got to know them. We didn't talk much more until we reached the house. It was getting chilly.

"Did you see *They Live By Night*?"

"Mom thought it was too adult for me. But I'd love to see that, too."

We went to our rooms to dress. Everything was going to work out swell, I thought. But I wondered if it was as hard for Dad to talk to me as it was for me to talk to him. There were such long silences.

I put on a white short-sleeved shirt, a pair of slacks, and the new pair of brown loafers I had worn for the trip, then went back downstairs. Dad was sitting at the head of the table, Gloria opposite him at the other end. The place in the middle, facing the ocean, was mine. Dad rang a crystal bell and Constance brought out a platter with an enormous roast on it. The meat was surrounded by potatoes, carrots and bite-size onions. She set the platter down next to Dad, who began carving. Gloria passed her plate to Dad and he served her. I passed my plate. Then Dad served himself. A bowl of green peas was passed around and we began to eat.

Boy, Dad made me nervous. I couldn't tell what he was thinking. He sopped up the gravy with a piece of bread. Gloria's foot pushed against mine and she gave me kind of an "it's okay" look.

There was a long silence. Forks tapping against plates, chewing, water pouring, table sounds, until Dad finally spoke.

"Tony, tell me about the schools you went to. What were they like?"

"P.S.3 worked out really well. I liked being at home. But all the boarding schools and homes I was sent to were pretty bad. I don't want to be sent away again."

"Your mother couldn't work and take care of you," Dad said. "During the war it was impossible to find help."

"I know," I said.

"Well, you're here now."

"Is there a riding academy in the neighborhood?"

"Gloria is the expert on local recreation."

"Tomorrow I'll take you where I take Tim to play with animals. It's not a riding academy, it's a small ranch. Have you ever been grunion hunting?" she asked. Dad got up to fix himself a drink.

"Who?" I asked.

"Not who, silly—grunion hunting."

"What are grunions?"

Gloria broke up. She tucked her legs under her and put her hands over her mouth to hold back the laughter. I wished she would stop calling me silly all the time.

"They're little fish." Gloria held her hands four or five inches apart to show me. "They come in with the tide when there's a full moon. You're funny."

She cocked her head to one side and squinted in a nice smile.

"What do you mean funny?"

"I don't know," she shrugged her shoulders again. "Anyway, you have to scoop up the grunion in a bucket after a wave breaks and before the next one comes in. They're supposed to be great to eat but I've never tried one. It's fun. We'll do it this summer."

"Grunions," I said.

"No, silly—grunion, like deer."

Dad came back to the table. "We'll call your mother now," he said.

"Okay, good." I got up. "Excuse me," I said to Gloria.

Dad and I went to his bedroom. He stood next to the bed, picked up the phone, and dialed the operator. The room smelled nice, of powder and cologne. "Operator. I'd like to place a call to New York. Watkins 9, 2..." Dad hesitated, then asked, "What's the rest of it?"

"One, two, six."

"One, two, six," he told the operator. Then he called out: "Gloria, bring me a drink."

"She's with Tim," said Constance, who came to the door.

"Scotch and water, Constance. Please."

"Yes, sir."

"Malibu 4359." Dad answered the operator. Then we got Mom. "Hello. Jean? Nick. Sorry if we woke you. Fine. Yes, Tony's here. He looks swell."

Constance came in and set the drink on the nightstand next to Dad. He reached for the glass, then stopped, deciding against it. "How's work, Jean?" Dad turned his back on me. "Don't be depressed. It's going to work out fine. Here's Tony."

"Hi, Mom." I flopped across the bed and took the telephone. "The trip was great. It's warm without being hot. Rain? That's funny. You've got rain, we have sun. Yes, we had a big dinner. Pot roast. You should see Dad eat bread and gravy. Oh, he did?" I smiled at Dad.

"I did what?"

"Always like bread and gravy." Dad nodded and picked up his drink. "We're going sailing with Humphrey Bogart next weekend.

It's going to be a great summer. Yes, I'll write. Here's a bear hug. Ummph. That felt good. And a kiss. Goodbye."

"You two men through?" Gloria stuck her head in the door.

"Yah," Dad grunted. "Is Tim asleep?"

"Constance must have let him nap too long this afternoon. He's asleep now."

There was a frozen moment between Dad and Gloria that stopped time in its tracks. The one lamp beside the bed cast a shadow that cut across Dad's face and left Gloria's in near darkness. I looked to the window and saw nothing but night. Dad's face was chiseled out of dark red quartz and his skin was rough. He clasped his long, manicured fingers under his chin and looked at Gloria without saying anything, just raising his eyebrows. His hair curled in black and gray specks like ocean spray hitting the rocks at the end of the cove.

The house was still. I was still. Gloria stood in the half open door and tapped her foot. She gazed at the dark black hole of the bay window as though searching for something. We're all strangers, I thought, and shivered.

"Well," Dad exhaled in a long breath. In three lumbering steps he was beside Gloria at the door. His head hung. "What happened to my little girl?" he whispered.

"She grew up," Gloria said softly.

"Didn't we all?"

"I guess I ought to go to bed," I said.

"It's 12.30 at night in New York. You're just excited." Gloria said.

"That must be it." I passed by her into the hallway. Then I turned to face her again. "It was nice meeting you." I was halfway to my room when I realized how stupid that must have sounded. But it was true.

I undressed and crawled between the fresh cool sheets. Dad came in and sat on the edge of the bed. He had to leave for work early in the morning and said if I wasn't awake, he would see me at dinner. He patted the blanket here and there and fooled with the sheets as though tucking in a baby. He started to put a hand on my head but stopped himself. I grabbed his hand and held it. At first he tried to draw it away, but then squeezed back. I looked him smack in the eye. I felt so good. Dad grinned back, but there was something sad in his eyes. Without saying anything, he got up and walked out the door.

I turned over, tired after all. Why hadn't he and Mom stayed together? The more I thought about that, the less I understood. There had been times when I backed Mom against a wall and demanded her to tell me why Dad wasn't with us all the time.

"Sometimes people who are perfectly wonderful separately don't get along together, no matter how hard they try," she once said. And: "Maybe if we had been older, we could have worked things out. It's a shame. We met during very difficult years for us both. Nick was struggling to find himself creatively and having a tough time earning a living. I sometimes wonder if we had a chance, or how it might go if we had another one. We were very young, son." But no matter what, she would never say anything bad about Dad. In fact, she never answered my questions at all. I wondered if Mom was still stuck on Dad, but I could never ask. She didn't have any boyfriends. I curled up around my pillow and closed my eyes.

"Tony?" It was Gloria.

"Come in." Although she had changed into a bathrobe and taken off all her makeup, she still looked as beautiful as when she was all done up.

"I wanted to say goodnight to you." She took one of my hands in hers. "You've got your father's eyes." She touched my eyelids with her free hand. "I've seen pictures of your mother. She's very attractive." Gloria paused, took her eyes away from mine, and looked down at the sheet. Her forehead wrinkled. She was sure prettier than my mother, and so much younger. "I don't expect to take her place, Tony. I'm not going to try. I don't want to. We'll have our own relationship" I was glad she said all that. I couldn't see her as my mother. She leaned over and kissed me quickly on the lips, then sat up again. I felt strange inside about her kissing me.

"Don't worry about the silences," Gloria said. "Nick goes off like that all the time. Sometimes it seems like he even forgets what he was talking about."

Gloria tried to find more words, but they didn't come. I wanted to ask if Dad always drank a lot, but decided I better not.

"Tomorrow I'll take you riding. These people nearby, the Archers, have two kids, 14 and 16. I love kids." Gloria smiled. "They're so much nicer than grownups." She got up and went to the door. "It was nice meeting you, too."

I listened to her walking down the hall and heard their bedroom door close behind her.

Between breaking waves, I could hear trucks racing up the highway. There was a steep hill just up the road from us and the trucks ground their gears as they approached it. The sound reminded me of my bedroom in New York when the whole building would shake when the subway ran under it. I wondered if everybody had their own fears.

2
A Queer Bird

Blades of hazy sunlight cut through the half-closed slats of the Venetian blinds and streamed across the floor. A huge yellow blob that looked like melting butter blended into the sky. I could barely make out the treetops through waves of fog. How far I had come. How far New York had already shrunk in my mind. "California!" I took a deep breath, put on a pair of jeans, and went barefoot to the living room. Gloria, in blue pleated skirt and crisp white blouse, sat at the dining table.

"Good morning," I said.

"Oh," Gloria spun around. "Hi."

"Excuse me. I'll get a shirt." The door to their bedroom was open, but I didn't see Dad. All I saw was the ruffled, empty, slept-in bed, and on the bed a red bathrobe lying across a pale blue nightgown. As I got to my room, I heard Gloria behind me.

"Did you sleep well?"

"Fine. Is Dad home?"

"No, silly, he left hours ago. Get dressed and I'll make you breakfast."

I pulled my favorite red polo shirt over my head and put on shoes and socks. I thought about how I would make my own breakfast at home before school. Gloria wasn't like a mother at all. Red bathrobe over blue nightgown. I could never imagine my mother and father together in bed. How sickening. But I couldn't see Gloria with Dad either. Even the idea of a brother was meaningless. He was only a baby. It was easier for me to picture Mom dying with me not there. How ashamed I would be for leaving her. I thought a lot about death, and it frightened me. Love and death. Nothing seemed very real sometimes.

Gloria had set a cup of coffee, cream and sugar, and a tall glass of fresh squeezed orange juice on the table. The juice was strained.

Mom used to do that, too, until I told her I liked the pulp best. Gloria brought a fresh cup of coffee for herself.

"Was Dad mad?" I asked as she sat down.

"Why?"

"Because I overslept."

"Lord, no. He wasn't expecting to see you. Please pass the cream."

"I saw Tim playing outside. What time is it?"

"About 8.30," she answered.

"What time does Dad leave?"

"6.30." Gloria took a sip of coffee. "What would you like for breakfast?"

"I don't care much about breakfast, but if you make juice for me again could you leave the pulp in? I love the pulp."

Gloria jumped up and ran barefoot to the kitchen. The swinging door whooshed behind her. I looked out the window, and couldn't see beyond the surf, not even to the bed of seaweed I knew was just beyond. White crests of waves crashed right out of the fog. Foamy bubbles sank into the sand, and the backwash ran a losing race with the next wave. No going back.

I would have to get up earlier, I thought. I was disappointed. I had imagined being with him all the time. But that was foolish. Fathers work. I tried to figure out when this moment, this exact vision, had happened before. It was nothing special, just the way a wave broke and how another one came up from behind. Their futile attempt to get out of the ocean, one of those tricks of mind and time that makes you think life is lived over and over again as an endless stream of frustrating dreams. I turned to see Gloria standing behind me with a silver tray on which was placed another glass of orange juice. She bowed, "At your service." Then, as she daintily set the new glass in front of me, she puckered her lips and said with a heavy English accent, "With pulp." Gloria grasped the rim of the old glass with two fingers as though it were something disgusting, put it on the tray, then covered it with a napkin. "Not fit for the eye."

"You didn't have to do that."

"You don't have riding boots, do you?"

"No."

"Old shoes?"

"No."

Gloria cocked her head and watched me drink my coffee. "What size do you wear?"

A mischievous glance flashed in her eyes.

"About ten."

"Oh good." She clapped her hands. "Promise not to tell?"

"Sure."

She got up, took my hand, and said, "C'mon."

We went to their bedroom. Gloria opened a closet. "Look," she said, pointing to two rows of shoes. "Pick a pair from the back. He never wears those."

"Wow! There must be twenty pairs." I chose brown loafers that were something like mine and slipped one of them on. "It fits."

"Let's get Tim." Gloria quickly closed the closet door, the way kids do when they're afraid of getting caught stealing candy between meals. She took my hand and we half ran, half tiptoed out of the empty room.

In the car, Tim sat between Gloria and me in his own high seat that had a red plastic steering wheel attached to it. I wished I knew how to drive. Maybe Dad or Gloria would teach me. I felt old enough. Gloria backed through the gate and onto our road. All the houses were built on the beach side. A small adobe building with a green bench in front of it had "Malibu Patrol" painted on the wall facing the road. "We have our own police," Gloria said proudly. "It's a safe place for children."

She turned right onto the highway and a minute later turned left onto a dirt road. A lumber company was on one corner and a row of beat-up mailboxes on the other.

"What kind of car does Dad drive?"

"An old Ford."

I was surprised he didn't also have a Cadillac, or a Lincoln Continental.

A creek ran along one side of the rutted road. The water line had been several feet higher at one time. A trickle found its way downstream around boulders and over the pebble bottom. Trees grew on both sides of the road. They were tall and thin. Sun-bleached bark hung in loose strips, like snakeskin, from the trunks. "Eucalyptus," said Gloria.

Flower fields seemed to stretch all the way to the mountains. As we came around a turn, a low branch brushed the windshield and a horse and rider came into view.

"Judy Archer," Gloria said to me. We stopped and the girl and horse stopped by the side of the car. "Hi, Judy."

"Good morning."

"I'd like you to meet Tony, Nick's son from New York."

"Figured that's who you were. Gloria said you were coming." She smiled showing buck teeth and leaned way over the saddle to extend a hand. We shook. I was sure if Judy didn't fall off, her big knockers would come pouring out of her shirt anyway. But nothing happened.

"We were on our way to your place," Gloria said. "Tony loves horses, so I promised to bring him."

Judy threw a moccasin over the saddle horn and chomped on a piece of gum. Long brown bangs fell over her eyes and tight jeans made her legs look heavier than they were. "We don't have enough kids who want to ride, except for the brats." She swung her leg back over the saddle. "I'm going down for the mail. Chris is in one of his moods and won't let me drive his wreck of a car. Be right back." Judy yanked her horse's head out of the grass. "C'mon, Liz." She tapped Liz in the belly and went down the road at a canter with her feet hanging loose out of the stirrups.

"Who's Chris?"

"Her older brother." Gloria put the car into gear.

The Archers' place was nestled in a thicket of oak trees. The barn and coral were neatly fenced and there was a hitching rail in front of the stable area. Two horses, their heads no more than six inches apart, munched on thick alfalfa. A boy who was a couple of years older than Judy leaned against the open entrance gate. He stepped aside to let our car pass, then walked off toward the barn. We pulled up in front of the house and got out of the car. Mrs. Archer, a short, solid woman in her forties, came out of the house followed by an army of cats. She was carrying two bowls of food that she set down by the door.

"Morning, Gloria. How's life treating you?"

"Fine, Nella. This is Tony."

"Happy to meet you." She shook hands like a man. "That's Chris, my boy. Maybe he will be polite enough to come over and get introduced," she raised her voice.

"Have to get the barn cleaned," whined Chris. "Can't let company stop the work."

"How well do you ride?" Mrs. Archer asked.

"Not very," I answered. "But how did you know I even wanted to ride?"

"Why else would you be here? Chris!" she called out. "Saddle up Misty for Tony here." A pitchfork came flying out of the barn, followed by Chris.

A couple of minutes later, Judy rode up to the house, dismounted neatly, and handed her mother a couple of letters and a magazine. Chris led over a black horse and handed the reins to Judy. She turned to me. "Get on up."

I put my foot in the stirrup.

"Not like that, unless you want a sore tail."

"I've always done it this way."

"Go on then," Judy shrugged a shoulder. I was facing the front of the horse. I held the reins with one hand, the stirrup with the other. As I lifted myself, the horse took off and I landed smack on my rear. Knowing what was going to happen, she caught the horse right away. I picked myself up.

"Are you alright?" Gloria asked.

"Sure." I was embarrassed in front of her.

"Face his tail, put your foot in, and climb aboard. That way, if he moves out, he's helping you instead of dumping you." Judy sounded like a record, as if she had told this to people a hundred times before. "Easier, isn't it?"

"Uh-huh. I forgot before, that's all."

"Tim and I will feed the chickens until you get back," said Gloria.

Judy mounted her horse and we walked toward the dirt road. "I don't want to sound mean, but these aren't hack horses." She took the red ribbon out of her hair and tied it to the forelock between Liz's ears. "A hack won't move unless you half kill it. Want a stick of gum?"

"Sure."

"Figured you might." Judy handed me a stick of spearmint. "The road goes straight for another hundred yards, then there's a gate. Can you handle yourself at a canter?"

"I can pull Misty in if I have to."

"Don't pull him in," she accented the word *pull*, drawing it out. "A jerk will stop him cold. Lean back a little when he stops or you'll go flying over his head. Understand?"

"I understand." I was scared out of my wits.

"Well, now, what did you have to do to make the horses you rode back east canter?"

"A hundred kicks in the gut and they might trot," I told her. "To make them canter, you had to beat them with the reins."

"Tell you what," Judy shook her head. "You do as I say or you're gonna end up killed. Whenever you're ready, loosen the lines a bit, tap Misty in the sides with your heels and lean forward." I followed Judy's instructions and Misty went right into a canter. Judy rode along beside me. She obviously disapproved. I don't know what about, but it sure griped me. I was doing what she told me to.

"Mind if I tell you things?"

"Go ahead."

"Keep your heels down and toes out. If you squeeze tight with your knees, you don't even need stirrups. Watch me."

She kicked her feet free, gripped with her knees, and shot out in front of me at a full run. That must have been her biggest accomplishment in life. Her rear never left the saddle. I had a lot to learn. I cantered to the gate where Judy waited, jerked in gently, and Misty stopped.

"Another thing," she said. "Stop beating the wind with your elbows like a wild Indian. Tuck them into your sides."

Judy led the way through the gate and we followed a narrow path up the canyon. We rode quietly for about fifteen minutes when Judy said, "Most of riding is walking, unless you're working a horse."

We came to a stream where we dismounted and sat on a rock.

"I don't think I'd care for the East, but I'd sure like to see it really snow someday."

"There's snow in parts of California, isn't there?"

"In the mountains, up north, but I've never seen it." Judy cupped her hands and drank from the stream. "You just out for the summer?"

"Nope, for good."

"Where are you going to school? All the kids around here go to Santa Monica High School. We call it Samo-Hi. A bus picks us up. It's about fifteen miles."

"I'll go to Samo-Hi then. I was in a special class in New York called 7-8 Special, so I don't know if they'll place me in eighth or ninth grade."

"There's a junior high school, too." Judy poked around the water with a finger. I skipped a rock to the other side of the stream. "You're a queer bird," she said.

"Why do you say that?"

"I don't know. Your eyes... they're sort of restless."

"I'm just trying to figure out where I am. I just got here yesterday."

Maybe I had seen too many Westerns, but Judy ruined something for me making a classroom out of her canyon. I had run away from a boarding school once with the school pony, Fanny, who didn't care if my elbows flapped in the wind. When Fanny ran through a woman's garden, she called the police.

"I'd like to look through one of those waves down there, just once, and see the whole universe. Then I could tell my Dad if there is a God."

"You're crazy," Judy whispered. "Of course there's a God."

"Are you afraid of death?" I asked.

"C'mon, we better go home."

From his perch in the hayloft, Chris was watching Gloria and Tim feeding oats to one of the horses. Mrs. Archer was feeding chickens. They had a lot of chicken houses. "How'd he do?" she asked.

"He's a little rough around the edges," said Judy, "but he bounces alright."

We rode over to the hitching rail and dismounted.

"Loosen the girth and tie him up."

Thank God I knew how to tie a clove hitch.

"We have to go home," Gloria said, "or I'll be late for an appointment in town."

Gloria signaled me to step aside with her. She handed me a $5 bill. "Give this to Judy."

"I didn't know this was for money. I'm sorry." It ruined the whole thing.

"Judy earns extra money in the summer giving riding lessons," said Gloria.

"I'll give it back to you when we get to the house," I assured her. "I've got $5 there."

"My treat," she said.

"I delivered groceries after school last year. Maybe I can find something here."

"Have you and Nick talked about an allowance yet?"

"We haven't had time to talk about much of anything yet."

Judy brought $3.50 change, which I tried to give Gloria.

"Keep it," she said, putting her hands behind her back.

We said goodbye to Mrs. Archer and Judy and I tried to wave to Chris, who stayed in the hayloft.

"I'm going to Santa Monica High School in the fall if I'm in ninth grade."

"Is that where Judy goes?"

"Uh-huh. Everyone does."

"I'll try not to be jealous," she joked.

The sun had burned off the fog and an ocean breeze played with Gloria's hair once we had left the dirt road behind. There was no comparison between Gloria and Judy. Gloria didn't think I was a queer bird. "I have a doctor's appointment," Gloria said as we stopped in front of the garage, "Want to go with me?"

"Yes."

I waited in the car while she delivered Tim to Constance.

"Nick thinks everyone needs to be analyzed," said Gloria as she put the car in gear and we pulled out.

"Mom's the same way. I went to a psychiatrist, but I know Dad paid for it."

"Nick goes, too. He wants everyone else to go because he does."

"What do you do there?"

"It depends on how much sleep I've had the night before."

"I asked the doctor how much he made, how much Dad paid him, and if he paid a lot of income tax." That wasn't altogether true. Sometimes I really poured things out to him, especially about being sent away to all those places and why I got into so much trouble at home. Gloria probably really talked sometimes, but neither of us were about to admit it to each other.

We talked a lot on the way to town. Before Dad, Gloria was married to a boy named Stanley. She divorced him because marrying him hadn't been the "right" thing to do. He was common. Gloria tried to explain what common meant, but all I could figure out from what she said was if you had no money you were common and if you had some you had class. Stanley was out of town and sent Gloria a telegram saying, "You're mine, ring or no ring," and Gloria went to him. "We spent three wild days, never leaving the hotel room except for hamburgers and beer, and got married on the fourth. Mother tried to give me the guilt for marrying for disgusting reasons like sex," Gloria said. "But she's old fashioned, and very British."

"Did you love him?"

"I don't know. That's one of the things I'm trying to figure out. I believe whatever the last person tells me. I can make a thousand lists of a man's good and bad points and not come up with an answer. He'll like children and be violent or not care about children and be so subdued you could die. One always cancels out the other. The doctor says I'm stuck between what I want to do and what I think I'm supposed to do." Gloria raised her sunglasses to her forehead and pointed a finger to the sky. "I have to make an adjustment," she said. "They all say the same thing." She dropped her glasses back into place. "It's part of their business vocabulary. The butcher sells meat, the analyst sells adjustments."

A new kind of smile crept over Gloria's face. She licked her upper lip with devilish pleasure. "You should know how I met your father. He was the hottest director on the lot. Mother met me at work every morning and begged me to go meet him. 'Knock at his bungalow door,' she'd say, 'All you have to do is introduce yourself.' Well, one night the boy in the picture I was working on called me to get some line changes he'd lost. I went to help him and Stanley thought I was cheating. So he hit me. I don't think I would have minded, but the boy was nothing, really nothing. Anyway, I came to the studio the next morning with a black eye. Mother's a great one for giving the guilt. She looked down her nose and said she'd told me so. *No class.* I was furious at Stanley because the picture had to shoot around me until my eye went back to normal. I thought they'd suspend me. Anyway, I was walking off the lot half in tears when Nick came up behind me. He put his arm around my shoulder and hugged me in that gentle, strong, way of his... you know that hug... and said, 'What are they doing to my little girl?' Well! That knocked me out. Nick made me feel I was protected against the world."

"Did he put you in a picture?"

"No, he married me instead. I divorced Stanley the same day I married Nick. Nick was everything a man was supposed to be. Even Mother was happy."

Gloria got the disc jockey on the radio. Her brows furrowed, pinching the bridge of her sunglasses, and she pouted. "Did Nick spend a lot of time with you when he was in New York on trips?"

"As much as he could, I guess. Not much."

"Nick's involved with work. Work, work, work. His opening remark to me when we were getting ready to go on our honeymoon—he packed a suitcase full of scripts and work—was, 'At last I've found someone I can relax with.' I wanted Nick to bring you out here so badly."

"You?"

"Sure, silly." Gloria's face really brightened, "I saw a picture of you right after we got married. I had to have you out here."

"I didn't know that."

"Yes, hon." She rested a hand on my knee. "My mother's a real stage mother. Unlike most of them, mine has a world of talent. She gave up an acting career in England to get married. I guess she wants to be sure I don't make the same mistake."

I told Gloria my mom worked hard all her life, and asked if she had bought her mother a house.

"Yes," she said. "It doesn't have genuine Victorian furniture in it, but it's hers."

"My mom's always wanted an apartment in New York with a backyard so she can have flowers and a dog. And she's going to have it someday, too, if I die trying to get it for her."

We listened to "Rhapsody in Blue" on the radio. Gloria asked me if it bothered me to talk so much. I said it didn't, that I liked it.

She was going to be a real friend.

"I'm not going to have anything left for the doctor," she sighed. I watched her drive.

I guess I wasn't the only one who didn't like their childhood. For some reason, Gloria made me feel strong.

"I don't know why I went on and on," she said as if she was sorry for having told me about herself. "All I wanted was to tell you I was someone you could talk to. And I hoped I could talk to you. After all, we're living in the same family now. If I said anything I shouldn't have, I didn't mean to."

"You're very pretty," I said.

She smiled beautifully, not half or kidding, but like I had given her a present or something. And she said, "Thank you." A moment later she looked at her watch.

"Oh, my God." She hit the gas. A mile or so down the highway the sirens started. There was one motorcycle behind us and another one alongside, waving Gloria over. They gave her a big fat speeding ticket with orders to appear in court. And they took their time writing it, too. When we got on our way again Gloria kept checking the rear-view mirror. She was steaming.

"Light me a cigarette, will you, Tony?"

"Sure." I took one from her purse.

"And one for yourself," she added.

"What?"

"You heard me," she said.

"But I don't smoke."

"Then you better find another place not to smoke."

"I'm not allowed to, Gloria."

"I know, and I'm not allowed to get tickets."

"What makes you think I smoke?"

"I was in our bathroom getting ready for bed last night after you went to bed. There's a window in it, like in yours. I almost choked to death."

"Gloria…" Boy, I was worried.

"I won't say anything about the smoking and you don't say anything about the ticket."

"Is that a deal?"

"Okay," I agreed. "It's our secret."

"Go ahead, silly."

3
Slaves of Mediocrity

At 7:30 there was still no sign of Dad, so we started dinner without him. Gloria told Constance we would clean up after ourselves and she could go for the evening. Neither of us were very hungry. "Sometimes Nick gets tied up and forgets to call," Gloria said five minutes after we sat down, but I could tell she was making excuses by the way she poked with her fork at the full plate of chicken.

"He must have had an important meeting," I said.

"He'll get here when he gets here."

Dad pushed through the swinging door into the living room, saw us at the table, and stopped to look at his watch. His black knit tie, still knotted, hung loose around his neck. He dropped his jacket, script binder and address book in a pile on the bar.

"Should have waited for me," he grumbled.

"We gave up," Gloria said.

"Busy," Dad said. "Busy."

Gloria asked him to come to dinner but he chose a glass and bottle instead.

"I let her go for the evening," Gloria said. She turned to me and said, "Eat."

"I don't want to eat," Dad said, thinking Gloria was talking to him. He finished his drink and poured another. Leaning against the bar for support, he kicked off his shoes. As he bent over to take off his socks, he lost his balance and fell to one knee. His glass tumbled to the floor.

Seeing Dad fall like a mountain suddenly crashing into the sea was as stunning as a car wreck. I couldn't move, only gape for several seconds in wide-eyed wonder. I jumped up to Dad's side and placed my hand under his arm to lift him. He pushed me away, hard. "I don't need any help." I went back to the table. My whole body was shaking. Gloria hadn't budged. Dad sat on the floor working off his socks. He got up and walked out the ocean door. Through

the window I watched him find a driftwood seat on the hard sand
near the water's edge. I pushed my chair out from the table. Maybe
I could just talk to Dad, I thought, to make him feel better.

"Stay here," Gloria ordered. "He's mad at himself." Then, as
an afterthought, "Not that it does any good."

"What's happening?" I asked. "Is Dad on a binge?"

"The longest lost weekend on record," muttered Gloria.

A few minutes later, Dad doused his face with water, came back
to the house, and sat down to dinner like nothing had happened.
I couldn't think of anything to say. I couldn't ask if he'd had a good
day or anything. Dad stuffed food into his mouth like a child being
forced to eat.

"Did you enjoy riding today," Gloria asked me.

"Yes," I said.

Dad didn't involve himself in the conversation. It was as if a
door had slammed, as if Gloria and I were at a restaurant sharing a
table with a stranger.

"Goddamned slaves of mediocrity," he grumbled to himself
before spitting a mouthful of food into his napkin and heaving
back and forth violently in his chair in a fit of coughing. He
choked, gagged and covered his mouth with a hand. I thought he
was going to be sick, but he finally got enough control to hold
his breath. He exhaled slowly, carefully, through his nose. "That's
what it is, getting them to trust you with their goddamned dollar.
They begged me to do films," he snorted. He focused on his food
again, wiped his mouth with the back of his hand, and took a deep
breath. "Yes, I said, I'd like to make my future secure. It's a seven-
year contract, my agent said, rushing me into the deal. Jean and I
had our share of waiting in line to use somebody else's bathtub
during the Depression."

Dad took a bite of his chicken and chewed it distastefully. "It's
a jungle out there." He gazed out the window and his face clouded
over with the look of a man betrayed by his best friend. "A house,
a name, a position, a career that destroys its own talent, that mush-
rooms into a great, giant, hollow image." Frustrated anger flushed
across his face and he held his knife straight up in a fist that could
turn either way, toward himself or out there at the ocean of invisible
enemies he cursed. "Self-satisfaction is death. Remember that, son."

"I will, Dad."

"Get me a pack of cigarettes from the bedroom, would you, Tony," Gloria said. There was a pack in the middle of the table, but I obeyed. As I left the room, Gloria said, "You're not getting off to a very good start with Tony, Nick." I listened from the hallway.

"I'll be alright."

"The rent is two months late and they're turning off the telephone."

"You'll have to lend me a thousand. My check hasn't come through yet."

"Get a business manager."

"I don't need anyone keeping tabs on me. I'm a big boy now."

"How many times have I heard that before? I can't afford you."

"What kind of crack is that?"

"You were out of the studio at noon today. So was Edna."

"So now you think I'm having an affair with my secretary. She had a doctor's appointment. I gave her the afternoon off."

"There's only one other place you could have been. The racetrack… *I can't afford to keep you*."

"Keep me?" Dad raised his voice. There was a long silence. Softly, he said, "Don't you think it hurts to have this happen, to have Tony see me this way?" Gloria didn't answer. "You can't understand, can you?" I wanted to yell out that *I* understood.

"Don't try to give me the guilt, Nick. That was the stupidest thing you could have done this afternoon, and you know it. You're weak."

"It'll never happen again."

"Will I get my money back? I never have."

"You'll get it," Dad said.

"Seven thousand and now this? Can I take it out of your salary?"

"You bitch!" exploded Dad.

Stay out of quarrels, Mom had warned. Nobody's perfect. I was about to go back into the room when Gloria started up again. I could have killed her.

"You gave up, didn't you, Nick?"

"How?"

"Your first picture was really good, but it lost money."

"That was the studio's fault. They changed the title and shelved it for a year. It wasn't a commercial film."

"Your next assignment wasn't *Hamlet* and you didn't give a damn. It was beneath you, so you retaliated by drinking on set. Or was that your way of making excuses for a lousy movie?"

"The producers wouldn't leave me alone."

"Do you plan to drink your way through the next one?"

Something crashed and broke. Then silence again. When I walked in, Dad was looking at his hand. He had slammed his coffee cup against the table so hard it had shattered and left the handle dangling on his finger. I put the pack of cigarettes next to Gloria, sat down, and pretended I hadn't heard a thing. It was none of my business.

"I've never done that in my life on a set," said Dad. "That's the kind of talk that ruins people."

He took the cup handle off his finger and dropped it into an ashtray. "We had a meeting this morning. They want me to do *Flying Leathernecks* with John Wayne."

"John Wayne!" I said, "I must have seen *Sands of Iwo Jima* a thousand times."

"What did you tell them?" Gloria asked.

"I've turned down two. Three strikes and I'm out. If I refuse this one, I go on suspension. I said I'd think it over and tell them in the morning."

Gloria put out her cigarette and lit another one.

"Income taxes are so damn high," said Dad, "I can't afford to be an artist in our society. I'll make this picture, son, and use the money to start my own company."

I couldn't understand the last thing Dad said. I mean, I understood what he said, but not how it made sense. "What about the taxes on this money?" I asked.

"Don't!" Dad snapped.

"I'm sorry, Dad."

"I have responsibilities," he explained. "You, Tim, Gloria."

Mom was right. I should have kept my mouth shut. Now it turned out I was partly to blame for Dad not being able to do what he wanted.

"Compromise to get position," he said, closing his eyes and rubbing his forehead. Then he got up, walked heavily out of the room, and left the house.

I was suddenly afraid of him. It's scary to be sure you're saying the right things and have them all turn out wrong. All through dinner I had wanted to tell him about Santa Monica High, but hadn't dared.

Gloria held her head in her hands and muttered, "Mirror, mirror on the wall." Then she looked up and our eyes met.

"I was only trying to help," I said.

"I know," she smiled. "C'mon, let's catch a flick."

"What about Dad? Shouldn't we wait for him?"

"He'll find his way. He's a big boy. Let's not be so morose."

Dad still wasn't at home when Gloria and I walked through the door. I climbed into bed and waited. Gloria probably went to sleep. She said it wasn't unusual for him to take off like that. I would never contradict him again, though, or say I didn't think he made sense. It was partly my fault that he left, butting in and saying the wrong things. How stupid could I get? I thought Dad had it made, that everything was great for him. He had the chance to make a movie with John Wayne, after all. Why was he drunk? Gloria was upset, too. And he owed her all that money.

This was going to have to work, no matter what. I had to find ways of making him happy. But how? I had been sure that Gloria was the one who would be hard to get to know, not Dad. But it wasn't working out that way.

I was groggy when I was awoken by the phonograph in the living room. I could have sworn I left my door open, but now it was closed. I heard the old sounds of a scratchy 78. Billie Holiday's voice penetrated the walls like a train whistle through a cold, damp wind. I wanted to go to Dad, but Gloria said the best thing to do when he was trying to figure things out for himself was to leave him alone. I didn't want to risk getting him mad again, so I curled up around my pillow and hoped he had just had a bad day, that he wasn't like this all the time.

Mom had boxes of old records Dad had left behind. I listened to them once in a while to bring him closer in my mind. But now Dad seemed far away, farther away than he had been when he was here in Hollywood and I was in New York.

> Then gay youth was mine,
> Truth was mine,
> Joyous, free and flaming life forsooth was mine.
> Sad am I,
> Glad am I,

For today I'm dreaming of
Yesterdays.

It was almost dawn. I turned over and tried to go back to sleep.
I was only scaring myself, I thought. And I did feel better now that
Dad was home. Home.

I cover the waterfront
I'm watching the sea
Will the one I love
Be coming back to me?

4
Empty Dreamland

I told Dad how badly I wanted to learn to drive, that I was nuts on the subject, but he said I would have plenty of time to learn when I was sixteen. He may as well have said sixty, sixteen was so far away. Dad was good about one thing, though. He said I would get $10 a week for riding, movies and other things. That was a lot of money for no work. Gloria must have talked to him about that.

"How old should a person be before he's allowed to smoke?" I asked after we had been driving quietly for a while. I was sure he would say something ridiculous like 21. He surprised me with "Never. It's a lousy habit. Research indicates smoking leads to cancer, and there's no cure. Deadly. Why do you ask?"

"Why do you smoke then?"

"Lousy habit."

"I had a real neat ride with Judy Archer. She's pretty slick with a horse. I'm going to go a lot."

"Do you know who Howard Hughes is?" he asked.

"No."

"Owns the studio, and TWA, the airline." Dad's forehead wrinkled. "Some time ago, Hughes and I had lunch to talk about the picture I was doing, the first one I tried to get out of. He was to pick me up at my house. I lived in the Hollywood Hills then, above Sunset." Dad rolled an unlit cigarette in his mouth. "Hughes arrived an hour late in his newest car, a ten-year-old Chevrolet. He was wearing a T-shirt, baggy old slacks, and tennis shoes. He always wore tennis shoes. We talked business while we drove. Regardless of how Hughes was dressed, we could have gone anywhere for lunch, but he stopped by the side of the road at the top of Coldwater Canyon. He took a wax-paper-wrapped sandwich from his jacket, which was rolled up in a ball on the seat between us, and offered me half. That was lunch." Dad looked for my reaction. He must have expected something that wasn't there. We drove on in silence.

Sure, I liked Gloria's car better, but if the owner of a movie studio could drive an old Chevrolet, why couldn't Dad drive an old Ford? As we went deeper and deeper into Hollywood, Dad stayed silent. He concentrated on driving, bumping back and forth across the trolley tracks on Santa Monica Boulevard. The upper part of Dad's jaw, just under the ear, throbbed as he clamped together his teeth over and over. The closer we came to the studio, the more alone and worried he looked.

"I'm sorry if I said anything I shouldn't have at dinner last night."

No answer.

"Dad?"

"Forget it."

"Judy Archer says everyone goes to Samo-Hi. That's the public school in Santa Monica. A bus picks up the kids in front of their houses. Can I go there?"

"I'll look into it," he said. "This is it."

We were driving past a long, two-story concrete building. A black iron fence surrounded the gray place. Across the street were a row of cheap bars and a Chinese restaurant. My mind was still on school. I wanted permission before another day passed. Once I was sure there would be no more boarding schools, I could relax and enjoy the rest of the summer.

"All the kids go to Samo-Hi, Dad."

"That's not true. Many of my friend's children attend other schools. Better ones."

We turned into the studio and stopped in the driveway next to a small guardhouse. A man dressed as a cop waved to Dad and a moment later the heavy rope that stretched across the entrance fell to the ground. We passed several huge box-like concrete buildings with white numbers painted on them. Each one had a single door with a red light above it, but there were no windows. "Soundstages," explained Dad. The studio was like a little city in itself: barber shop, restaurant, newsstand, cigarette and cigar stores. Joan Crawford crossed the street in front of us! A double row of Cadillacs, Chryslers and limousines were parked in front of the administration building. Names were painted on the cement at the head of each parking space. "You've got your own reserved place!" I was impressed.

"Very expensive," said Dad with a smile.

We climbed a flight of wide stone steps which reminded me of those in front of the New York Public Library at Fifth Avenue and 42nd Street. Then we passed through a revolving door. Gold framed pictures of stars lined the walls of the foyer. "Is it okay to get autographs?" I asked.

"Poor taste," Dad said. "Rather you didn't."

"Good morning, Mr. Ray," the guard behind the reception desk said.

"Good morning, Harvey." A buzzer release sounded and we went through another door to a long, dimly lit hallway. "Harvey was in silent pictures." We walked briskly by all the closed office doors with gold nameplates on them. Once in a while I heard the tapping of a typewriter, but we were pretty much the first ones there. I think Dad was proud of himself for having gotten past the guards, into the studio, and to a private office of his own, in spite of all the complaining he did. The administration building sat like a ruler over the streets and soundstages, and Dad walked with his head straight up like he owned the place.

Photographs of Dad riding camera cranes, on the set with stars, and a few of other people covered a large bulletin board. There were real paintings and framed posters of Dad's movies on the other walls. And that couch! It was more like a living room than an office. "I had it made and sent the bill to the studio," Dad said. He sat behind his large desk, and even though the door to the outer office was open, and Edna, his secretary was in plain sight, Dad used the intercom to ask if there had been any calls the afternoon before. Then he opened up *The Hollywood Reporter*. There was even a telephone with four buttons. Dad looked very important. Edna brought in a flask of coffee and a mug.

"I decided to give you your black before the bad news." She placed the flask before Dad on a painted tile.

"Where's your cup, and one for Tony?" Dad poured for himself while Edna got the extra cups.

"You have a meeting at 10:30," said Edna when she came back. She fingered one of the blue flowers on her white dress and half closed her eyes as though bracing herself for an explosion.

"I know," Dad said almost too softly to hear.

"Are you going to put me out of work?" Edna asked good-naturedly but meaning it.

"Uh-uh." Dad shook his head. "Not yet."

Edna, visibly relieved, sank into the chair in front of Dad's desk and poured coffee for us. "When you finish, let the monsters know I'll be a half hour late."

"Late!" Edna gasped. "It's only eight o'clock."

"Don't call," Dad said. "Maybe I won't go at all."

"Oh, Nick," Edna laughed when she caught on Dad was kidding her. "You'll give me a nervous breakdown."

"Have you read the script?"

"Yes."

"Well, what did you think of it? Really."

"It'll make money," said Edna.

"Yeah. I know." He turned on his swivel chair to face the window behind his desk

"Want to give Max anything today?" Edna asked. Dad turned back to the desk and opened a newspaper to the sports pages. Edna went to the outer office and came back with the *Form*, which she put on Dad's desk.

"How much am I in for?" Dad asked.

"I haven't seen yesterday's results yet myself and Max doesn't come in until 11."

"I know we took a beating in the east." Dad frowned as he made notes on a memo pad. "Damn parasites," he muttered. "Agents and bookies. Everybody gets his cut." He tore the sheet from the memo pad and crumpled it up. "$340." Edna said nothing. Dad opened the *Form*, and as he turned the pages, after studying each carefully, he made a short list of horses on a fresh sheet of paper. "Give this to Max," he said when finished. "Say I'll settle up at the end of next week." Dad handed the sheet to Edna and paced back and forth across the office. "Call Warner and ask if he's trying with Sweet Sue today." A full smile broke across Dad's face. "You know what that son of a bitch did with a horse last year? He spread it all over the studio he was running a four-year-old named Gallant Warrior for the first time. He kept the horse under wraps so he could make a killing, but he let it leak he'd worked him six furlongs in 1.09 and three fifths. I've never seen a studio so dead. Even the bookies disappeared."

"I remember that day," said Edna. "Every secretary on the lot went home with a headache. The guy I was working for asked if we were trying to corner the aspirin market."

"The odds went down to three to five. On a first-time starter!" Dad's voice grew more and more excited. "Warner ran the horse eighth."

"A fourteen to one shot came in," Edna said.

"The next day I was told Warner had a grand on the winner. That son of a bitch. Next time out he won at eight to one."

Dad came back to the desk and picked up the *Form*. "Call that S.O.B. and see what he likes today," he told Edna. "Not that it matters."

Dad really enjoyed his gambling. It must be exciting, I thought.

Dad told Edna they would have to start keeping regular office hours, from nine in the morning until six at night, instead of coming in at 7.30 and leaving at noon. He was settling down to work now that the fun was over. Dad gave me $5 and said I should have breakfast at the commissary, then walk around the studio. There was a lot to see, he said, and I could go onto the soundstages and watch them making movies as long as I went in when the red light over the door wasn't on. When it was on it meant they were shooting and needed quiet.

I walked to the far end of the main street. There was a whole Western town there: the Last Chance Saloon, a hotel, Dodge City railroad station. None of the buildings had insides, only fronts held up by a network of wooden braces. How different things turn out from the way you imagine them. It was sad to find out they didn't use real old towns, to see how empty dreamland was. Listening to my footsteps on the plank sidewalk, I tried to believe the town was real. I kicked a stone. It clattered along the planks and came precariously close to falling into the dry mud street, into a time-hardened rut left by a wagon that could have been bringing a boy and his father to town. The stone stopped against a bench in front of the general store. The father would have had an isolated ranch in the mountains and the mother would have died long ago of a mysterious disease. The man and his son, who was probably my age at the time, worked the ranch alone together. Once a month they would come to town for provisions. There weren't movies then so they went to the square dance down there at the corner, at the livery stable, on Saturday night. And if his Dad got drunk it was alright. The boy would help him onto the wagon and drive all night and all the next day to get home. They were very close. "Nonsense," I said as a new station wagon let two workman off at the sheriff's office. They took down the Dodge City sign hanging over the door and replaced it with one that said Laramie. "Nothing's real that you want to be."

"Has Max come by?" asked Dad when he got back from his meeting.

"Next Friday's fine," Edna answered. "How did it go?"

"Lousy," Dad said, "but I'm going to make that the best damn war picture to come out of Hollywood in years." He picked up a script from his desk, turned to me, and said, "Let's get out of here."

"Bit of advice," Edna said.

"Sure."

"Don't break your heart if your hopes finish down the track behind their reality. It's a war picture."

"Enough said," whispered Dad. He pulled a check from his jacket pocket, the one Gloria must have given him, and said, "Deposit this for me." He handed the check to Edna.

"C'mon, son."

"I was supposed to quit today," Dad said as we drove off the lot. He parked behind one of the bars across the street from the studio and we went in. He ordered a drink of scotch for himself and a Coke for me. Then he stuck a nickel in the jukebox.

"You sure like music, don't you, Dad? I heard you listening to records…"

"Shh…" he said.

> I was walking down the street this morning,
> I heard someone call my name and I could not stop.
> I was broke and I was hungry
> On my way to the pawnshop.
>
> I went to the pawn shop
> 'cause the man done come and took my car.
> I'm going to the pawn shop in the morning
> to see if I can pawn my old guitar.
>
> I asked that pawnshop man,
> "What are those three balls on the wall?"
> He said, "Two to one, buddy,
> You won't get your things back out of here at all."

Dad drove hard and quiet on the way home.

5
Flower or Animal

How nice to have happy friends like Judy and Chris. I had always made enemies of kids in short order, but not this time.

Once I got to know Chris, he was okay. I paid the dollar and a half to ride like everybody else until, after a couple of weeks, I offered to help with chores, like cleaning stalls, raking the yard and feeding the horses and chickens. In exchange, I rode free and Judy gave me lessons. I did everything the Archers didn't like to do and enjoyed every minute of it. They were a real family. And, to top it off, Mr. Archer taught me how to shoot his .22 rifle. I suppose Chris was tired of hunting hawks with Mr. Archer because he never came with us. Chris didn't spend much time with his father at all. "Boy," I thought. "If my father were home at five o'clock every afternoon, I wouldn't leave him alone for a minute."

I asked Dad a hundred times to go shooting and riding. He kept saying he would try, and smile, but he never did come. He was always too tired during the week and too busy "taking care of social obligations" on the weekends, so after a while I stopped asking.

The Archers had an old Studebaker which no one in the family used. Mrs. Archer taught me how to drive it. Not the way Gloria did, just letting me hold the wheel, but really drive it. There was no law against me driving on the dirt road to the highway because it was private property. "Tony," Mrs. Archer said after showing me how everything worked, "go on out there and drive that thing. There's nothing around here you can hit to do any harm. You know where the brakes are. If another car comes along and you don't know what to do, hit 'em hard and don't be scared. Let the other fella figure it out." Driving around those fields like I owned them sure was fun. I planned to surprise Gloria once I drove perfectly and would have enjoyed showing Dad too, but I didn't dare.

Sumner Williams, Dad's nephew, my cousin, was working for Dad at the studio. He was about 21, a tall blond with a pompadour and a duck's ass. He came to the house on weekends and stayed in my room. I watched Sumner making telephone calls, mixing drinks and taking notes from Dad. None of that looked very complicated and I didn't see why, if I worked hard, I couldn't do the same things, at least on the weekends. But Dad said no and told me not to argue with him. On Saturday mornings we watched Dad play tennis with Mr. Kazan, another director who lived in Malibu. Then, in the afternoon, he went to the racetrack. On Sunday afternoons he played canasta at the Bloomingdales' house.

Sumner tried to teach Gloria and me to play tennis, but we weren't very good. I practiced a lot by myself, hitting the ball against the back of the garage which faced the tennis court. At least Dad was home late Sunday afternoons in time to barbecue steaks on the beach. He took me to the Bloomingdales' twice. He won the first time, but the second time he had to write a check. He was all smiles until we were in the car, then he got real morose. "That isn't really gambling," he said, "only a necessary afternoon's relaxation. I could as easily have spent that much money in nightclubs over a year. And I don't go to nightclubs."

When I wasn't at the Archers doing my chores or riding, I stayed home with Gloria and she did voice exercises, read, let me brush her hair a hundred times, or we lay on the beach. She was more of a movie star than I had realized. People stopped her in stores and on the street for autographs.

Gloria and I exploded into conversation whenever we were together. There wasn't any difference between us. "For all I know, the way we talk, we could be the same age." She said that, not me. I didn't get all pent up and panicky inside with her the way I did with Dad. If it hadn't been for Gloria, I think I would have lost all hope. One afternoon, just as the sun was falling into the sea and we were wrapping ourselves in a blanket to keep warm, Gloria said that being with Dad before they were married made her believe she was going to have an ideal combination of the excitement and intensity of her first husband Stanley and all the protection and comfort she remembered getting from her father before he left.

"It was as if I had seen an extraordinary store window and had gone inside only to find the toys didn't work."

I thought of Dad's smiles, the ones he gave that were wonderful promises, that seemed like invitations to much more, but never were.

"The toy store sounds like the Western town with the phony fronts at the studio," I said.

"Oh no!" Gloria gasped. "Acting is a thrilling game. All your dreams come true in some parts. And the others... well... then it was only a game." She shivered and snuggled up close to me. "You can't get hurt."

"You're right," I said. "I had a great daydream on the Western set, and I believed every minute of it." I studied the sandcastle we had built and watched the tide creeping closer and closer to it. Then I pulled the blanket up over our heads so we were in total darkness. "Everything real dies."

"We'll never die," Gloria said.

I went to court with Gloria to pay her speeding ticket. We had kept our secrets about the ticket and the smoking, and she still gave me cigarettes when I needed them. It didn't embarrass me or feel wrong to smoke in front of Gloria, but it bothered me a lot that I was shorter than she was. I thought a boy should be taller, or at least as tall, as a girl. "My God, Tony, when did you get so big?" she asked on the way to the car. I bit my lip and didn't say anything. She looked me up and down trying to figure out exactly how tall I had been but ended up shrugging her shoulders and leaving it at that. I didn't tell her I had stuffed socks in my shoes. It was hard to walk though, with a whole pair under each heel.

The fog lifting from the water, the sun when it first broke through, the brief moments with Dad before he went to work, brushing Gloria's hair while we planned the day. Those were my favorite times.

In the morning, I often found Dad stretched out on the couch, snoring, with one arm hiding his unshaven face and the other hanging over the side of the couch as if reaching to put out the cigarette that had burned out hours before in the ashtray on the floor. A half-filled glass, a bottle of whiskey and a script were always spread before him on the coffee table. If Dad woke when I came through the living room on the way to the kitchen, we had more time than usual together over a cup of coffee. It was on one of those mornings I learned he was going away on location for three months beginning in September. "It's no different than being the son of a traveling salesman," I told myself, "or anyone else who has to travel for work." But I had to grit my teeth over the prospect of my time with Dad being reduced from little to none. As cheerfully as I could, I said, "Gloria and I will manage okay."

"You and Gloria get along well, don't you?"

"Oh, yes," I said. Dad glowered into his cup and said nothing. "Why, Dad—didn't you think we would?"

"No, no," he shook his head, "I only hoped you'd find companionship with people your own age."

"There's Judy Archer," I offered, "but she's sort of a tomboy. Not too sharp." Dad smiled. "The first day I met her I said I wasn't sure there was a God. She's been scared of me ever since."

"Never mind, son." Dad looked at his watch and gulped his coffee. "Have to get dressed."

"I'd much rather go with you," I said, as Dad disappeared into his bedroom, but I don't think he heard me.

After seeing Dad off to the studio, I went back to the house and turned on the hi-fi.

"Is that you, Tony?" Gloria called from the bedroom.

"Who were you expecting? Marlon Brando?"

"Bring me some juice and coffee."

"Sure." I fixed a tray, went to her door, and knocked.

"Tony?"

"Yes, stupid." I opened the door.

"Has Nick gone to work yet?"

"He just left."

Gloria propped herself up against both pillows. I put the tray on the nightstand and handed her the orange juice. Gloria patted the spot on the bed next to her, and I sat down. "Hey, lie down. Relax." She reached over and mussed my hair. "What are you doing today?"

"I don't know yet." I was thinking about what Dad had said. "I might go to the Archers' or hitch a ride into town. I've been saving up my allowance." Dad's half of the bed hadn't been slept in. The jar of face cream next to the bed had been left open.

"Come with me," Gloria said. "We'll have fun. I have to make a deposit at the bank, then we'll go shopping. We'll find something for you, too."

"I should go to the Archers'."

Gloria finished her juice and leaned over me to put the glass on the table. Her face hovered right over mine. She set the glass down. Then, instead of going right back where she had been, she lay across me, put a finger on my nose, and said, "I really want you to come with me, silly."

"Okay," I said. I wanted her to get up. My whole body was tightening. The way Gloria made me feel inside wasn't right, like a butter churner in motion. She kissed the end of my nose, then bit it, and bounded out of bed. Her white nightgown barely covered her.

"You're awfully cute," she said from the bathroom. "I wish you were ten years older. Come keep me company. Talk to me while I shower." I went to the bathroom and sat on the john. "Turn around."

I felt her nightgown floating down behind me. I thought of her standing there nude, fiddling with the hot and cold water. I wanted to spin around, and at the same time I wanted to run out of the room. She stepped into the shower and closed the door. I picked up the nightgown and crumpled it into a ball.

It smelled good, of flowers mingling with the animal base of Joy perfume. Gloria had told me all about perfumes, how the flower perfumes were for innocent girls, and the animal ones for women. She told me Joy was her favorite. I watched the lithe silhouette behind the opaque shower door. I couldn't really see anything, only Gloria's outline.

"Are you flower or animal?" I asked.

"Animal, silly. I told you that."

I hadn't thought of Gloria this way before, except for an instant that first night when she kissed me goodnight. I wondered what she meant by saying I was cute and that she wished I were ten years older. "How much older than you is Dad?" I asked.

"I haven't got enough toes and fingers to count that high." Then I heard her subtracting. "My God, Tony. Nick's seventeen years older than I am." The shower stopped. "Hand me a towel, doll." Gloria held her arm over the door and I gave her the towel, which she wrapped around herself. Then she stepped out of the shower, took a smaller towel from the rack, and lowered the bath towel to her waist as she turned her back to me. "Dry my back, dollface." The full part of her breasts was white next to the rest of her skin where the tan line ended. I had never dried a girl's back before and I took my time, but tried to think about something else at the same time. I couldn't help it—I was getting excited. I draped the towel around her neck. Gloria pulled the bath towel up high again and I went back to the bedroom. My forehead and hands were covered with beads of sweat.

"Doesn't Dad want us to be friends?" I called to her.

"What makes you say a thing like that?" Gloria came out of the bathroom in a pink bathrobe and her hair wrapped in a towel like a turban. She sat down at the dressing table.

"He said something when we were having coffee this morning."

"Oh?" Gloria caught my eye in the mirror. She poised her mascara brush between two fingers. "What?"

I repeated the conversation almost word for word. Gloria said nothing when I finished but she seemed pleased. The corners of her mouth turned up in a knowing half smile when I said Dad had dropped the subject. I said I would much rather go to the studio with him. Gloria laughed at the age thing. It was sort of funny when you thought about Dad telling me to find companionship my own age with Gloria being 26 and Dad about to turn 39. "He doesn't have to know everything we do," Gloria said, "if it's going to bother him."

Gloria went to the bank, then bought a pile of Stanislavsky acting books for herself and stationery for me. It was blue, rough-edged paper with matching envelopes, exactly like Dad's, except his was gray. Then she took me to a Western store and bought me a pair of cowboy boots. I wore them out of the store and I was as tall as Gloria. "Nick's birthday is less than a month away, in August, so if we want to order a special present for him, we should do it now." For the rest of the morning, we walked from shop to shop in Beverly Hills. At one point, as we left a leather store, Gloria laughed and said, "Look at us, we're holding hands like a couple of teenagers." At lunch we discussed all the gift possibilities we had seen. Gloria decided on a beautiful silver cigarette case. I thought it cost too much, but Gloria had her heart set. When we finished our hamburgers and chocolate malts, we went back to the jewelry store. The salesman asked what we wanted inscribed on it. Gloria glanced at me, then wrote something on the piece of paper the salesman had given her. "Do you approve, dear?" she said with an English accent and handed me the slip. "Would script or print be fitting?" I was pleased to read: "To Nick. Happy Birthday. Love Gloria, Tony and Tim."

"Script, I should say." I tried to imitate Gloria's accent. So it was settled. I insisted on giving Gloria $20 toward the price. I had saved the money from my allowance. I could never have bought such a wonderful present myself, and this way it would be from all of us. Mom always said it was nicer to have one good thing than a lot of junk.

At dinner, Dad asked what I had done during the day. I told him I had gone to the Archers.' Gloria said she went to get her account straightened out at the bank and had her hair trimmed. When Dad got up for a second to hang up his jacket, I asked Gloria why she said she'd had her hair cut. "I could take it all off and wear a man's toupee," she said, "and Nick wouldn't know the difference."

After dinner I went to my room and wrote Mom.

Dear Mom.

We haven't decided on a school yet. As a matter of fact, we really haven't talked about it. But I'm so glad there won't be any more boarding schools. I don't mean that I blame you or anything, it's just that I'm happy I'll be coming home every night. I'm planning on going to Samo-Hi. That's in Santa Monica. I'm worried about what Dad has in mind because he said there were better schools, but that's the only school around here that has a bus to take us back and forth. It looks like Dad has to go away to work for a few months pretty soon. He's making a big war picture with John Wayne. Isn't that keen? I've made friends with some people who live near us. They have horses and all, and I ride a lot. I even get to shoot guns. They have kids who go to Samo-Hi. Why can't I go there? Will you talk to him about it? I'm sorry I haven't answered all your letters, but I've been so busy getting to know my father I just haven't had time. He's wonderful. Everybody likes him where he works. He's taken me there a few times.

How are you? Are you happy, and all? Gloria and I got Dad a beautiful cigarette case for his birthday.

We're going to let it come from Tim, too. We hope he likes it. Please write soon.

Love and Kisses, your son, Tony.
XXXXXXOOOOOOXXXXXXOOOOOO

P.S. Gloria bought me this stationery. Isn't it exclusive? This is just a sample. The store is having my name printed on all the rest of it. It's just like Dad's. We don't call each other Mom and son, and all that stuff. We're real great friends. Love, again.

6
Running Was Useless

Dad shook the cigarette butt after digging it out of the sand where I had tried to bury it with my foot. Then he rolled it around in his fingers to the brand printing. The way his lips tightened in a hard angry line and the blood drained from his face when he saw that it was a Pall Mall made me sick. "I suppose Gloria gives you these."

"No," was my dry-throated, almost inaudible, reply. "I take them." I couldn't even look at Dad when I said it. He took a deep breath and sighed heavily.

"I'll have to punish you, you know," he said, as though resigned to the situation.

His large hand took a firm grip under my elbow and pulled me toward the house. I couldn't blame Dad for being sore. He had caught me dead to rights. *How stupid can you be?* I asked myself when I thought of the mistakes I had made. I switched off the record player which I knew woke Dad. I hadn't brought the cellophane-wrapped blob of toothpaste I usually used to kill my breath. Then, knowing Dad was awake, I gave him plenty of time to get dressed while I screwed around in the kitchen before going out. If I had wanted to get caught, I couldn't have planned it better.

I could tell Dad was completely absorbed in thought about me—not smiling to appese me while his mind was off in some strange world, not trying to concentrate on something else when I talked to him, but focused entirely on me.

Splinters of driftwood, clusters of kelp washed up on the beach to die, the ocean itself... They were all small and meaningless. The whole world was filled like a giant glass of wine running over with the importance of Dad thinking about me, and I wanted to drown in it. I felt more a part of him, in trouble, than ever before. In that instant I almost forgot I had been caught smoking. Dad jerked me through the gate and into the yard, then led me along the side of the house to the garage.

"I'll never do it again," I pleaded. "Really, Dad." But he wasn't having any of that.

My mind flooded with outs. I had been good except for the smoking. I hadn't asked Dad to take me to the studio again, or to fish with me, or anything, for weeks. I even told him to get the money back on the rod and reel he had bought me if he wanted, and I knew how important the money was to him. What about all the times he said Gloria and I didn't understand him? Why couldn't he understand this *one time*? I was getting scared and didn't know what to do. I hated taking a beating like any other kid, but the idea of running was useless. It would only make things worse unless I made up my mind to never come back. I started undoing my pants.

When Dad returned carrying a heavy belt, I panicked and got dizzy. Everything around me—the walls, and Dad, and the lightbulb—began spinning. I tried to fasten my eyes on Gloria's car to keep from falling to my knees. "What a chicken shit I am," I thought to myself. My hands, which had been holding up my pants, went to my head and the pants fell down.

Dad told me to lean over the fender. His voice sounded like it was coming through a filter or from under deep water. Then, by magic or an act of God, Gloria walked in.

"What's this all about?" she asked.

"Keep out of it," Dad said. "You're responsible for this. If you were his age, I'd..."

"You'd what?"

"Go back to the house."

"No. Nick, he isn't a child. He's all grown up."

"Please go away," I said. I raised my pants to my waist. It wasn't that I was trying to get out of the beating, I just couldn't stand having her see me like that.

"I won't go. I want to watch big Nick hit you."

Dad's face flushed and he threw the belt as hard as he could to the floor at Gloria's feet. Then he got into his car and started it. "Tony," he breathed only loud enough for me to hear, "never again, understand?" Dad threw the Ford into gear and tore off.

Gloria rushed over and tried to hug me, but I wouldn't let her.

"Do you want to come with me? I'll give you a grand tour of my studio."

"No thanks," I said as I hurried past her. "I want to be alone today."

By four in the afternoon the sky had filled with a mass of black clouds. Wind sliced the tops off the breakers and slapped the shutters back and forth on the ocean side of the house. The radio said it was going to be the first August storm in years. Gloria came home drenched around six, and Dad called shortly after. I couldn't hear what was said because Gloria closed the bedroom door, but I bet he was darn sore at her. I wasn't anymore. After all, she had saved my skin. When they finished talking, Gloria called me to the phone. Dad said he was sorry about the "smoking bit" but I had to learn right from wrong. What was he sorry about? Then he said he was staying in town overnight.

After dinner I built a crackling fire, even though it wasn't cold. I lay down on the rug in front of it with *Twenty Thousand Leagues Under the Sea* and the Sunday newspaper. Gloria went to the little house to play with Tim and put him to bed. When she came back an hour or so later, she fooled around in her room for a while, then came out to the living room and tried to read a book. But she was in no mood for it. She stalked around like a caged animal, marching back and forth between the fireplace and the rain-pelted bay window, pulling the drapes closed to shut out the storm, searching the room for something to do. One of the bedroom shutters slammed and Gloria almost jumped out of her skin. "Jesus, I'm bored." She threw her arms up in exasperation, then stood over me twiddling her thumbs.

"Sit down," I said. "You're making me nervous."

"Bored, bored, bored," she sighed. Then, at the end of her breath, as though a last resort, she asked, "Do you know how to dance?"

"No." I hid behind the newspaper.

"I'm going to teach you," Gloria said with grim determination.

"No, you're not." I kept reading. "I'm not making a fool of myself so you can have a good time."

Gloria snatched the paper out of my hands and threw it on the fire. "Whether you like it or not," she said, "a boy has to dance." I watched the funnies going up in smoke. What a crime. I'd been saving the Sunday comic section as a treat for days.

"What did you go and do that for?"

"The world is dull," Gloria answered as she pulled me to my feet.

"But now I'll never know if Dick Tracy caught…"

"Make us a drink," she cut me off. "That's an order."

"I'd rather play canasta," I grumbled on my way to the kitchen for ice.

Gloria was screwing around in her room when I brought the ice bucket back to the bar, so I went ahead and poured the drinks. She liked vodka and orange juice. At least she was letting me have some, too. That was pretty neat. I filled two glasses with half orange juice and half vodka. I had tasted liquor plenty of times. I must have been seven or eight when I starting sipping from my mother's bottles at home, even though she marked the labels. All I had to do to fool her was add water when I finished. But I never had the chance to mix a drink as strong as I wanted.

I tasted one of the drinks. Nothing. It wasn't strong like Dad's Scotch, and I decided it might taste better if it was sweeter, so I hurried into the kitchen and dumped a heaped spoonful of sugar into the glass, stirred it up, and drank it down. Then I went back to the bar and refilled my glass. I was afraid Gloria wouldn't allow a second drink. When Gloria came back to the living room, I was sitting on one of the stools with my head on the bar. It was swimming. The vodka had surprised me. Gloria put a bunch of records on. The thought of dancing made me sick. I didn't think I could walk let alone dance.

"You're not tired, are you?" Gloria asked.

"Heck, no." I turned to face Gloria, but I couldn't quite focus on her. She had changed into two blue cashmere sweater shirts and a couple of white pleated skirts. She had four bare feet.

"There's a box of candy in the cabinet above the stove," Gloria said. "Go get it, will you?"

"Sure." I climbed off the bar stool and made my way to the kitchen, keeping my hand on the wall for balance. When I got there, I stuck my head under the cold water faucet and dried myself with a dish towel. It helped.

Gloria held my hand and we tapped our feet to the beat of different kinds of music. Then, when a waltz came up, she told me to try walking to it. "One, two, three, four," she counted as I walked across the room. As stupid as it made me feel having a girl teach me how to dance, I was excited about learning.

"You've got it!" Gloria said at the end of the number. "Now take off your boots and come here." She put the needle back to the beginning of the same record, held one of my hands in hers, and placed the other on the back of my neck. I held her around the waist. "Find the beat again," she instructed, "and I'll lead you."

"One, two, three, four," I counted.

"It's a box, that's all. Right, back, left, forward."

I made my feet follow hers. Once in a while I stepped on her toes, but she didn't get mad. I did, though. It drove me nuts. That was the worst thing a boy could do. Whenever it happened, I stormed off to the bar and took a gulp of my screwdriver. Gloria patiently convinced me to try again every time. After a while I was leading her. It was fun and I didn't want to stop. I made Gloria play the same record over and over until we were sick of it. During a break we finished our drinks and made another. Gloria warned me about making them so strong. She opened the box of candy when the next record turned out to be a Lindy. "Let's sit it out."

"Did you hear footsteps?" I asked. It was cold and black and the wind kept howling. We moved from the bar where it was dark to the floor in front of the fire.

"Umm, good." Gloria barely got the words out of her half-closed mouth. She searched the box for another candy like it but didn't find one. "I'll share this with you."

"How?" I laughed. We were pretty drunk.

"Stand up," she said, "and I'll show you." Gloria tilted her head back and took my face in her hands. "Open your mouth and close your eyes." I did as she said. "Not that wide, silly, only a little bit." She kissed me and I tasted the candy. It lasted a long time, until there was no sweetness left. While it was happening, I tried to tell myself we were like children sharing a piece of gum, but it was no use. It was nothing like that at all. "That was good," Gloria said when she drew away.

"Yes." I went to the bar for my drink. Gloria was staring into the fire.

"I've been wanting to do that ever since I saw a picture of you playing stickball on the street." Gloria turned toward me and smiled. "You were so dark and intense."

We danced a lot and shared a lot more candy, and had some more to drink, before Gloria went to her room and I went to mine. I thought of how afraid I used to be of lightning and thunder. One summer a long time ago I went to visit my father's mother and sisters who lived in a spooky old house in LaCrosse, Wisconsin. There were bats in the attic and one of the kids I played with told me they came swooping down into the bedrooms and made nests in your hair. I believed him.

"Are you awake?" Gloria was at my door.

"Yes."

"What's wrong?" she asked.

"Lonely, that's all. We don't have an attic, do we?"

"No, silly. Come into my room. I'm feeling the same way."

Gloria pulled down the covers and got into bed. I watched her spreading night cream all over her face.

"What's wrong with Dad," I asked. "Is he always so miserable?"

"Most of the time."

"But he's successful and all, and has a family. My mother doesn't have either of those things."

"Climb in," Gloria said.

"What?"

"Hop into bed. If you think I'm staying alone tonight, you're daffy."

"Do you trust me?" I asked.

"No one's touched me in so long…"

"I didn't mean that way."

"Oh," Gloria laughed. "I only trust children. They're so honest. But I'm not sure you're a child anymore." She patted the bed. "Let's get some sleep. We're going to have terrible hangovers as it is." I crawled under the blankets and snuggled up close to Gloria. "It'll be alright, Tony. I promise."

I was banging tennis balls against the garage when Dad came home late the next afternoon. He just waved hello and nodded on his way past the court to the house. I waited a few minutes hoping he might change his clothes and come out to play with me. Then I decided to take the bull by the horns and ask him to play. He couldn't stay mad at me forever. I was just about to knock on the bedroom door when Gloria stopped me. "He's taking a nap," she warned. I put away the racket and balls, washed up, and played solitaire until dinnertime. After dinner, Dad got up, stopped in the hall door on his way back to bed, and said, "We'll find a school for you this week or next."

"How about Samo-Hi?" I asked.

Dad squinted his eyes and frowned as though he resented being reminded that I knew where I wanted to go to school. He had told me to find one, after all. And I had done really well in public school last year. "I can only say…" Dad took a long drag on his cigarette, then exhaled and started over again. "I can only say I don't think Santa Monica High School would work well." That was that. He turned on his heel and disappeared into his room.

"I wish he hadn't come home," I mumbled.

Gloria and I cleared the table, rinsed the dishes, and stacked them in the sink for Constance to wash in the morning. We didn't say a word to each other. I sat at the kitchen table building a house and fence of sugar cubes. "What's wrong with Samo-Hi?" I asked.

"He better explain that one himself," she said. I could always tell when Gloria was burning by the way she pursed her lips and the clipped manner with which she said things. I had tried to start a conversation with Dad at dinner, but he didn't want to talk.

Sometimes I thought Dad just didn't care for me much. I could never suggest things for us to do because I didn't know what he enjoyed except playing tennis and cards. Neither did Gloria. I wondered how people could get married who didn't really know each other. Did they just imagine what it would be like?

"How about a glass of wine for a lift?" asked Gloria. I didn't answer. She poured two glasses anyway, and even though wine was the farthest thing from my mind, I drank it and enjoyed it.

"Is Dad mad at you, too?"

"He's sore at the whole world."

"That's stupid," I said. "I started smoking a long time before you knew me."

Gloria shrugged her shoulders and poured us each a little more wine.

"I'll tell him you had nothing to do with it."

"Don't bother," said Gloria. "He likes to think people are conspiring against him."

"Why won't Samo-Hi work?" I asked. Gloria said nothing. I knocked over my sugar house. "The bus picks up the kids in the morning and brings them home after school. It's the only school around here." Gloria turned her glass in her hand and shook her head. I went on trying to convince her. My voice cracked. I got up and paced back and forth. I knew if I said anything else I would cry. When I regained control, I tried again. "Except for catching me smoking, I haven't been bad at all. He won't let me near him." Words rushed out faster and faster. "What should I do? How do you make him happy? It's a great school!" Gloria turned me around and held me.

"He doesn't let anyone near him," Gloria said. "Not even me. Sometimes I think there's nothing to get to."

Gloria held my shoulders while they shook. I could have killed Dad at that moment, actually gone up and beaten him to death for not being what I wanted him to be. Why couldn't I stay with Dad and Gloria? There was always someone at the house. It wasn't like with Mom having to go out to work with no one to look after me. But even then I did okay. I got my own breakfast, bought a sandwich for lunch at the Italian deli, and played with friends after school. They had Constance to take care of Tim. She could look after me, too, if she even had to. I wasn't any trouble. And Gloria would be there, too.

"I've been counting on this, Gloria. All my life I've wanted Dad to make it stop. I've dreamed of getting to know him, of living at home, and doing stupid little things with him. Nothing special, just little things. Why couldn't he play cards with me?"

"Simple things," said Gloria, "aren't always easy to get."

"And no more of those schools. They're terrible, and there isn't anyone to talk to. Mom sometimes left me there for months. She'd come visit once in a while. Please, please…"

Gloria wrapped her arms around my shoulders and hugged me, but I couldn't stop crying. "Dad promised."

"Your father loves you. He must be doing what he thinks best."

"Do you love me?"

"Yes." Gloria hugged harder. "Of course I do."

"Then whose side are you on?" I broke loose and went running to my room. When I woke up, I heard Dad yelling. "Tony has done everything from stealing to burning down a barn!"

"That was years ago. He's been perfect for a long time."

"Now this smoking episode, and you supporting it. If you think I enjoy seeing him miserable, tell me why I brought him out here."

"Out of guilt, and because I wanted you to."

"Oh, come on."

I waited for Gloria to say something, but she didn't. There was just silence. Then Dad said, "This is hardly the environment for Tony."

I bounded out of bed and into jeans and a sweatshirt. Out of my room, through the living room, the screen door, the yard, out onto the beach. Walk, walk, walk… run. Bare feet digging into the cold night sand. Black sky, horns blowing on the steep blind hill. Feet running nowhere, tears falling everywhere, spray. Run, run, run, until I fall out of breath, drained. Dull, aching. Lie on the sand and go to sleep folded in the arms of night, of warmth, of love. Mother, your petticoat makes a nice noise, like bacon. I'm sorry, Mom. I'm sorry. Rip out the rotten badness. Rip it out so I'll be perfect. Star light, star bright, where are you? Black sky, sleep. Die there, smothered by the tide, if he doesn't come. Hate him for letting me die. He must come. Will come. Sleep.

"Wake up. Tony. Wake up." I was being shaken.

"Where's Dad?"

Gloria held my head in her lap and lit a cigarette.

"Why are you here? Where's Dad?"

"Asleep, I think." Gloria gave me a drag of the cigarette. "I haven't gotten over my father," she said. "Nick's father died in a barroom when he was sixteen. Your image was full of hope. Losing hope is worse than anything."

I got up and walked to the water's edge.

"Should I go home?" I asked.

"It's chilly out here."

"No, I mean back to New York. He'd be happier if I went away. Where's the moon and stars? The night is so black and lonely."

"We'll have weekends together," she said. "Just you and me. Come on, let's go in." She took my hand. "Tomorrow is Nick's birthday, remember? Let's give him a good time, see if we can make him smile for a change. Maybe he'll even laugh a little, okay?"

"Sure."

"I don't want you to go. And you don't want to lose those hours with the time change."

We went inside to our rooms. Maybe if I went along with Dad's ideas for a while and got Gloria to keep working on him, I could come home to live when Dad returns from location, I thought. Three months isn't so very long. I hadn't even undressed when Gloria burst into my room.

"Nick isn't here?"

"Isn't he in the house? I thought he was asleep."

We went out to look for him. His car was gone. Dad must have known Gloria was with me. Something else for him to be furious about. Nothing ever worked out right. I closed the gate.

"Does Dad often just take off?"

"When he's drinking a lot."

"Has he been?" I asked.

"It's hard to tell sometimes. He drinks most when he can't kid himself about his own illusions anymore, when he makes a mistake and knows it, the way you ran out of the house tonight." She looked for my reaction but I was confused. "Don't you know what I mean?"

"No."

"He likes to think of himself as an artist," Gloria explained, "but he won't take the risk of not making much money for a while. He always needs money. He won't wait for the right script." She cupped her face in her hands and yawned. "I think he's driven by his habits."

I took her hand.

"C'mon, we better go inside."

7
Happy Birthday

Gloria and I tried to see who could blow up the most balloons. Red, yellow and blue balloons for Dad's birthday. Tim tried to squash them. We hung crepe paper wall to wall, crisscrossing it in every direction. We set the table with noisemakers and favors. The chocolate cake was hidden in the closet in my room. By two o'clock, the house was cheerfully decorated. Then we drove into Beverly Hills to pick up Dad's present at the jewelry store. It sure was beautiful. I had never seen my name engraved on anything before. On the way home, we bought steaks, potatoes, salad stuff and lots of ice cream. We were going to give Dad a barbecue to which no one was invited but us.

It was a wonderful day. I was already beginning to convince myself that Dad might change his mind about school. There were still three weeks of vacation to go. Maybe if I could be really good, not get caught smoking, try hard the rest of the summer, maybe he would let me stay home. Whitecaps danced in the sun, the car radio played happy music, and I leaned back and watched billowing white clouds float past. "Gloria," I said. "Gloria, I love you." Her eyes crinkled with pleasure and she smiled. "I'm not kidding," I said.

"I really, really, love you."

"I love you, too, silly." She put her hand over my mouth and I kissed it. "Don't you forget it," she added.

Gloria called Edna to make sure that Dad was planning to come home. She said Dad had come to the studio late last night and wandered around the lot. She found him sleeping on his pride and joy, the couch in his office. The guards told Edna they had seen him sitting on the sidewalk in front of stage seven humming songs to himself. They thought that was pretty funny, but I felt sorry for him. I remembered the time I sat on that lonesome back lot.

"He's coming home," Gloria announced.

"Good! Good!" we began to chant. "Party! Party! Get ready for the party!"

I lit the coals in the barbecue while Gloria made the salad. Constance fed Tim. We were all ready to put the steaks on at seven o'clock. I waited in front of the garage for Dad. I was to warn Gloria when his car pulled up so she could get Tim and Constance into the living room in time to sing Happy Birthday when we walked in. The way we planned it, I was to lead Dad around the house and make him come in from the beach side. Gloria was posted at the living room window.

When Dad stopped in the driveway, I opened the car door for him and bowed like the doorman at a fancy restaurant. "Good evening, sir," I said.

"Hi." Dad gathered his books and papers from the seat. He had a sour look on his face, like someone who had just eaten a whole lemon, and I could have sworn he was plain ignoring me. Maybe he didn't know it was his birthday.

"Did you have a good day?"

"Okay," he said. Dad got out of the car and brushed past me toward the house. I hurried alongside him.

"Want to walk on the beach?"

"No, thanks, son."

"Oh, come on, Dad!" I grabbed his arm and turned him around. "I want to talk to you."

"What's this all about?" I led him back to the garage and onto the road. "Suddenly you want to talk to me?"

I would take him through the neighbor's yard, onto the beach, then back to the house. But I did also want to talk to him.

"What's on your mind?" Dad asked.

"Nothing special." Dad put his arm across my shoulders. It felt good. I put my arm around his waist. I would do anything if it could be like this more often. "I'll try anything you want, Dad." I stopped walking and looked Dad straight in the eye. "No matter how I feel about boarding school, I'll try. If that's what you want." Dad set his jaw. He stared at me like an angry sun fixating on a weed in the garden—not with obvious harshness, but with a warmth that grew hotter, a look that acknowledged my dependence on the sun's light while hinting it could just as easily kill me. I realized at that moment that he didn't know I knew about boarding school yet. I tried to go on through our neighbor's yard and onto the beach, but Dad didn't budge.

"Has Gloria been relaying private discussions to you?"

"It wasn't her fault, Dad," I explained. "I know that Samo-Hi is the only school around here."

"What were you doing on the beach in the middle of the night?" Dad sighed heavily, as though he figured I was beyond hope. "Smoking?"

"No, Dad. I was upset. I went for a walk. Gloria came after me, that's all."

"What were you upset about?" he asked. That really burned me up. All the good cheer of the day was getting away from me. I could feel myself getting mad, a tantrum building up inside like a pressure cooker. I was trying to get along. I was even letting him know I would forget about his promise, but Dad probably didn't even remember making it.

"Because you promised," I exploded. "You promised there wouldn't be any more boarding schools."

"I see," Dad said as he turned away from me and started through the neighbor's yard. I followed after him.

"Say something, Dad."

"I can't explain all my decisions," Dad muttered. I caught up to him. Dad looked troubled but it seemed like whenever something like this came up with Gloria or me, something important, he would get very quiet and not want to talk about it. That was infuriating. It was the kind of thing that made me want to break something or do something bad.

A man was sitting in a beach chair reading a book. He was surprised to see us coming through his property but he recognized Dad. "My son," Dad explained, "is taking me on a mysterious journey. Forgive the intrusion."

"Be my guest." The man smiled and went back to his book. Dad and I walked out onto the beach.

"I wish we had talked this over ourselves," Dad said. "Perhaps the emotionalism could have been avoided." The way he said things was so final. We got to the gate to our yard and Gloria rushed out to join us. She put her arm around Dad's waist and kissed him on the check. "What the hell is all this?" he asked Gloria.

"Just greeting the tired man back from the coal mines." We went in. Constance was holding the cake and Tim was at her feet.

We sang "Happy Birthday." At the end of the song, Gloria took the cake and carried it to Dad, who was blushing. "Make a wish," she said. Dad looked at each of us separately, then closed his eyes. "One, two, three—blow!" we all said together. He blew out the candle. Dad was funny. First he seemed embarrassed and uncomfortable, then as happy as a child. He truly hadn't expected a party, or for us to even remember that it was his birthday.

Dad lifted Tim, who was really much more interested in the balloons, to his shoulder and put an arm around me. Gloria held our gift out to him. He gave Tim to Constance, and opened it.

"It's beautiful," Dad whispered. Then he looked at the case for what seemed a long time before saying anything else. "Thank you very much. Really, thank you." Dad stood very near me. The expression on his face changed and I could tell he wanted to say something serious, but before he had a chance I gave him a bear hug, the kind my mother used to give me.

"Happy birthday," I said. Dad broke away and held my arms. "What wrong Dad?" He didn't answer. Instead, he went to the bar and fixed himself a drink. Constance hauled Tim off to bed.

"Are you ready for steak and salad?" Gloria asked.

"Not yet," Dad dismissed her and beckoned for me to come to him at the bar.

"Son," he said, "please excuse Gloria and me this evening. We have private matters to discuss."

"What about our party?"

"Look," he reached in his pocket, "here's five bucks. Get yourself some dinner at the Malibu Inn."

"We bought steaks and all," I urged. Dad set his jaw in that way that meant don't argue. "Did we do something wrong?"

"No," he smiled. "Thanks for the party." I looked to Gloria to see what she was thinking. She was furious. There was nothing for me to do. Dad turned me around and slapped me on the rear. "Now get going."

I was passing through the kitchen on my way out when I heard Gloria say, "Boy, Nick, you stink."

A beach town at dusk, stuck at the edge of the highway, is like a canceled stamp on a dead letter. Dinners are being eaten, flowers are crawling inside themselves for the night, and cars, some with lights on, some without, stream past like guided missiles heading toward their meaningless targets, blind to the towns whose heartbeats stopped when the sun went down. Malibu is as lonely as a tombstone. The grind and clack of my boots on the highway pavement sounded the same as shoes on the streets of New York, looking for something, anything, not knowing what. Giving up. New York had died for me, had become a place without hope, of bad memories. Now Malibu was becoming empty, too, and I wondered who drove those cars going home, if all towns were lonely towns, if all people are forever alone. Having decided to skip eating and save the money, I walked briskly past the gas station, crossed the highway, and continued along the edge of the Japanese flower fields. I had decided to visit the Archers for a while, then go home. They wouldn't mind. I turned up their road. Darkness swept over the countryside like a giant cold wave and the ocean breeze blew dusty day through the bark of the eucalyptus trees. It sounded like wind blowing through a haunted house. I zipped my leather jacket.

Dad had been pleased with his gift, but the party had been a bust. If I could have shown him how much I wanted to make him happy, I thought he might change his mind about boarding school. What did Dad have to talk to Gloria about that couldn't wait until after dinner and ice cream? Dinner… All those coals dying in the barbecue and the salad wilting. It wasn't right. Dad was wrong to ruin our party. I passed the bunkhouse where the wetbacks who worked the flower fields lived. Why was Dad sleeping on the couch or at the studio? Was it work, or liquor, or that he didn't like Gloria anymore? They hardly ever talked the way I imagined people talked. Why was it hard for me to think of Gloria as Dad's wife? Most important, what were they talking about that Dad wanted to be sure I didn't hear? I had to know. Light from the Archers' house flashed through the trees a couple of hundred yards up the road. I wanted to go home, but Dad would get mad if I went home early. Could it be Dad asked me to leave so he could be alone with Gloria? I closed my eyes and tried to picture them together in bed. The idea made me sick. It made me unbearably jealous and angry. But there was no one to be mad at. Who? Dad? Gloria? They were married. Myself? It wasn't right for me to be jealous or feel the way I did about Gloria.

I decided to go back to the house. I turned around and walked quickly back. I couldn't have been gone more than half an hour. I crossed the road and trotted toward our garage. I closed the gate behind me and edged past Tim's house, then the tennis court and the kitchen door. Where could I hide and still hear what was going on? By a window? No, I might be seen. Try to sneak into my room? That was a dumb idea. Under the house pilings. From the darkness of the trees I surveyed the space between the house and the sand. It was about three feet. I could move under any room and be safe. I darted across the lawn from the tennis court to the house, then crawled slowly, ever so slowly, underneath. There were no sounds from the kitchen or living room but I heard the hollow thumping of footsteps to my left. I crept across the sand and sat with my back against one of the pilings underneath Dad's and Gloria's room. They were there. I couldn't hear a word. I decided to wait about fifteen minutes before going in. That would have given me time enough to have had a hamburger or something. I lit a cigarette. I would have to go to the Malibu Inn soon so I could buy some. It wasn't good taking them from Gloria. She would get in trouble. I should get another brand, too, so if I got caught she wouldn't be blamed. A few minutes later there was silence in the bedroom. Then the kitchen door opened. When Dad finished coming down the steps I could see his legs. He was carrying a suitcase. I waited, then heard the garage door open and Dad's car start. Headlight beams flashed across the house, then retreated. Dad's car pulled away. I waited until I was sure Dad wasn't coming back, finished my cigarette, and crawled out from my hiding place. I went into the house and stopped in the kitchen for a glass of milk. "Is that you, Tony?" Gloria called from the bedroom.

"Yes," I tried to answer happily, but I could hardly hold the glass in my hand. I was so nervous. What was going on?

"Want a glass of milk?"

"No, thanks."

"Do you want one, Dad?" I asked as if he were home.

"He's gone out," Gloria called. "Tony, bring in a bottle of vodka, some juice, and ice, will you, doll?" I poured my milk back into the bottle, got a bucket of ice and a container of orange juice, then went into the living room to find the vodka. "Bring a glass for yourself, too." I went to the bedroom. "C'mon in," Gloria said, "and play personal bartender for me." I set the tray on the night-stand and kneeled beside it to make the drinks. Gloria was lying down. She was wearing a pale blue nightgown that had dozens of layers of thin material. You could see through each layer, but not through the whole thing. "Like it?" Gloria asked.

"A lot."

"You're the only one around here who's noticed it," she joked. "I'll have to wear it whenever we sleep together."

"How many have you had?" I asked.

"You're asking the wrong person," Gloria tweaked my nose and smiled. "I tried to keep up with Nick. It drove him crazy." She leaned back against the pillows. "Put on the Edith Piaf record and I'll finish making the drinks."

I did as she asked. "I've made a nightclub for us," she said when I got back to the bedroom. She had taken the bright white bulb out of the lamp by the bed and replaced it with a soft red one. The drapes had been pulled closed. She was sitting cross legged on the bed with a drink in her hand. Mine waited on the nightstand. "We have drink, song, and soft lights."

"Where's Dad?"

Gloria shrugged her shoulders. "We had another fight. The studio gave him a bungalow—that's like an apartment—on the lot. He's going to spend two or three nights a week there. He took a suitcase."

"What did you fight about?"

"About you, among many other things." I took a big gulp of my drink. It was strong. Gloria smiled at me. "Do you like Judy Archer?" she asked.

"She's okay."

"I mean, do you like her as a girl? "

"She's alright." I had never thought of Judy in any way other than as someone to ride with.

"Are you attracted to her?" Gloria pressed on. The truth was that except for one girl in New York, I had never kissed anyone except Gloria. And then it wasn't a French kiss like Gloria showed me.

"I'm not attracted to Judy," I said. "There was one girl I liked in New York."

"Tell me about her."

I closed my eyes and remembered. "She had long brown hair and worked at the 8th Street Playhouse after school and on weekends. She was the manager's daughter." It made me smile to remember. "Her breasts came to a point. She didn't wear falsies or anything. I know because I met her at the movie house whenever I could. She stopped meeting me when she found out I was only twelve." Although the room was beginning to spin and my body was sinking into the bed like a sultan riding a cloud, I thought I had complete control of myself.

"Refill, please." I held out my glass.

"You're drinking too fast," said Gloria.

"I have to catch up with you. You were keeping up with Dad and I have to catch up with you. Anyway," I buried my head in the pillow, "it makes me feel good. It's sexy."

"Then make us both one. You're closer to the bottle than I am. We'll get drunk."

I lifted my head and looked around.

"Is it true you burned down a barn?" asked Gloria.

"Did Dad tell you that? It was an accident. I was playing with my magnifying glass on a stack of hay and the hay caught fire. I wanted to see how big it could burn. It didn't burn down the whole barn. It was an accident. Why did Dad have to tell you that? Why did my mother have to tell Dad? Boy, I am getting drunk... How did I get up on the bed? I was sitting on the floor before." I dropped my head back on the pillows and lay there for what seemed a long time. The music was sounding so good. Everything started to get soft and fuzzy. I peeped at Gloria through my fingers. "You're a big white teddy bear," I said. I got up to go to the bathroom. The liquor hit the back of my head like a rock. I stumbled into the bathroom and had to work real hard to take a leak. Then I went out and flopped down on the bed again. Gloria caught me and laughed. I laughed, too, but I prayed she hadn't seen my erection.

"We sure have fun," Gloria said. I was lying on my stomach. Gloria hugged my shoulders. "Do you like me a lot?"

"Do I like you?" I leaned back against the headboard. "Do I like you?" I didn't know what to say. I already felt so lousy for liking her too much. But, hell, I thought, when would there be a better time for me to be honest? "Yes, I like you. It's there so strong and hard. I love you. Oh, boy..." I laughed self-consciously. "What did I just say?" A blurred Gloria was smiling down at me. "Did I say I love you? I must be out of my head. But it's true." I let my empty glass fall to the floor and turned my back on her. "Don't laugh at me." Gloria touched my head, ran her fingers through my hair.

"Don't feel bad. I'm glad, silly."

Her cool fingers worked their way under my sweatshirt and rubbed my back. Then her lips, warm and moist, brushed my neck.

I didn't move. I didn't even dare open my eyes. Gloria rolled me over so I was facing her. Her hands held my chest and waist and she kissed my stomach. The muscles flexed and drew away. "Relax," she said.

"I can't. I want to, but I can't. I need about twenty more drinks."

"Here, finish mine." She handed me her glass. I drank it down. "It was funny the way you kissed me with the candy."

"Funny?" I opened my eyes. She was so beautiful. It made me queasy to look at her. She was propped up on one elbow, leaning over me. The warmth of her bare legs penetrated my pants. That was terrible. What should I do? She touched my cheek gently. The way her yellow hair fell against her nightgown with beams of red light bouncing off it looked like cotton candy. A few strands of hair were on my lips.

"You kissed me that night. What did I do wrong?" I asked.

"Kiss me and I'll show you." I did, and when we were finished, she looked disappointed. "Is that how you kiss? After I showed you?" She made me feel stupid, as though I had made a fool of myself. It's true I wasn't as free with my mouth and tongue as she was, but I was unsure. "Someone has to teach you. Try to relax and do everything I do," she whispered in my ear as she pinned me down by putting one of her legs between mine. "Take off your boots."

I could still feel the moisture of her breath in my ear as I did what she said.

"Come here."

Gloria kissed my ear. I kissed hers. Her mouth hovered over mine. Her lips were parted. I parted mine. I followed every move she made, tensed and relaxed every muscle she did. Something inside began to tell me what to do, began to give me impulses. We kissed many times. I wanted to touch her, to let my hands wander. During a kiss I untied the bow at the top of her nightgown. I took her breast in my mouth. She stroked the back of my head. Tasted, touched, caressed. It was all gentle, delicate and clean, in the beginning. But then the need to envelop, to consume her, rushed over me as though my whole body screamed to be released from a red-hot furnace. Gloria pulled away.

"We have to stop," she said. "It's time to stop."

I picked up my boots and went to my room, then lay down on my bed and tried to calm down. Gloria came in about ten minutes later. She had a bathrobe on over her nightgown. "Tony, did you eat dinner?"

"No. I just took a walk."

"It's only nine o'clock. Let's eat. We'll feel better if we eat."

"Okay. That sounds good."

"Turn on the outside lights and put on the charcoal. I'll try to save the salad."

8
No Place to Hide

The air was damp and heavy. Fog blankets rolled like clouds of smoke down the slopes of the hills. The sun peeked sleepily through the hazy sky, suspended there by some magical force. We had to be at Harvard, a local military academy boarding school, at 8.30, so we left at seven. Dad drove in silence. Harvard was only an hour or so from the house, he had said — only a hop, skip, and a jump. *Only an hour or so from home*, I thought as I watched the telephone poles skip by. But not *at* home.

Dad's steel gray eyes negotiated the road automatically. He appeared distracted, as though seeing the road at all meant forcing himself to work through a dense screen which separated whatever it was that preoccupied his mind from the rest of the world. I would have asked what was bothering him, but I couldn't stop thinking about Gloria. I was afraid anything I might say would give me away. It was all I could do to say good morning to Dad when he came to pick me up. I went to the car without another word and never met his eyes straight on. I always kept to myself when I was upset or ashamed. I allowed the things that worried me most to build up and explode inside. That's when I got into trouble, when they exploded. There were times when I poured everything out though, like the night Gloria found me on the beach after Dad said I couldn't go to Samo-Hi. I wasn't taking any chances of having Dad lead me into talking about Gloria. *If I get away with it this time, I'll never do it again.* That's what I usually said to myself when I did something wrong. But right there in the car with Dad, the hunger for Gloria gnawed at my stomach. He turned off Pacific Coast Highway and drove into the hills.

"When are you going away?" I asked.

"What?" Dad snapped. He kept watching the road.

"Will you be gone a long time?"

The veil of thought that had been shading Dad's eyes lifted and his attention focused crystal clear on me.

"Gloria told you that, too, I take it."

His driving became pointed. He jerked the car in and out as he went around the cars he passed. Going into curves he hit the brakes, coming out of them he hit the gas. He couldn't get rid of me fast enough, I thought. Then it dawned on me. I had goofed again. Before his party, Dad found out Gloria had told me his decision on school. Now I had let it out I knew he was leaving soon. Couldn't I do anything right? But I didn't see why Dad was mad at Gloria for telling me things. Why was everything supposed to be a secret? I propped an elbow on the window ledge and held my head.

"I made her tell me, Dad." He said nothing. "I made her tell me because I didn't know why I had to go away to school." I looked to Dad for his reaction. He nodded his head slightly, which made me think he might have understood. He wasn't driving quite so fast anymore.

Trees, shrubs, rocks and a stretch of bare black limbs which must have been scorched by fire whizzed past. The sun shined warm and the sky was clear as we drove along the high ridge of the canyon I knew must be near school. We had been traveling over an hour. My breathing became short and my chest was aching. There was nothing I could do about it. I wiped my forehead with the back of my hand and fingered the knot of my tie. It was tight. The mountain side dropped sharply on my side of the road.

I hated Dad at that moment. I wondered what it would be like to jump out the car door as we went around a curve and go plummeting head over heels down, down, all the way to the valley below. I tried to remember the first place Mom had sent me to. It wasn't even really a school. It was just a home in the country where they took care of about ten kids. Then, when I was six, Mom sent me to my first real school, Hession Hills in Upstate New York, where they had the pony, Fanny, that I loved to take care of and that I ran away with. That place had been "only a little more than hour away from home" too.

"Are you giving me away?" I remember asking.

"Oh, no. God, no," she whispered, holding me tight. "You mustn't feel like that." Through her tears, she told me how she had once felt the same way. She and her brother were orphans who were brought up by foster parents. They were threatened that if they were bad, they would be sent back to the orphanage. But I mustn't think that way, she said. I only had to go because she couldn't find help to take care of me. There was a war on.

"You're mad at me because I hate you for making Daddy go away," I had said to her. "That's why you're giving me away." No matter what Mom said, I blamed her for everything.

I looked at Dad for a minute. He must have sensed I was watching him.

"Are you okay?" he asked.

"A little nervous," I said. He nodded his head and concentrated on driving again. I tried to remember the day Mom took me to Hessian Hills. I was scared then, too. We rode up on the train and took a taxi from the station to the school. Once there, it took a long time of walking around the school in mid-winter for us to say goodbye. We walked and walked, and eventually found ourselves in front of the dormitory. We both knew it was time. Mom bent over and kissed me. I hugged her and tried not to let go. I guess that's where our bear hugs started. Mom walked down the hill to the taxi stand. As she got further and further away, turning around every few paces to wave, her small figure which was wrapped up in the blue coat that wasn't quite warm enough, her brown hair with the slight gray streaks, and her thin mouth and tired pale eyes that reached out to me, grew smaller and smaller. I wanted to run to her but my feet were frozen in place.

Dad wound down the valley side of the canyon. Even though I had my hand on the door handle, I knew I didn't have the guts to jump out, just as I knew better than to run away anymore, and that I was getting too old for bear hugs. We came to a large red sign with black lettering on it that read "Harvard," and below, in smaller letters, "Under the auspices of the Episcopal Church." We had arrived.

Dad turned off the canyon road and passed through an open gate. A row of tan barracks ran the length of the football field. We passed a gymnasium, swimming pool and tennis courts. Everything was fenced in. The chain-link fence ran the length of the football field, keeping people away from the canyon road. Or was it there to keep the kids in? At least the gate wasn't locked. There was a chapel, a two-story building, and a parking lot at the top of the hill. Everything was the same color, tan with red tile roofing. It actually looked nice. I had never seen a place like this before. Dad pulled into a parking spot for visitors.

"Can I come home when you get back?"

"You should really finish out the school year where you start it."

It was always the same. If you were good, everyone thought you were happy and you should stay. If you were bad, or somehow managed to get kicked out, the answer was always another—worse—school. A squad of uniformed boys were marching in step toward the chapel. They looked like regular army men in summer khakis, but younger. They must have been juniors and seniors, I thought. The one marching to the side of the squad wore a shiny silver saber that hung from a wide garrison belt. "Hup, hup, hup, two, three, four," he counted.

Dad and I followed the signs to the administration building, which overlooked the football field, where more than two hundred cadets, divided into four platoons, were standing absolutely still. One of the commanding officers shouted "A... ten... shun!" The "shun" came like the crack of a whip. Then there was the single thump, as the cadet's heels came together. They stood straight as arrows with their rifles held firmly to their sides. The only things moving were the blue and gold company standards and the boys' pants legs in the breeze. The uniforms and rifles looked really sharp. What was the use of feeling lousy? I tried to cheer myself up. Maybe it wouldn't be so bad after all.

"Dad," I said softly.

He didn't answer. He kept watching the formation. *I'll make him proud of me*, I said to myself. I even pretended I was going away to the army.

"Dad," I said again. He turned to me. "It's alright. I don't mind."

Dad told the receptionist who we were and that Father Chalmers was expecting us. He asked us to have a seat on the brown wooden bench facing his desk, then went down a hall. A few moments later he came back. "Father Chalmers will see you first," he said to me.

"Alone?" I asked.

"Yes."

I picked up my legs and followed the receptionist to Father Chalmers' office. When I got there, I felt the confidence I had built up drain out onto the floor. Father Chalmers rose from his chair and leaned over his cluttered desk. "Hi, Tony," he said. We shook hands. I was surprised to see the combination of turned-around collar and Madras sport jacket.

"How do you do, sir," I said. He sat down.

"Relax," he smiled. He motioned to the chair in front of his desk. *Fat chance*, I thought. A file with a bunch of official papers in it had my name on it. What did he have to meet me for if he had all my records right there in front of him? "Tony." Hell, what kind of chance do I have if Father Chalmers knows I've had trouble before? I felt like a cockroach with no place to hide. "Tony," he said again.

"Yes, sir."

First, he'll ask why I've been kicked out of schools, then about the head doctor in New York. I could see it all coming.

"Do you like California?"

"Very much."

"The last school you attended was P.S. 3 in New York, wasn't it?"

"Yes, sir."

I was dying to ask if he had seen me there, or if he had memorized everything in that file on his desk.

"One year. I was in 7-8 Special. You already have my records. Why don't you just look at them?" I asked. Then I felt bad. "I'm sorry." I told him.

"The records," he chuckled. "Is that what's upsetting you?" His voice was so kind it made me sick. He picked up the file and put it in the side drawer of his desk. "I can't make the gesture of destroying them," Father Chalmers explained. "They follow you all the way through school. As you get older, you'll find you carry a more complete set of records. They reflect your relationships with people, the kind and quality of work you do, your moral reputation."

"Yes, sir. I'm sorry."

Sometimes I wondered why I lashed out at people who had nothing to do with what was bugging me. I could see the parking lot and chapel through the window behind Father Chalmers' desk. Dad was walking back and forth behind the car. His hands were in his pockets. A cigarette dangled from his mouth and his head was bent over in thought. "Why are the parking spaces numbered?" I asked. Father Chalmers said the juniors and seniors were allowed to have cars and were assigned their own parking spaces. "That's great," I said. Our eyes met. His were such a clear, icy, blue. Maybe his steel-rimmed glasses made his eyes seem bigger. "I almost know how to drive," I said proudly. "I've been learning this summer. These people who live near us let me practice with an old car. Their road is private," I explained, "so it isn't against the law. I'm going to surprise my father when I know how perfectly, so I would appreciate it if you wouldn't say anything."

"I promise not to mention it."

"Father Chalmers, can I ask you something?"

"Go ahead."

"How come you're not dressed all in black?"

"Episcopal," he smiled. "I may dress as I wish, have a drink once in a while, play cards, marry."

"That's neat," I said. "I thought you couldn't do any of that. I thought you walked around in black suits and counted beads all day." That got a laugh. "Why are there so many kids here before school starts?"

"We take great pride in our ROTC.," he answered. "When we're invited to march in parades during the summer, we get together as many of the students as we can. Then there's summer session, of course." There was an empty moment after he finished during which neither of us had anything to say. Father Chalmers broke the silence, but now he was more businesslike. "Tony, whenever a student comes to us from another state, we ask him to take some placement tests."

"Like what?"

"English and math for the most part, and an aptitude test."

"I've had the aptitude one before. Sure, I'll take them."

Father Chalmers leaned back in his swivel chair, then set his glasses by pinching them to the bridge of his nose. "Now let me tell you some things about Harvard." The speech was coming. The famous sales pitch. While he talked about all the sports and how many of the graduates went to good colleges, I let my thoughts drift back to when I had begged my mother to let me go live with my father. One time when I was pretty young came to mind. Mom and I were walking up Sixth Avenue toward the restaurant on 8th Street where they had my favorite Sunday breakfast of waffles. It was Spring. I had asked Mom when I could go live with Dad.

"*Someday*," she answered.

"Next Sunday, Mom? Next Sunday?"

"Not Sunday, son," she corrected. "Someday."

"When is someday?" I asked. She said she didn't know, that I would have to learn to be patient. All the rest of the way to the restaurant I stepped on the cracks in the sidewalk and muttered over and over to myself, but loud enough for her to hear, "Step on a crack, break your mother's back." Now I wondered if Mom in New York, or Dad, had ever found their somedays.

"Tony."

"I'm sorry, sir. I must have been dreaming."

"I suppose we all daydream now and then," he said smiling. I liked Father Chalmers.

"Sir," I said, "you don't have to tell me any more about Harvard. Dad says it's a very good school. I've never seen anything like it. I mean it's so big, and you have so many things to do. It must be very expensive. I can find out more about it later, if you'll take me." Father Chalmers got up. I got up, too, and we shook hands.

"Thank you for coming in to see me," he said. "It was nice talking to you."

"Thank you, sir."

"Would you have your father come in for a minute?"

"Yes. Right now." Our hands parted and I said, "Goodbye."

Dad looked relieved when he came out. I opened the car door for him. A smile was breaking on the corners of his lips. "You'll take the placement tests next week and move in the Sunday after Labor Day."

"He liked me?"

"It seems so," Dad said as he started the car. Then he took a bunch of lists out of the side pocket of his jacket and handed them to me. "You'll have to be fitted for these uniforms."

I read aloud as Dad drove down the hill. "O.D. uniform consisting of olive drab pants, 3; olive drab Eisenhower jackets, 3; khaki long sleeve shirts, 6; black ties, 2…"

9
Cry Havoc

The day Dad had to go away drew close. So did school. He still stayed in town a lot, but when he was home, Scotch mixed with milk replaced orange juice at breakfast. I think he thought no one knew what he was doing. At night he wandered aimlessly around the house, not saying much. One evening Gloria was giving him a massage on the living room couch. He was lying there, almost dozing off, when he said, "Tony. Harvard called today. Ninth grade." I was overjoyed. It meant I had skipped. I knew I had done well in school last year, that 7-8 Special had worked. Ninth grade! That was great.

Gloria took me to Desmond's, a big department store on Wilshire Boulevard where the uniforms were made for all the kids who went to Harvard. While I was being fitted, she kept bringing sweaters and sport shirts over to ask if I liked them. She was having as much fun looking for clothing for me as I was having pretending I was going into the army. It was true in a way, though. ROTC stood for Reserve Officers' Training Corps, and the brochure from Harvard said there was a real army captain in charge of it. The tailor asked if Gloria was my older sister. "She's my mother," I said. He turned the cuff, glanced up as if to say "fresh kid," and took a pin from his mouth, which he jammed into my pants. "Well, you see," I explained, "she was eight when she had me."

"Sexy," Gloria whispered in my ear when I tried on the Eisenhower jacket. She sang a little of "When Johnny Comes Marching Home." When I told her to be quiet, she said she was going to the women's department.

I was finished at four o'clock but had to wait until closing time for Gloria. As we walked across the parking lot to the car, everything—discarded paper bags, a piece of Kleenex, old candy wrappers—was blowing in the wind. Gloria carried her packages.

"What did you buy?" I asked.

"Presents."

We drove quietly for a few minutes, then she asked, "Feeling blue?"

"I guess so." Gloria drove through town, then down the ramp to the ocean. The water was choppy. Today is Friday, I thought. I only have until a week from Sunday before reporting to school. Gloria slowed for a light and reached over to stroke my head. I wanted to pull away but didn't. I was still really mad about having to go away to school.

"I had a terrible time in school," Gloria said. "My mother made a lot of my clothes. They hung like sacks. They were just terrible. I always sat in the back row so no one could see me. I couldn't hear a thing."

Horns honked behind us. The light had changed and we were just sitting there, holding up traffic. As Gloria drove off, I sat back against the door and stared at her. She hated to be stared at. Then I slid over, and before she could do anything about it, kissed her. The car swayed back and forth, but I wouldn't stop. Gloria yanked her head away. "You'll get us killed!"

"So what?"

"Do you want to park?"

"Yes, yes, yes," I said.

Gloria turned up Topanga Canyon. When we were high above the ocean, she turned onto a dirt road and we bumped along to the edge of a plateau. Hundreds of feet below, the ocean pounded against the rocks. We were in a hay field. The hay would be cut and fed to cows and the cow's milk would be used to feed babies. Children became men, grew old, died, and were planted in the earth to nourish the next crop of hay. So it was with all things, forever changing, living, dying, being reborn. Could that be how God worked?

"We never die," I said.

"What?"

"We might come back as a clump of grass or a tree, but we never die."

Gloria peered out of the car. "I don't know how I found this place."

I asked if she was afraid of the dark. She was. I asked if she was afraid to be alone in the house. "Yes," she said. Dad called her a hopeless baby for locking every door and window whether it was day or night. She wanted to know if I was lonely. She said she had been until I came to live with them. We kissed.

"Tony, this is all between us, isn't it?" Gloria asked while we were still holding each other. "Nick must never know."

"I'm not a baby," I said. "Do you really like me a lot?"

"Of course," she answered.

"How?" I asked. "I mean why do you bother with me? I don't mean anything to you."

"Yes, you do, but Nick wouldn't appreciate how we feel about each other."

"I'll never tell," I insisted. Why did she keep bringing Dad into it? It had nothing to do with him. "Believe me, I don't want him to know." Nick, Nick, Dad, Nick. Always him. "Gloria? Do you and dad make love much?" Gloria didn't answer for a long time. My head was on her breast, waiting. She ran her fingers idly through my hair, then unbuttoned her blouse.

"No, we don't," she said finally. "I hoped it would be different, but our sex life went from occasional to nonexistent as the number of Scotch bottles I threw away increased."

That it made her unhappy to talk about it was almost as bad as if they had sex all the time. All I could think about was that Dad was somewhere else, and Gloria and I were together on top of a hill. It had nothing to do with him. If I had all the things my father had, if I was a movie director with a house on the beach and a great wife, I wouldn't do the things he did. "I don't want to go to that goddamned military academy."

"Tony, I love you," Gloria said as though she meant don't be afraid, or like a mother saying, "It'll be alright." It wasn't like saying I love you the way I pictured a boy and girl saying it. She made me feel stupid, like a baby again.

"But I don't have you," I said.

"You have as much of me as I can give."

"To a child, huh?"

"No," she said.

I couldn't question too far. I couldn't risk losing as much of her as was mine. She was the one who let me sit on the edge of the bed and talk about anything I wanted. We could be ourselves together, not like the game we had to play in front of Dad. But I couldn't have her the way I wanted. And I couldn't have Dad, either. Dad and Gloria were half real, half shadow. I wanted to latch onto the real part of each, but I couldn't choose between them. Did I have to?

"Do you like your new sweater?" Gloria asked. "It's in the back seat."

She pointed to one of the packages and buttoned up her blouse. I opened the box and held the dark gray cashmere to my face. It was soft and warm. Gloria started the car. God, I thought. I would give anything to be a man and have a woman like Gloria.

Gloria went in to see Tim. I went into the house. Dad's car was home. His suitcase was sitting by the door and he was playing solitaire at the dinner table. I couldn't tell if he had brought a suitcase back from town or had packed another one to take with him.

"Hi, son." His face lit up warmly. "How did it go?"

"Real good. Gloria bought me a sweater and the uniforms are fine. They'll be ready Thursday."

Maybe I shouldn't have told him about the sweater. It was getting so I never knew what I could say and what I couldn't. There were so many secrets. I hated that part of it. Dad pushed together the neat rows of cards from his unfinished game.

"How about a glass of milk?" he invited. I didn't know if I was hearing right. Dad led the way back to the kitchen. He eyed his suitcase. I was glad he didn't ask what took Gloria and me so long. I hated the idea of having to lie. I don't know why I didn't come right out and ask if he was leaving. It was obvious— his suitcase was by the door. But I just couldn't. Maybe he was waiting for Gloria, to tell us both at once. He got the milk. I got the glasses.

"Would you like to take a trip?"

"Sure."

"We could drive up the coast to San Francisco," he said enthusiastically. "It's one of the most scenic drives in America."

"That would be a lot of fun. All of us together." It didn't take much convincing to like the idea. "I haven't seen you too much this summer."

"I'm sorry."

"Would Gloria come?" I asked. In a way, I hoped that Dad would say no. It would really be a great trip if he and I went alone.

"Yes," he said.

"Not Tim, though. We couldn't take him on such a long—"

"Constance will take care of him here," Dad said. "Go pack."

"If it's so scenic," I asked after gulping down my milk, "shouldn't we wait until morning?" Gloria came in before dad could answer. "Hey, Dad says we're going on a trip. Let's get packed."

"Aren't you working, Nick?"

"Tony has only ten days before school. I can take a long weekend before I go on location." I could have killed Gloria. "Work comes second to family now and then. We'll leave as soon as you two are ready."

Half an hour later we were all set to go. Dad had been calling into our rooms every five minutes. "There won't be any point of going if you don't hurry." He even threatened to leave Gloria behind because she was taking so long. Dad was marching around the house like an expectant father. On the way to the car he put his arm around Gloria's shoulder. He was sure in a good mood. I couldn't remember the last time I had seen him touch her. We took Gloria's car. She sat close to Dad, which left a gap between Gloria and me. I knew it was crazy, but somehow I felt like Dad didn't belong with us. I had spent most of my summer with Gloria, not with him.

I had a nightmare of being trapped in an airless steel ball that shrank smaller and smaller until I couldn't breathe. Dad stopped the car in front of a roadside diner. There were a lot of big trucks. Gloria told me we had been on the road for three hours, about a hundred and fifty miles. The smell of coffee and hamburgers filled the crowded diner. We found a booth all the way in the back next to a window. There was a lot of laughing and loud conversation and a jukebox playing. The waitress twisted and twirled her way down the aisle of booths, through arms that struggled to get into leather jackets, sidestepping small groups of *goodbye-* and *good luck*-bidding truck drivers. She wore a broad, never changing, smile, and yelled "hot stuff" as many times as needed to get to her destination. A man who I guessed was her husband worked feverishly behind the counter, only taking time out for a jealous glance at his wife or to shoot a warning look at some driver whose eyes grabbed her as she went by. Maybe I was just making it all up in my head, but I was sure Gloria looked at every man in the place. Any minute I expected Dad to tell her not to stare at people.

"Waitress," Dad called impatiently as she sped past us to another booth. He was exasperated and acted as though she had personally offended him by not stopping. Why was he in such a hurry? On her way back to the counter for another load, the waitress screeched to a halt at our table like a racing car at a red light.

"What'll it be, folks?" Her face was beaded with sweat and her big breasts filled the upper half of her grease-smeared apron. She seemed nice.

"Coffee, black," Dad ordered, "and a Danish."

"I'm starving, Dad. Can I have a hamburger and a Coke?"

"If it doesn't take too long."

"I'd like a hamburger and a Coke, too," Gloria said. Then she asked, "Are we stopping at a motel?"

"No," answered Dad. "I hate stopping on the road."

"We can't see anything at night," I said.

"Must you make a marathon out of this trip, Nick? Think about it. If we drive all night, we'll end up sleeping all day."

We slept at a motel after all, though only for a few hours. When morning came, we could see that we were winding along ocean cliffs that were hugged by redwood trees. The sky was picture-book blue, perfectly painted, perfectly clear. Every time Dad spun around a hairpin turn, we could see the breakers crashing against the rocks hundreds of feet below. We had breakfast in Monterey, a small green, red and brown town. People wore crisp summer outfits of bright yellows, blues, and whites. Some had lightweight sweaters on. It was cooler here. Dad took pictures of me, then of Gloria. I wanted one of Gloria and me together but didn't ask.

Mountains of grays and blacks, of smoke and railroad freight cars, bumpy crossings and traffic lights, marked our approach to San Francisco. Tall, wide billboards advertising everything from toothpaste to hotels to tires made the buildings of the city seem small in the background. *I will write a composition one day*, I thought, *about all the people, signs and cars that race along this highway, and I'll say all of them lived in a dark historical wilderness in which man challenged nature's laws of simplicity and beauty, in which man was blinded by the bright lights and empty promises of the neon age.*

We checked into the Fairmont Hotel. It was very fancy. I even had my own room. That was pretty neat. I stuffed some of the stationery with the fancy letterhead into my suitcase. It would be fun to write Mom a letter about the trip on it. I found the gift shop, where the lady behind the counter was selling an old couple some postcards. Next to me was a display of perfumes. I don't know what got into me, but my hand shot out and in a split second the bottle of Joy perfume was in my jacket pocket. I pretended to look around and left. The lady never even looked at me.

I knocked at Dad and Gloria's room, but there was no answer. Maybe they were taking a nap. From the window of my room I could see the Golden Gate Bridge. Or maybe it was some other bridge. I wondered what I would tell Judy. She would say I was just another movie brat, going off to boarding school like all the rest. I had been so sure I would be able to stay home and go to Samo-Hi. I could picture myself getting on the bus, going to classes, and coming home at night to find Gloria waiting for me in the living room, even when Dad was away.

A little while later Dad called to say he was in the bar and why didn't Gloria and I join him. Gloria answered the door in her bathrobe. "Sit down. I'll get dressed in the john." I sat on the edge of the ruffled bed. Gloria came out wearing a pretty dress and combed her hair at the dresser.

"Gloria?"

"Yes, love."

"I don't want to go to that damned school."

Gloria looked at me through the mirror and said, "If you go, Nick can tell all his friends his son is at Harvard." She dug through her cosmetics case. I was sure she was looking for perfume.

"Here." I held the bottle of Joy out to her.

"Where'd this come from?"

"I bought it for you."

"I bet."

"I did. I had some money from my mother and some allowance money."

"Listen," Gloria said, "things are bad enough. For God's sake don't get into trouble." She opened the bottle and dabbed some on her wrist. "It was sweet of you, anyway."

We found Dad at the bar having a drink and reading a newspaper. He folded the paper as we sat down. He seemed full of energy.

"What's the plan?" Gloria asked. "Do we get to see San Francisco night life"

"There's nothing happening. Dead season, I guess."

"We could go to a club. We never go out."

"I'm not really interested in city lights and low life. It's like a wax museum. Why don't we drive to the High Sierras and get some fresh air?" I hoped he would take us to a nightclub, but I said nothing. Neither did Gloria. "It's my vacation," Dad said with finality. He ordered another drink. Gloria and I finished ours in silence.

The car clock read nearly 10pm when, out of the darkness, a large neon sign appeared. It read "Cal-Neva Lodge." There was another sign below it that said "Hotel-Casino." We pulled up in front of a large redwood building. A doorman rushed to the car doors. Two more uniformed men followed, a bellhop and a parking lot man.

"Where are we?" I asked.

"Lake Tahoe," said Dad. "You'll love it. A famous resort."

"Checking in, sir, or just for the evening?"

"Checking in," said Dad. At first Gloria refused to budge. Dad and I got out and Dad opened the trunk to get our things. The parking lot man got in and looked at Gloria as though asking a question. She slid out. "Don't worry," Dad said happily, "a few spins of the wheel. Then we'll get a good night's sleep and sightsee tomorrow. We'll give Tony the grand tour and go back through the desert."

Inside, Cal-Neva Lodge was full of bright lights, wood paneling and thick carpets. From the registration desk I could see an almost empty restaurant that overlooked the crowded casino floor. There was a bar area with a bandstand. The band played loud music. A sign between the restaurant and casino hung above a split-rail fence. "You are now leaving California," it read. "Welcome to Nevada."

"How are you this evening, Mr. Ray? Did you have a good trip?"

"So, so," said Dad. He signed the register and glanced over at the Nevada side. "Your cabin is ready, sir."

A moment later we were outside, following the bellhop who had loaded our suitcases onto a cart. The night air was chilly.

"This is great, isn't it?" I said to Gloria.

"I knew Nick wouldn't let us down. He always saves the day."

"Should I wear my suit?" I asked dad.

"Of course," he answered.

The two-bedroom cabin was also wood paneled and had thick red carpet. The bellhop explained how all the lights and gas heater worked. Then, at the door, ready to leave, he said, "The cabin is on the house for the length of your stay, sir." Dad gave him a tip.

"They're going to lose on this one," Dad said. "Come on, wash up for dinner."

"'Bring your black dress,'" Gloria said sarcastically. "'We'll go to the theater.'"

"Oh, stop bitching."

"You planned this all along. You had reservations."

Dad was the first to be ready. He left, saying he was going to get us a table for dinner. I changed into my suit. When I came back, Gloria was wearing a beautiful low-cut cocktail dress. Dad was waiting for us in the restaurant. The only other people there were two tall showgirls who sat with a group of George Raft-type men. A waitress came over to our table.

"Steak, medium rare, salad with house dressing, baked potato," said Dad. "Tony? Gloria?" He was rushing us. Gloria ordered lamb chops and I ordered the same as Dad.

"The air here is marvelous, Nick," said Gloria.

I couldn't help staring at the showgirls. They kept talking and laughing, but there was something hard about their eyes, and they wore so much makeup. We didn't talk much. Gloria was really morose. When our food came, Dad finished quickly and asked the waitress for the check, which he signed. Gloria and I were only halfway through our meal. Dad took a $10 bill from his pocket and gave it to me. "Play the slot machines. If you stick to the nickel and dime machines, the money will last longer."

"How do you play?"

"Just put in a nickel and pull the handle." Dad grabbed his coffee and rose from the table. "I'm going to watch the suckers for a while before I turn in."

Gloria, sitting with her elbows on the table, watched Dad as he made his way to the gate leading to Nevada and disappeared into the crowd. "From the way he's acting, you'd think he was a saint looking in to see what the sinners are doing."

"Is he going to gamble?"

"What do you think?" Gloria pushed back her chair and stood up. "I'm going to the bar. Want to come with me?"

I followed her. It felt good being with such a beautiful woman. The bartender looked at her as though he knew her from someplace. She ordered two Brandy Alexanders, telling him that both

were for her. Then she took out her compact and pinched the skin
under her chin.

"Do you think I should have this nipped in a little?" I had no
answer. She gazed into the compact mirror. "I look terrible. I didn't
get enough sleep last night." The bartender set the two drinks in
front of her. She pushed one in front of me. "It's sweet. You'll like
it." A few minutes later she said she was going back to the cabin.
She asked if I wanted to come with her. I said I wanted to try the
slot machines.

I crossed over to the Nevada side and saw a woman wearing
a change belt. My $10 bill was converted into five $2 rolls of
nickels. She also gave me a large paper cup to hold my nickels in.
Then I went up and down the rows of slot machines until I found
a nickel one that wasn't being used. I sat down in front of it,
then dropped in a nickel and pulled the handle. The wheels spun
around fast, then slowed and came to a stop. An orange, a lemon
and a bell. Then silence. I had lost. Mine was the third machine
in a row of ten. Had I picked a good one? I studied the chart
of payoffs on the face of the machine, decided it must be okay,
and dropped in another nickel. Two cherries and a bell! I had
won. Five nickels fell into the tray. The next time I lost. There
was an old lady on my left wearing a pink evening gown and
about a million strings of pearls. She got her nickels from a red
plastic coin purse. If it wasn't for her strong-smelling perfume,
you would never know she was there, she was concentrating so
hard. A tall, thin man stood on my right. His machine was silent.
He went through his pockets, stared at the machine for a minute,
then walked away. A cherry. A plum. A bell. Two nickels fell.
I felt like I was the only one coming out ahead.

I heard the loud roar of about thirty excited people. "Yes!"
"Seven!" I turned to look. Behind me, past the roulette wheel and
blackjack tables, was a crowd standing around the crap table. In a
pool of light, I saw Dad. He was shaking the dice in his fist. Then
he threw. I smiled to myself. It was as though my father and I were
doing something together. I turned back to my slot machine. A little
man and his wife took over the machine next to me. "We stopped
here for breakfast and we've been here three days," she whined.
"Don't you love it?" he said.

I thought of Gloria sitting in the cabin and wondered why she
couldn't have a good time. I knew she hated it when Dad gambled

and that it caused trouble between them, but she could have gone to see a show or something.

A bell. A bell. A bell! Eighteen nickels tumbled into my tray.

"Are you Tony?"

A sleek, dark-skinned man, his black hair plastered down, tapped me on the shoulder. He was smiling from the corners of his mouth.

"Yes," I said.

"How are you doing?"

"Pretty good, I think. I've lost track."

"My name is Manino. I'm the manager here. You're too young to be playing, but if you stay right here, nobody will notice. Your father said I should give you this."

Mr. Manino handed me three rolls of nickels.

"Thanks," I said, and stuffed the rolls into the side pocket of my jacket.

"You can't have much fun around here without money." He rested his long bony hand on my shoulder. I saw his shiny polished fingernails. He made me feel weird. After watching me play two nickels, he said, "Let your father alone, okay? He's having a good time." He moved away, his black mohair suit disappearing into the crowd.

I kept on playing. but something had changed. It was as if Mr. Manino had stolen my good luck. I felt sad and alone. I didn't feel like I was with Dad anymore. An image of the old, black-suited undertaker on Houston Street, standing in the snow outside his store front funeral parlor, flashed into my mind.

The machine ate my original $10 in about half an hour. I opened one of the rolls Mr. Manino had given me. That lasted only a little while. The second roll lasted a little longer. I fed the third roll into the machine mechanically, knowing I was going to lose. Five nickels left. Four. Three. I wanted it to be over. A cherry paid two, but that just annoyed me. Four. Three. Two. I put in the last nickel, pulled the handle, and turned away before the machine stopped whirring. Then I heard the clunk, clunk, clunk of the three discs. Then nothing. I stood up and a new player sat down at my machine. "Come on, baby," she said. I had the sick feeling that it would give her my $16, and all the rest. I moved away quickly, not wanting to see it happen.

I worked my way through people to the California side of the club. There were tables with comfortable chairs in the bar area. An announcer came out onto the bandstand. "Ladies and gentlemen: Louis Prima and Keely Smith!" There was a round of applause and a minute later the loud music began. Maybe Gloria had come back. I weaved through the tables looking for her. Plums. Oranges. Bells. I took a seat at an empty table near the back of the lounge. A dark-haired waitress wearing a very short skirt and high heels moved quickly through the crowd with her tray of drinks. She stopped at my table. "Get you something?"

"No, thank you. I'm broke."

"I'll treat you to a Coke." She smiled and went off to deliver the drinks to a table of very drunk soldiers. At the table to my left, a group of four off-duty dealers were drinking coffee and talking about the World Series. Behind me, Al told Bernice not to worry, his brother would wire more money from the store. Next to me, I saw two very pretty girls, about Gloria's age, but they had too much makeup on. One of them had her hair dyed a grayish blonde and done in hundreds of fancy curls. The other had long, dark hair. Her mascara had run a little, and, looking into a rhinestone-studded campact, she brushed it away with a fingertip wet with spit. I could hear every word they said.

"Who's working Labor Day, besides us?"

"I heard Denise and some friend of hers."

"Denise? I thought she was in a house in Reno."

"Don't kid yourself. Denise looks after Denise."

"What'd she do with that jerk she used to live with? Juan. That was some piece of work."

A bell captain tapped Fancy Curls on the shoulder and whispered a few words in her ear. "See you later," she said. She took her purse, but left her coat hanging over the chair. The girl with the long brown hair caught me staring and smiled at me. I was embarrassed and turned away. I looked up to see Gloria standing before me.

"Have you got any money?" The words were out of my mouth before I could think of what I was saying.

"Lose it all?"

"It was only $16."

"You're going to be as bad as your father." She took me by the hand and pulled me up. "C'mon. Let's see how the big shot is doing."

We walked to the Nevada gate and looked down into the casino. Gloria pulled me behind her. She seemed drunk and dangerous. I hoped she wasn't going to make a scene. We had to fight our way through the people coming out of the show. I wondered what time it was. There were no clocks anywhere. I stole a look at my slot machine as we passed it. There was another new player. I wondered if I could find out if anyone had hit the jackpot. We pushed our way past the roulette wheel and blackjack tables, then to the crap tables.

Dad had not changed position. He was leaning against the table at the front of a noisy crowd of men and women, three deep, who reached over each other to place their bets. "Snake eyes!" The dealer's voice was loud enough for all to hear. Many groaned, but an older lady, clutching her purse in one hand and a bunch of silver dollars in the other, cried, "I won, Harold! I won!" She shoved her way forward to be paid. "Can I have it in silver dollars? Oh, I just love it. It's so exciting. Let one ride for the dealer." A young man in a white shirt and string tie stacked the silver dollars in piles of ten, then knocked one gently off the top of the last stack. Another man, using what looked like a hockey stick, cleared the table of Dad's black chips along with all the other multicolored chips on the pass line. An older man wearing a gray suit seemed to be in charge of the game. Gray temples framed his gray face. He sat in front of racks of chips of all different colors and rows of silver dollars, putting away the losses into the racks and then paying the winners. He had no expression on his face, but his eyes watched every move of the game.

Gloria managed to squeeze herself in behind Dad. A cocktail waitress pushed shoulders aside to get a tray with a Scotch to him. Gloria snatched the drink off the tray and drank it down. I studied the dice table, but couldn't figure out anything. It was all just a bunch of numbers to me. A fat man next to me said to his friend, "Getting into his tray is more exciting than getting into a woman's pants."

"How much are the black chips?"

"Hundred bucks a pop. I've been watching him, too. High roller, bad gambler."

Dad had two and a half neat stacks of blacks. He pushed the short stack onto the table. "Coming out," the stickman said. "No more bets." A bald, sweaty man bounced the dice across the table. Two ones. "Snake eyes. Spit in your eye. Came right back. What did the little lady do?" Dad's chips were taken away. I wanted him to win as much as I had wanted my slot machine to make me a winner.

"Hi, Nick. How are you doing?" said Gloria.

"I was doing great till you showed up."

"Why don't you come to bed?"

"Leave me alone." Dad shook off her hand as if it were a pesky fly.

"Another Vegas honeymoon."

"Get out of here. I can't concentrate."

"Faggot," Gloria said pleasantly.

"Jesus Christ. Leave me alone."

"Give us something to play with. We're broke."

Dad slammed a black chip into her hand. Gloria reached to the table and took another one. "One each." I put out my hand for the chip, but both disappeared into Gloria's purse.

"Seven," the stickman called. "Pay the front line."

"Goddamn it! Get her out of here, Vic," Dad said to the man next to him. "Did you see that? I never got my bet down."

Vic rolled a toothpick in his mouth. "Never bring your own. Can't sleep, take a pill or buy it here, right? No offense, ma'am."

"So that's how it's done," Gloria said. Her smile was sickly. "You won't sleep with me but you'll sleep with the whores around here." Dad pushed the rest of his chips on the table. Gloria lunged toward them and grabbed some chips. Dad snapped at her wrist and squeezed it, trying to make her let go of them. "You owe me eight thousand, you bastard."

"You'll get it later."

Two very big men moved to the edge of the crowded table. They wore tan uniforms and big tin stars that said SECURITY on them. The dice were rolled and the last of Dad's chips were taken away. "Satisfied?" he said.

Dad signaled to Mr. Manino. "Another five thousand." Mr. Manino signaled the man with the tray that it was okay. He slid five stacks of chips and a slip of paper to Dad. He signed it and passed it back.

"Another five thousand. That's a hot streak all right," Gloria said. And then. as if she really understood it, she shouted, "Another five thousand! Are you crazy?"

"Get them out of here." Dad said to Mr. Manino.

"I've got as much right to be here as anybody else," said Gloria. The game came to a halt. Mr. Manino took Gloria by the shoulder and tried to draw her away from the table. "We're pleased to have you as a guest, Miss Grahame, but the boy is too young to be on the casino floor, and you're interrupting these people's entertainment. If you'd like to play…"

"All right, I'll play." Gloria grabbed at Dad's pile of chips. "This is my money. He owes it to me. I want to play, all right?"

One of the security men jumped forward and grabbed Gloria's wrist. Mr. Manino nodded. The other security man took Gloria's other arm. Gloria dragged her feet, refusing to walk, so they lifted her up an inch from the floor. People made room as they took her out. "I won't pay the phone bill," she yelled. "Bastard! You can take care of Tim. He's losing all my money. Robbery!"

As the guards neared the exit with Gloria, Dad flung his arms wide toward her and shouted, "CRY HAVOC!" I caught Mr. Manino's eye. "I'm leaving," I said.

"Place your bets, please. New shooter." The casino returned to its normal noise.

Outside the air was cold. Gloria must have gone back to the cabin. I buttoned my suit jacket and pulled up my collar. A bank of billowing gray clouds passed before the full moon. One time when Mom was working as a crime reporter, she told me that the New York police doubled its guard on train stations and airports when there was a full moon because there was so much more violent crime.

Gloria was hanging up the telephone when I walked in. She went to the bathroom and slammed the door. "Who did you call?" I asked.

"Room service. The bastards." The place was upside down. A sheet and blanket from the bed had been thrown over the sitting room couch. The contents of Gloria's suitcase were spilled on the floor. Her black dress was crumpled in a ball on a chair, a nightgown and robe thrown over it. Gloria's phone book lay open on the coffee table. Beside it stood a half-empty bottle of Smirnoff. Gloria had probably called her friend Julie. She always did when she was upset.

"Should I get a cleft put in my chin," Gloria called from the bathroom. "I love clefts."

"How do I know. How could you, anyway?"

"Plastic surgery. Marilyn Monroe does it all the time."

"I don't know." I took a cigarette from a pack lying beside the bottle. Then I took a big swig. The vodka burned my chest, then made me feel warm.

"What are you sitting around for? Why don't you go to bed?"

I took the cigarette with me. I was too tired to search for pajamas, so I turned down the covers, stripped to my jockey shorts, and got in. The vodka undid the knot in my stomach. They had certainly made a scene. After I finished the cigarette, I put it out in the ashtray and slid the ashtray under the bed.

> I ain't got nobody
> And nobody cares for me…

The casino band was a whisper, like a radio turned down to its lowest volume. It must have been very late. The apartment on Houston Street, Mom never having any money, the horse betting at Dad's office, the unpaid bills. Dad had lost the money gambling. That was why he stayed in town, so he could gamble. Cherries and bars and oranges and lemons. Dice landing on the green felt and chips being handed out and taken away. Dad was winning. The chips piled higher—then he was losing. Another five thousand. Ten dollars swallowed by the machine. Gone forever. Or until I have a chance to win it back… someday.

I was asleep when Gloria came into my room. She sat on the edge of my bed. It was like a dream. I tried to put my arms around her.

"Lie still."

She pushed back my hands and rolled me over on my back. I could barely make out her face in the dark, but I felt her breath, then her mouth. I raised my head toward the kiss and lifted my hands to hold her.

"Keep your hands to yourself."

Her fingers ran over my shoulders, then my chest and stomach. They stopped at the elastic of my undershorts. She was still kissing me. Then her hand slipped into my shorts and she wrapped her fingers around my penis.

"Gloria…"

"Shh…

I didn't know my own voice. It felt so good. She stopped kissing me and I could see her in the dim light. She was lying beside me with her head propped up by her other hand. I didn't know what to do. I just lay there and let her. Her eyes were half closed and her mouth half open. I wished she would kiss me again. Then, in one giant explosion, it happened.

Gloria got up and left, walking past me in the dark. I hoped she would come back, just to talk, but she didn't. I went to the bathroom to wash myself, then put on a pair of pants and a shirt. The sitting room was dark, and only a small lamp burned in her bedroom. The shower was on. A cart with covered dishes was next to the table. I lifted them and found two shrimp cocktails and a lobster untouched. I remembered she had called room service. I was starving. I ate one of the shrimp cocktails. Gloria came out in her robe and her hair wrapped in a towel.

"I must be the world's biggest idiot. I really thought Nick was taking us to San Francisco."

I waited for her to say something else, something about what had happened, but she didn't. She sat at the dressing table and turned on a light. Then she opened a jar of cold cream.

"He brought me here a couple of years ago when I was expecting Tim. Another fiasco."

"Did he win?" I really didn't want to talk about Dad. It felt so strange.

"When he does, he just loses it back."

I stood behind her at the mirror, but I couldn't get her eyes to meet mine. I wanted her to tell me everything was okay, to tell me I shouldn't feel ashamed. She gave her hair a couple of brushes and turned off the dresser lamp. You would think nothing had happened.

"I'm going to bed," she said. "You'd better go, too."

"You can always sleep with Marilyn Monroe. I know you've been having lunches at Lucy's with her. It was in Hedda Hopper's column."

"For God's sake."

"Did you offer her a part in a picture? She always sleeps with her directors. Is that why you've been staying in town?"

"Just give me the damn chips."

"They're mine."

"I'll tear this place apart."

"You'll just throw them away."

"What the hell is going on around here? Shrimp, lobster. Look who's talking about throwing money away."

"You're not paying for it."

"That's not the point."

"Here they are, Nick. Take them and leave me alone." The cabin door slammed. Then there was silence.

When I woke again, the cabin was still. I went outside to the porch. The lodge was beside a lake. It was a peaceful morning, the air cold and fresh, the sky blue. High, snow-capped mountains surrounded the lake, and there were narrow beaches lined with pine trees. A few motorboats were floating on the water. I caught a glimpse of a line being thrown out. It felt like there was a world separating me from Mom and Dad and from the people of the world who went out on lakes and fished, the world I so badly wanted.

The restaurant was almost empty. The casino looked the same as it had the night before. Maintenance men were vacuuming. It sounded so loud. Dad and Gloria were having coffee at the end of the bar. Dad was in his thinking position, head bowed, eyes squinting, a cigarette dangling from the corner of his mouth. I went across the restaurant and joined them.

"We're having coffee," Gloria said, "Want some?"

"Go get breakfast at a table. I'll tell them to put it on my bill."

"All I want is some juice and coffee," I said.

"We're busy." Dad replied.

I walked off to the other side of the restaurant. The waitress took my order. I could still see them at the bar but couldn't hear them. Dad stood up and stared at the empty casino, then turned and put his hand on Gloria's arm. She didn't seem mad anymore. Then they left, hardly looking in my direction. After breakfast I went out and sat on the dock. I wished that I wouldn't have to talk to Dad. I watched the lake's small waves splash up against the white wood at my feet and thought of Gloria. I wished it hadn't happened. When I finally returned to the cabin, Gloria was packing her suitcase.

"Where's the camera?" she asked.

"Dad's camera? The little one?"

"It's missing."

"I don't know. I didn't see it."

"Look, tell him where it is so we can get out of here. Nick's on a rampage."

It took me a few seconds to remember the picture-taking in Monterey, but I hadn't seen it since. Gloria started picking up cosmetics from the dresser.

"You stole this." She held up the small bottle of Joy perfume. "And I don't know what else you've been up to, but if we don't settle this thing…"

Dad walked in, slamming the door behind him. He looked at me like I was some kind of disgusting roach. "Please take my shoes out of your room and bring them here. You don't have to steal my things. You have your own things."

"I only took them because…"

"No excuses, please. You've had them for a long time. You no sooner get to my house than… Oh, Christ. Just go get them."

I looked at Gloria, expecting her to say something, but she didn't. What was wrong with her? I went quietly to my room and got the shoes. I dropped them at my father's feet.

"Did you sell the camera in the casino? It was expensive. How much did you get?"

"I didn't take it. I don't know where it is."

Dad half-smiled at me, a strange smile. Then he went to the door to leave. "You'd better think it over and come up with some answers." Gloria went to the bathroom and closed the door. I pounded on the door. She must have forgotten that she was the one who had told me to take the shoes. "You told me to take them. I wouldn't have done it if you hadn't told me to." She turned on the sink faucet as if to drown me out. "Gloria, you have to tell him you told me to take them."

The water was turned off. "Listen, Tony, I've got more important things to worry about than shoes."

"Well, then tell him the truth."

She opened the door suddenly. "I can't stand up for you if you're going to steal. I mean, the perfume and now the camera. You're sort of a one-man crime wave lately. Maybe you should just go back to the streets where you came from."

I ran outside, then to the lodge. Dad standing at a cashier window with Mr. Manino, who was looking as freshly pressed in his sport jacket, slacks and shiny black shoes as he had the night before. He smiled at me.

"Dad?"

"Not now."

"Why don't you stay a few days, Nick," said Mr. Manino. "Go out on one of our boats, do a little fishing. The cabin is yours."

"No, thanks. I have to get back to work."

Dad wrote a check and gave it to Mr. Manino. He took the check, gave it to the cashier, and handed dad some bills. "Sorry we can't extend your credit any further, Nick. It's probably just as well, don't you think? Maybe you'll have better luck next time."

"Dad, I don't know where the camera went. I haven't seen it since you used it, and Gloria told me to take the shoes to go riding in. Then she got me some boots."

"Don't interrupt," Dad snapped. He thanked Mr. Manino and they shook hands. We were outside, alone on the gravel driveway. Dad looked directly at me and stopped walking.

"You are a small man," he said. "I am a big man. I hold the cards in this game. Okay?"

Words came to my lips, but I couldn't say anything. I didn't even know what he meant. A boat on the lake zipped by close to shore. Dad walked toward the cabin and I followed. My leg muscles felt tight. "Get this straight," he said. "I'm glad you're going to military school. It'll do you good. But right now, Tony, if you don't mind, I'd like an hour alone with my wife. Don't disturb us."

Two minutes later, I was on the highway.

10
Wonderful Vacation

There was a gas station about a hundred yards down the road. I asked the attendant which way Los Angeles was. "South," he said, and pointed down the mountain. I thanked him and started on my way. "Hey, kid," the attendant called.

"What?"

"There's two ways of going. You better cut off toward Frisco at the bottom of the hill. There's a junction there. Take the right fork. Can't miss it."

"Why that way?"

"The desert's awful hot this time of year. You might not get a ride through."

"Which is the shortest way?" I asked.

"Through the desert."

"Thanks."

He probably thought I was nuts, but I decided to go through the desert. It didn't scare me. So it was hot, so what? I would get a ride somehow, even if I had to lie down in the road. And Dad had said he was going home through the desert. I stuck my thumb out every time a car came around the curve I was on. It didn't take long to realize a car might not want to stop because the driver could never tell what was coming from behind. Mrs. Archer had taught me never to stop on a curve. I waited in the middle of the next straight. One car. Two. Three. A Cadillac! I jumped into the brush by the side of the road. It drove by. I could tell by the fins it wasn't Gloria's car. It wasn't even a convertible.

Would Dad ask the gas station attendant if he had seen me? They might not even leave together. Maybe they had broken up. Dad would have to take a train or a bus home. I stuck out my thumb again. An old blue pickup truck screeched to a stop a few yards ahead of me.

"How far, son?"

"Los Angeles." I was panting after running to the cab of the truck. The driver must have been a farmer. His hat was worn and dirty and he wore faded blue overalls and a plaid shirt.

"I can ride you as far as Mojave."

"Where's that?" I asked

"'Bout half-ways to Los Angeles. There's a truck and bus stop there, out in the desert. My place is there."

He threw the truck into gear and we were on our way. He was about sixty. The wrinkles in his sun-cracked lips curled around the stem of a pipe. We bounced onward, down the mountain. Something about the way he looked was out of place, peculiar. Then I figured it out. His beat-up gray hat was the kind businessmen wore in New York, not the straw or Stetson I would have expected.

"What kind of place do you have?" I shouted to be heard above the rattling of tools in back and perhaps because I suspected all old people were a little deaf.

"Trees," he answered, after thinking about it. He didn't explain. He was probably thinking about his trees, or a good winter. Whatever it was, his eyes showed he was pleased. It's funny how much you can tell about a person when you first meet them. I knew I would like Gloria from that first second at the airport. We took a couple more curves and bounces when, finally, I ventured to break the silence.

"What kind of trees?"

"Orange."

"Orange," I nodded.

"And lemon," he added, smiling.

I looked over my shoulder at the road behind. I expected Dad and Gloria to catch up with us at any minute. If they didn't hurry, it would be only a matter of luck if they found me at all. That worried me, but I decided if worse came to worse and I changed my mind about running away, I could always find my way home, or ask the police to get me there.

"Where ya from, boy?"

"New York."

"New York! I've been to New York City. Yup. Let's see…" He half-closed his eyes, as if they were binoculars scanning the distant past, trying to bring into focus a vague memory. "Back around… '30… Yup." He snapped his fingers. "'32, to be exact."

"That's before I was born," I said.

"Busy place, New York. Yup. No time to think. Got this hat there. You like it?" He ran his weathered fingers over the brim. "I've worn it every year since. Wears real good. Pays to buy good things." He took his pipe out of his mouth and raised his eyebrows at me as though that had been an important lesson. Then he chortled, "Don't think I'll be getting back there anymore now," and poked me in the ribs with the stem of his pipe. "Do you?" There was a moment of silence, then he said, "No place for me."

We drove into the noon hour but there was still no sign of Dad. The sun was high above a mountain. The peaks glistened with ice and snow. It was inviting compared to the heat of the desert, which made breathing hard. Lakes in the middle of the road disappeared into clouds of heat vapor as we drove through them. The gas station attendant had been right. What would I do if I got stuck in Mojave?

"Sure is hot," I said.

"Get used to it after a spell."

"Is there a gas station at the bus depot?"

"Yup," he said. "Got a post office and a store, too."

At least I could wait at the station and ask people filling their tanks for rides. A couple of hours later we passed signs that advertized orange juice. The first one read, "Ice cold juice. Five miles." A picture of an orange was painted on the sign. My tongue almost stuck to the roof of my mouth. I couldn't even gather enough saliva to swallow. The signs were placed closer together as we drove on until, finally, the last one said, "Orange juice, 500 feet." I kicked myself again for losing all my money. We stopped in front of a wooden stand that was sheltered from the sun by a canvas top. Guthrie, as he had finally introduced himself some time back, slid from his seat to the ground. He stretched his arms over his head and walked up to the stand on stiff legs. I liked Guthrie. Everything about him was nice. He got up in the morning, took care of his trees, was his own boss, ate well, and went to bed early.

"Hiya, William," Guthrie said to the man behind the counter.

"How was the family, Guth? Have an agreeable trip?"

"Fair to middlin'. Fair to middlin'."

They seemed to be friends of many years, maybe even longer than I had been alive. While they talked trees, irrigation problems and government land leases, I surveyed the vast desert. Behind the wooden stand were an orange grove and a cabin. The trees grew out of sandy soil and lost their pale green, parched tops in the bright afternoon sky. The wheel of the windmill behind the cabin creaked and groaned but didn't move more than a few inches in either direction. William set up three cups. Cubes of ice rattled as he lifted the tall jar of orange juice from under the counter. I wondered where he got ice.

"None for me, thanks," I said as William poured.

"Son," he said. "You realize what you're passin' up? This here," he poked the bottle, "is fresh squeezed, grade A cold California orange juice."

"Thanks just the same," I said. "Maybe a cup of that cold water you have down there would be nice." William frowned. He was even older than Guthrie. There was a short impasse. Then Guthrie said it would be his treat and insisted I have the juice. Either he knew I was broke or he didn't want to hurt his friend's feelings. I supposed it was unusual for someone to stop at a juice stand in the middle of the desert and say, "No, thank you." Either you stop, or you don't stop.

As the sun began to fall behind the mountains, the snows reflected a myriad of colors that changed from fiery reds to the almost purple shades I had seen the night before on the way to Lake Tahoe. The sky was flooded with pale oranges and white, turning to gray, clouds. It was getting cooler.

"Purty, ain't it?" Guthrie asked as he drew on his pipe.

"Scary, too," I said.

"No. I don't think I'll be seein' New York again. But no matter, this here country's been good to me. Given me a full life, it has." Even after Guthrie had parked in front of the bus depot and restaurant at Mojave, my eyes were glued to the sky. The clouds had turned to an almost black against a pale blue sky. "This is it, boy," he said. I turned abruptly. I had been dreaming again. I was suddenly afraid of being alone. I opened the door.

"Thanks, Mr. Guthrie."

"It's alright. Been my pleasure ta have you for company." He put out his hand and I shook it. I slid down from the truck. There was something in my hand.

Guthrie threw the truck into gear and rumbled off down the highway leaving a cloud of dust behind him. I opened my hand. A $5 bill was crumpled in it. He had given me a $5 bill to eat on or something, and hadn't even waited long enough for me to notice or thank him. I wondered how far $5 would take me on the bus. Boy, I thought. I'd like to live the way Guthrie did for a while, working with trees, getting all that sun and warmth, visiting his family. I wished I had asked him for a job.

It wasn't really a depot at all. There weren't any benches, waiting rooms or ticket windows like in the city. It was a large, barn-like restaurant with rows and rows of counters and booths with windows that looked out at the gas pumps. It was where Greyhound buses stopped to get gas and let the passengers stretch their legs and get something to eat. Tickets were sold at the cigarette and cigar counter. There weren't any buses parked outside, so I wasn't surprised that the restaurant was almost empty. I sat at the counter and ordered a cup of coffee. After I had sipped enough off the top of the cup, I dumped in my customary three spoons of sugar and filled the cup up the rest of the way with cream. That was how I liked coffee, and it was sure one way of getting your nickel's worth.

I was halfway through and very worried about what my next move would be with night coming on when in walked Dad and Gloria. I was facing the door but they hadn't seen me yet. They must have tracked me down through the gas station attendant at Lake Tahoe after all. I turned on my stool so my back was to them.

I shouldn't have run away. I shouldn't have. Now there would be hell to pay. I had to get out of there. I had to beat them home. I headed for the souvenir counter. There was a side door behind the postcard racks. What would I say if they did see me? How could I explain? It would be alright if they found me at home. Then I would probably just get a bawling out and it would be over. But the idea of having them catch me, of having to ride all the way home like a prisoner, was too humiliating for words. I hadn't even wanted to run away. Not really. But I had to.

"Hey, buddy, your check!"

I froze in my tracks, then turned around. The first thing I saw was my father's face. He was all the way across the restaurant at the farthest counter, but his eyes were focused directly on mine. I went back to pick up my check.

"I'm sorry," I told the waitress. "I was afraid I'd miss my bus."

Dad didn't get up or say anything. He just watched. I felt like a trapped animal. What was he thinking? That I was trying to steal the coffee? I decided I would act like I was minding my own business. "Hi," I said, and half-raised my arm in greeting. Gloria was staring, too. I started to cry. I couldn't control it. I ran out through the side door. Dad ran after me. Once outside I slowed to a walk, but a fast walk. *I'll keep walking*, I said to myself. *Keep moving, as though I have someplace to go.* It was getting dark and chilly. God, I wished Guthrie had been there waiting to take me somewhere, anyplace away from there.

"Tony." Dad was calling out to me. His footsteps were about ten yards behind me. He wasn't trying to catch up. "Tony," he said again. His voice was calm and smooth. I stopped. He stopped when I did.

"Let me go, Dad."

"We found the camera in the spare tire wheel well in the trunk."

"I tried to tell you," I said.

"I know."

"Can I go now?"

"You didn't finish your coffee," Dad said.

"I don't want it."

I'll be damned if I was going to let Gloria see me that way, caught running away and brought back by Dad like some sniveling brat.

Why didn't Dad get mad? He had caught me. "Aren't you sore?" I asked.

"No."

"Why not? For Christ's sake, why don't you do something?"

"Are you hungry, son?"

"No," I said. "I'll wait for you in the car." I didn't budge until I was sure Dad was back in the restaurant. Then I went to the car and curled up in the back seat. I would pretend to be asleep. Then I wouldn't have to face Gloria and it would be almost the same as if I had gone home alone. They came out a few minutes later. Gloria said hello, but I didn't answer. What did I want to talk to her for, anyway. She reached back and tousled my hair. "You nut," she said.

Dad and Gloria talked about everything from the weather to movies that friends of theirs had made. They had a long talk about acting, and Dad said he had to give her credit for being so dedicated. There wasn't one mention of the money Dad had lost or the fight. Gloria sat close to Dad. They weren't mad at each other at all. Even though the camera had been found, I felt I had lost something. In fact, I felt like a complete fool.

A letter from my mother was waiting for me when we got home. Constance had put it on my pillow. *It was sure good to hear from her*, I thought, as I tore open the envelope. It was almost as if Mom knew when a letter would do the most good.

My dearest son,

I am so proud about the ninth grade instead of the eighth. You'll have to work hard at first to keep up. The coming school year should be a most important one for you. Please send the address of the school so I can write to you there.

It's hot and muggy here. On weekends I fight the crowds to find a little spot on the beach to sun myself.

Please remember some of our talks, darling. I want you to feel free to give your love and friendship. I know you have plenty for all of us. Loving people are always happier than people who don't love so much, and they make other people happier, too.

I hope you remembered to ask Gloria if the teddy bear should be cleaned before you gave it to Tim. I bet he loved it. I'll write to you often, and I'll give you all the news of myself. In the meantime, all my love to you, and remember to enjoy everything, especially the beaches. Give my regards to everyone. As always, with all my love,

Mother

I wanted to write back and tell her everything that was happening. I took the stationery from the Fairmont Hotel out of my suitcase and sat down at the desk.

Dear Mom,

We got home just this minute from a wonderful vacation. Dad took us all the way up the coast to San Francisco. As you can see, we stayed at the Fairmont Hotel. It was really fancy. Then we went even further north to Lake Tahoe. I saw the gambling there, and the mountains were bigger than any I had ever seen. The desert was beautiful. We all had a wonderful time.

How are you? I guess it is pretty hot this time of year. The desert was hot but you get used to it after a while. So I didn't mind it.

I start school very soon, and Dad will be going away at about the same time. It's funny. I want to hurry up and get started because I want to do well, but at the same time I hate the idea. It is another boarding school. But it's supposed to be a good one. I've never been to one as fancy as this. I'll get to come home every weekend, from Friday afternoon at 3pm until Sunday at 4pm, even after Dad leaves. He promised. That makes it better than any of the other schools.

Please write, write, write. And, if you can afford it, would you send me a little money to spend? I can't ask Dad or Gloria for anything right now.

I love you. XXXXXXOOOOOOOXXXXXX and a bear hug. Your son, Tony.

11

Reveille

Gloria didn't invite me to go to town with her or come into her room to talk after Dad went to work in the morning. I don't think she gave a damn about me anymore. And, to top it off, Sumner, Dad's nephew, moved in the day after we got back from Lake Tahoe. Into my room! Boy, that pissed me off. He either went to the studio with Dad or hung around the house all day. It was murder because, by some coincidence, Sumner was always home when Gloria was and he always went to the studio with Dad on the days Gloria had to go to town. I never got a chance to talk to Gloria alone. Not that she seemed to want to.

The one thing Gloria did tell me was that Dad had sworn off drinking and gambling. I could tell she didn't quite believe him, and I remembered the last time Dad had said something similar, when he borrowed that $1000 from Gloria at the beginning of the summer. The one person who thought Dad was a saint was Sumner. He would have believed Dad if he said he could jump off the Empire State Building, land on his feet, and bounce back to the top, all with a smile. I admit that after a few days I really thought Dad was going to change. But at dinner on Friday night, he lashed out at Gloria and me for no reason at all. He shot us a scorching look and said, "You all think you're so perfect. I'll show you what discipline is." Then he smiled warmly at Sumner. "Won't I?"

"Sure will, Nick."

Dad's jacket was hung over the back of his chair, and through the whole meal the silver gleam of a flask top could be seen sticking out of the inside pocket. When Gloria and I said nothing, not because we were being mean, but because we were disappointed, Dad got up in a huff and stormed out of the house to the yard. Then, at breakfast on Saturday morning, he announced he was going to the track and that on Sunday he was playing canasta at the Bloomingdales'. That meant Gloria was going to have to take me back to school on Sunday. Every time something important came up, Dad managed to disappear, like that first day when he hadn't come to the airport to pick me up and sent Gloria instead.

Sumner was faithful. Either he never got a day off or he had no friends. I decided he had no friends. After Dad left, he, Gloria and I went out to the beach. Sumner was in rare form. He made fun of military schools and asked if I was going to enjoy playing tin soldiers. When he suggested I go riding at the Archers', I knew he wanted to get rid of me. But I said no. Sumner had brought two beers and a Coke. As he and Gloria were spreading the towels on the sand, I made a quick but not too obvious grab and took a beer for myself and Gloria. I asked Gloria if she wanted to take a walk along the beach with me. Sumner got up to come, too. Gloria was great. "We'd like to be alone for a few minutes," she said. "If you don't mind." We left Sumner, who thought himself the great blonde Adonis of all time, sitting alone on the beach with a Coke in his hand, like a kid.

"You do love me, don't you?" Gloria asked out of a clear blue sky.

"Why have you been so mean?"

"I didn't think you liked me anymore," she said. "But I had to keep things cool between us."

"Why?"

"You're so serious about me." Gloria held my hand. "I didn't dare let it go on. I think Nick has Sumner here to watch us, or me anyway."

"That's funny."

"What is?"

"He's here to watch us and I've been watching *him*."

"Nick's so blind. Sumner has been trying to make it with me since the day we met." Gloria spotted Sumner trotting along the beach behind us. "Here comes hound dog man," she said. "Quick, kiss and make up."

Gloria picked up her friend, Julie, on the way to school. She was very tall and wore high heel shoes. Her dark hair flowed down her back and she wore too much makeup. She reminded me of the girls who sat talking about their friend Denise at Cal-Neva Lodge. I kind of resented that Gloria didn't let it be our time together, alone, but Julie was nice. Gloria explained that she and Julie were meeting a realtor later to help Julie pick out a house.

"I hope I find something today, before the offer is withdrawn, if you know what I mean," said Julie.

"Was he stoned when he said it?" asked Gloria.

"Believe it or not, it was in the morning."

"Then he probably meant it."

"He made a big pile on a cattle deal, so he was in a generous mood. I think he wants to save me for himself. You know—set me up in a house and have me there waiting for him when he comes to town."

"It still sounds like a great deal. Brentwood would be nice. I've thought about getting a house there if…" Gloria stopped herself. We drove quietly for a while, then Gloria and Julie started rating people they knew on a scale of one to ten. Movie stars, from three to five. A Chicago gangster, four. "What about me?" Gloria asked.

"Ten," Julie said. "Me?"

"Ten, naturally."

"We can talk. That's the difference."

"You can't talk to men," said Gloria. "I found that out years ago. It's always an act." Julie reached across me and patted Gloria affectionately. Then she smiled at me, and patted my knee.

At school, Gloria gave me a real kiss goodbye. It didn't bother her in front of Julie. They were real good friends. I watched them turn around in the parking lot, then drive away.

My roommate was lying on the lower bunk reading a Dracula comic book when I came in with my black trunk. There it was. I had the upper bunk again. I dropped my trunk with a crash. He looked up over the top of his comic book.

"I'm Roth. My friends call me Sy. You'll call me Roth."

"Ray," I said.

"I hate it here. I hope you're not going to like it. I can't stand brown-nosers." Roth squeezed one of many pimples on his face between two nail-bitten fingers. White junk oozed out. I didn't wince. He shrugged and wiped his fingers on the school blanket. "I tried to flunk every subject last year, but they wouldn't let me."

"This is my first year," I said.

"Freshman?" Roth asked.

"Yes."

"So am I. But I'll probably always be a freshman. I never study. I have a high I.Q., but I refuse to apply myself. Once in a while I read a classic comic book to break the monotony."

Roth's suitcases were in the middle of the floor, still closed. "Are we supposed to unpack now?" I asked.

"Of course," he said. "Someone will be around to snoop in our dresser drawers. If you have any contraband, you'd better hide it. Those are yours." He pointed to a dresser and closet. "What does your father do?"

"He's a movie director."

"The Industry. You'll find a lot of that around here." He turned a page. "Where'd you go to school last year?"

"P.S. 3. New York."

"A public school? Don't admit that. No one here has ever been to a public school."

"I've been to other kinds, too. What does your father do?"

"Plumbing supplies," Roth said. "It's a good business because Los Angeles is so full of shit. Have you noticed that?"

I was already getting tired of listening to Roth. I opened my trunk. Roth slipped the comic book under his pillow and got up. He opened his suitcases carelessly, dumping everything on the floor around his feet, and stood right on top of a pile of freshly pressed uniforms. He scooped an armful of clothes from the floor and piled them on top of his dresser. All schools had their own rules about arranging closets and dressers. Even though Roth didn't fold anything, I figured I could at least find out where things went. Roth forced an overfilled drawer closed. After he brought me up to date on his whole life story, which wasn't that different from mine except that his parents were still married, he stopped talking long enough to notice I was arranging my gear the way he was. He threw his hands to his face and peered through two fingers, the way a kid watching a movie looks at something scary and horrible that's about to happen.

"No, no, no," he groaned. "Don't do what I do. I make a point of not doing anything right."

Lieutenant Lewis, the student officer in charge of our cabin, sent a sharp-looking kid from room to room to order us to meet in Lewis' room with paper and pencil.

"Right away," Roth said with a mock bow. "We do as the chief flunky commands."

I didn't like it. I wanted a different roommate.

Lewis, straddling a chair in front of his desk, took a pencil out of his mouth and called out everybody's name, checking each off a list. A sick smile crossed his face when he came to Roth's name. "I drew the booby prize," he said. A couple of the older kids snickered. Roth smiled brightly. He was in his glory.

"I'm glad I made the grade, George," Roth said.

"Lieutenant Lewis," the officer snapped.

"Yes, sir," Roth said with false crispness, "Lieutenant Lewis, sir." He saluted.

"I was about to give you your schedules," Lewis said. "Do you all have pencils?"

"No, sir." Roth spoke up immediately.

"Dismissed for thirty seconds." Lewis went ahead without waiting for Roth. "Reveille at o-six hundred. Calisthenics at o-six fifteen in front of the bleachers on the football field. Uniform: white T-shirt, khakis and tennis shoes. No outer jackets." He paused briefly while we wrote. "Return to barracks o-six forty for clean-up and change into uniform of the day. Assembly on the upper parking lot, o-seven hundred. You'll have to run to make it."

"K...h...a...k...i...s," Roth spelled out. He was way behind us. "Would you hold on a minute, George?" Lewis ignored him and kept going. We got the times for sick calls, inspections, classes, drill periods, study halls, meals and, finally, taps.

"Most of you will be in my company," Lewis said when he finished with the day's routine. He ran his finger down the roll sheet. "Abel, Burton, Decker," he mumbled to himself. "Ray?" He raised his voice to seek me out. "Cadet Ray."

"Yes, sir."

"You'll be assigned to one of the lower school units." Every eye in the room turned toward me.

"But I'm a freshman," I protested.

"Sir," Lewis corrected.

"Sir," I repeated

"What the hell does the United States Army care if you're a freshman? You're under ROTC age, are you not?" I didn't answer. I knew you had to be 14 in ROTC. "Speak up, Ray."

"Yes, sir," I said. There was nothing in the world worse than being the youngest in a group of guys. Maybe it wasn't so hot that

I skipped, after all. I glued my eyes to the heels of the boy in front of me.

"Dismissed," Lewis said.

"They're real bastards when they get to be seniors," said Roth on the way back to our room. "They go power mad."

"How about showing me the right way to do my clothes?" I asked.

"I'm terribly dense that way, but I can ask one of Lewis' flunkies to help you. They're do-gooders of the first order."

Roth flopped across his bed. He took the comic book he had started earlier out from under his pillow and found his place.

"What does Sy stand for?"

"Seymour," he grimaced. I could tell he felt the same way about his name as I did about my age. "I can't stand Seymour." I laughed. "What are you giggling at, Baby Fats?"

"Nothing," I said, "Nothing at all."

"Hey!" Roth screamed at the top of his lungs. "Baby Fats needs help putting away his diapers!"

"Shut up, Seymour!" a voice threatened from across the hall.

Roth was a total mess. His shoes were scuffed and his hair was greasy. Whether I could figure him out or not, I knew I wasn't going to like him.

After lights out, my mind wandered to other schools. Roth was asleep. As I thought about the things that had happened, I came to the conclusion that I had given people a hard time. I wondered if the "foolish rebellions" and "always finding fault in others" I had been accused of by Mom and Dad meant that I was like Roth. I had never looked at it that way before. I knew I hadn't been liked at school. I was a loner. What a fool I had been to think that Dad could make life perfect for me. I didn't even know him. I knew Gloria, though. She wasn't a dream. Boy, was I glad we had made up before she brought me to school. Going through the first week with nothing to look forward to would have been awful. I hugged my pillow and thought how great it would be to see her when I went home for the weekend. I cursed Sumner, and even Dad, for being there. I wanted Gloria for myself. So I came to live in California. So what? What had I gained? I didn't know Dad much better than I did before. But I had met Gloria. That was good. Good? Don't think about that. I let my pillow go. I tried to lie absolutely still, very straight on the bed. I stared at the ceiling. I tried to make my mind a blank.

I made a thousand resolutions about becoming an honor student, a star football player, anything to keep from thinking about Gloria anymore. I twisted and turned trying to get comfortable in the strange bed. The night was black and hollow.

What's it like to grow up blind, to stumble over strange objects, not to know what you want or where you're heading? To reach from a sucking whirlpool for a hand but not know whose hand, where it is, or if it will save you?

Roth ripped off his blankets and threw them violently to the floor in his sleep. He yelped a couple of times, then whimpered, and was quiet again. *Oh Dad!* I buried my head in the pillow. *I don't know what I'm doing.*

At 5.30 in the morning, a half hour before Reveille, I slipped on my khaki pants, T-shirt and tennis shoes. I went out into the damp morning and sat on the cabin steps to watch the first deep red curve of the sun make its appearance over the tiled roof of the chapel. The highest stained-glass window shined like a sheet of gold mica. It would be a hot day. The grass of the football field was almost hidden under a giant mass of fog that had settled into the valley overnight. I decided to walk through the fog and have a cigarette. Cold air seeped through my shirt and crept up my back. I cupped the cigarette to keep my hand warm. The smoke tasted good. A few minutes later I heard someone coughing, then footsteps coming in my direction. I strained my eyes trying to see through the fog.

I stepped on the cigarette and kept walking. But before I had taken ten paces, this cadet appeared. I stood still, stupidly hoping he might walk right by without noticing me.

"Mornin'," he wheezed from about twenty feet away. He wasn't dressed for calisthenics, but in the darker wool pants that went with the Eisenhower jacket. He had a long red scarf wrapped about five times around his neck. As he got close, I could see the sergeant stripes on his jacket. He was much older than me. I thought of myself standing there in a T-shirt. Maybe it wouldn't seem strange to him that I was cold. He trampled the grass like an elephant and quietly muttered to the bugle which he held tucked firmly under his arm. "What in the Lord's name are you doin' outta your nice warm bed, little boy?" the sergeant asked as he stopped before me.

"I woke up early, sir."

"The name's Wallah, Billy Wallah." We shook hands. "Man," he complained, "I can't see gettin' up this time o' day. Why should men and boys rise before chickens and dogs?" He took a pack of Luckies out of his pocket. "Smoke?"

"No, thanks. I'm not allowed."

"You smoke, though, don't you?" Waller asked as he lumbered on beside me. I shook my head to his question and quickened the pace toward my cabin. "Then don't let me see hot coals stickin' outta your face, hear?" I didn't say anything, but he went on. "Don't try to kid ol' Billy, kaydet. We all smoke. We ah' all afflicted by this nasty habit." Waller inhaled deeply. "And if we're not allowed to indulge, we find a way anyhow. Isn't that so, kaydet?" He blew a giant stream of smoke out through his nose and mouth.

"I guess so," I said. We were almost at the cabin steps.

"What's your name," he asked.

"Ray," I said. "I'm new."

"Ray," he grabbed my arm to make me stop walking. "You don't have to be scared o' me," the sergeant chuckled, "I'm like you, no different, wanna get through schoolin' as painlessly as possible. Only reason I have these stripes here," he patted his shoulder, "is 'cause I've stuck it out three years without gettin' into serious difficulty. And 'cause they found out I could blow this here piece o' tin."

"Are you the bugler?"

"Now what do you go askin' a stupid question like that for?" Waller adjusted his earmuffs. "Do you suppose I'd be outta my cozy bed if I didn't have ta be?" He shook his head. "Don't try to get away from me with a stupid question like that. I'm gonna tell you somethin', Ray. I don't wanna see you puffin' away out here like a smokestack. It's no offense to me, understand, but if I see you and don't report it, and someone else sees you, too, then it's my skin. I'd have ta go through the same punishment as you." He poked my chest to make his point. "That's what I mean by difficulties," he explained. "I don't want ta spend my precious weekends on campus. You wouldn't want ta get ol' Billy into trouble, would you, Ray?"

"No, sir. Of course not, sir. Please don't report me this time. I don't want to be campused, either. Please."

"Okay, Ray. Simmer down, simmer down. We understand each other. Now don't you go tellin' anybody you saw me smokin' on the football field. We seniors are only allowed to smoke in the smoke shack, up on the hill. Fire danger. You understand?"

"Yes, sir."

Waller found the mouthpiece to his bugle in a pocket. "Gets cold," he said as he massaged it. When he was satisfied with the temperature of the mouthpiece, he fitted it into the hollow stem of the bugle. Then he consulted his watch. "O-five-fifty-five." He put the bugle to his lips and blasted Reveille. Then he went to each window of the cabin and pounded on the glass, "Reveille. Reveille," he shouted. "Get your fannies outta those nice warm beds." I followed him from window to window. "You hear me? Reveille. Rise and shine, chickies!"

"Where do you go now?" I asked.

"Run like a fool to every other cottage, barracks and chicken house on the grounds. Look at me," he protested. "My size, and they make me bugler! I have eleven minutes to get every kaydet outta the sack." Waller made a wide sweep of his arm indicating the large area he had to cover. "See you 'round, Ray," he said as he began trotting to the next cabin.

"Thanks." I called after him. I was thinking how lucky I had been that Waller caught me rather than someone like Lewis or Roth. Roth would have announced I was smoking to the whole campus just to prove nobody was any better than he was. Waller half-trotted, half-ran, his head bowed like a locomotive, cursing his weight under his breath. Our cabin was jumping. I could hear everyone talking, water splashing on sleepy faces, Lewis ordering everyone to hurry. I hid my cigarettes under the porch steps and went inside to brush my teeth. A minute or two later, Reveille blew up above. The grounds were coming to life.

12
Forever Alone

I sat on a bench along the sidelines when football practice was over. Sumner had answered the telephone when I tried to call Gloria after breakfast. I hung up without saying hello. If he was watching Gloria for Dad, I couldn't let him know I was trying to reach her. There hadn't been another chance to get to a telephone all day. Every second was carefully planned at Harvard. Planned? Ha! Regimented. You answered roll call about twenty times a day.

I wanted to do something to make Dad think I was great. I couldn't blame him for sending me back to boarding school, even if he didn't know about Gloria and me. Mr. Green, the coach, and his assistant walked across the field toward the gym. A minute later I was alone. I wished Dad had seen that tackle I made and heard the coach saying how good it was.

Billy Waller's bugle announced a half hour until dinner formation. "Sumner," I spat. "I'd like to smash his head in with my cleats." I wrecked my toe kicking a stone as hard as I could. "Damn it," I said over and over. When I reached the spot where the stone stopped, I threw my helmet at it, then made two fists and shadowboxed a short, vicious, fight with Sumner. I punched his face about twenty times, until his nose was bashed in and bloody and he couldn't see, then I kneed him in the groin as hard as I could. When he fell at my feet in a pile, I kicked him in the ribs. I stood panting over him. I was more tired from that than I had been from playing ball, but I had the same good feeling that came over me after making the tackle.

It's a funny thing, though, when you're fake fighting like that. You always see the punch coming that would have killed you if the fight had been real, and you know damn well it would have been you lying on the ground in a bloody heap instead of the other guy. In my heart I knew I couldn't beat Sumner. But I could pretend. It made me feel better.

"Tony loves Gloria," "Gloria loves Tony," "Gloria and Tony." I wrote each hundreds of times, first the whole phrase, then a column of Glorias, a column of loves, and a column of Tonys. I spent most of study hall hunched over my half-closed notebook trying to look like I was working. A cadet officer monitored the aisles to be sure nobody was sleeping, reading comic books or writing letters. Every time he passed my desk, I turned to a fresh page and scribbled an algebraic equation. But even when I tried to do the ten assigned math problems and the composition on "Why I wanted to come to Harvard," it was no use. I couldn't keep my mind on school.

I went through the next day like a robot. Mr. Sherman, the English teacher, asked why I didn't have a composition to turn in. I told him study hall was over before I could finish. He lectured on the importance of getting off to a good start at school. I couldn't get my heart into football practice either. What was the point of working your ass off to get a ball from one side of a field to the other? I had missed so many tackles, thrown so many blocks all wrong, it was hard to keep from thinking I was a complete failure.

A letter from Mom was waiting for me when I went to my room. I flopped down on the bed to read it. Maybe Gloria would write, too. Wouldn't that be wonderful, if she sent me a letter? I lifted the typewritten page out of the envelope. A $5 bill was paperclipped to the top.

Dear Mugwump,

Please send details about school, and let me know all the new things that are happening to you. Try to work hard and don't worry about catching up. Why can't you ask Dad for anything? Are you two on bad terms? Enclosed is $5 I pray you won't spend foolishly. It is hard, bless your heart, as much as I want to, for me to send you money. You know my budget.

You say in your letter how much you enjoyed the gambling in Nevada. Don't allow yourself to get the impression that a person can get anything for nothing in this life. It can be a very serious mistake. I'm sure Dad is supplying you with enough for your needs. Although things may be hard for you at school for a while, try not to complain too much. Just do your best and everything will be fine.

Remember, we are all trying to do what's best for you. Sometimes, when you think that everyone's against you, and have put you in school or some such thing because they don't want you, remember it is only because they are trying to do what's best. I still think about one time when you were very angry with me for placing you in boarding school when my only other choice was to have sent you all the way to a distant relative in Canada. Bless your heart, I wanted you near me, but couldn't have you home. I wouldn't have traded my visits with you, or the vacations, for anything in the world. You have given my life meaning.

Well, back to work. Let me hear from you soon.
OOOOXXXXOOOOXXXX and a bear hug.
Love, Mother.

Mom was always nagging me about the way I spent money. Just because Dad had thrown away all his money didn't mean I would, too. Maybe I should tell her that when I wrote back. And all that hogwash about not being able to have me home. She sent me to boarding school because I was a pain in the neck. Mom really burned me up.

I took a chance and answered her letter in study hall. As much as I was tempted, I wasn't a wise guy, after all. I knew she wanted me to be happy, so I wrote her the kind of letter I thought she wanted. I said everything was peaches and cream, and that I certainly wouldn't complain about anything. Then I told a small lie. I said it wasn't that I couldn't ask Dad for anything, but that I was saving up enough money to buy him a nice present. I wanted it to be a surprise. "So," I asked mom, "if you can afford it, please send another $5 when you get the chance." Sometimes, when things weren't going very well, it made me feel better to have a lot of money in my pocket.

The next morning after breakfast I made a beeline for the telephone booth outside the administration building. I didn't want to take a chance of some other guy getting there first. I planned to wait until the last minute before class to call Gloria. Maybe she would be awake by then, and if I only had enough time to say hello, it would be okay. I had a few minutes to kill, so I carried on a fake conversation with Dad. "School's fascinating," I said. "I miss you, too." Every minute a cadet came up to the booth, looked at his watch, and went on to class. "I wish we could spend more time together. We'll have time to visit this weekend." I paused as though he were speaking, then acted real elated for the benefit of this cadet who had decided to wait for the telephone. "We're going sailing with Humphrey Bogart? That's tremendous!" I checked the time. It was 8.15. "Okay. Okay. I have to get to class," I said. "Goodbye." I hung up, then took the receiver right off the hook again. I held up one finger to let the cadet who was waiting know I had one more call to make. He waved a fist at me and took off. I lifted the dime I had been fingering through the whole phony conversation with Dad to the small round slot, but fumbled trying to put it in and dropped it. When I finally got the dial tone, my knees were shaking and I was all choked up. I dialed the operator.

"Operator. May I help you?"

"Yes, yes," I said. "Oh…" I hung up. I hadn't taken out enough money for the call. I fished a quarter out of my pocket and put it on the stand under the phone. I dialed "0" again. *I don't know what to say to Gloria. That's what's wrong,* I told myself.

"Operator."

"I'd like to call Malibu 4586, please."

"What number are you calling from?"

"State 26691."

"Twenty cents for the first three minutes," she instructed. "Signal when through."

"I'm putting in a quarter," I said. "I mean, I already have a dime in, so that'll be thirty-five. Okay?"

The phone was already ringing. It sounded far away and muffled, as though it were in another country.

"I'll give you credit for the extra fifteen cents," the operator said.

"Fine. Okay," I tried to say politely. Get your nosey ass off the phone is what I wanted to say. I pictured the phone ringing on the nightstand next to Gloria's bed, and her stirring in her sleep. It was like calling a stranger. How do you call a stranger and say you love her? Maybe it's easier with someone you don't know too well. Maybe it's better not to let yourself get all screwed up over someone. If you don't expect anything. whatever you get is gravy. But why hadn't Gloria written me a letter? It was awful soon, I guess.

Don't answer, Sumner, I said to myself. *Don't be there. Be dead.*

"Hello," Gloria picked up on the fifth ring. Her voice was faint, filtered through a dream. I had woken her up. "Who is it?"

"Tony," I said. "I've been trying to reach you for days, but Sumner keeps picking up the telephone."

"Oh, hi, doll."

"I'm sorry I woke you. Is Sumner there?"

"He went to the studio with Nick. What time is it?"

"8.30. I had to call early."

There was a short silence. Then, as though someone had thrown cold water in Gloria's face, she said, "Tony. How are you? Miserable, I bet."

"I got a letter from my mother yesterday. I thought it was from you when I saw the envelope on my dresser. Why haven't you written?"

"I can't!" Gloria gasped. "I never write anything. Hang on. Let me get a cigarette. She was on the line again in a few seconds. "Tony?"

"Yes, go ahead."

"I've been reading about Nordic types in this psychology book. Nick's Nordic, you know. That's why he's withdrawn and detached all the time. They never show any emotion and success is very important."

"I don't know about all that." I wanted to change the subject. "What have you been doing?"

"I may go back to work. There's nothing to stay around here for and the studio may have a wonderful part for me."

"I hope you don't go away, too." I could feel it coming. It would be like always. I would be left at school to rot.

"Hey, you know what happened?" Gloria snickered. "We were walking on the beach last night and the little girl from next door said, 'Look at Mr. Ray, he's a big old chocolate bar.'" Gloria laughed. "Isn't that a panic?" Then she became real serious again. "I can't believe he isn't even 40, can you?" Gloria waited a moment for my answer, but I had none. "I think he acts like 75, the way he sits like a silent Buddha pretending to be so wise."

"I miss you."

"I miss you, too, silly." It didn't mean anything. She was only saying it because I did.

"Do you think Nick's smart?" she asked.

"I don't know, Gloria." She was driving me nuts with all the talk about Dad. "Let's not talk about him." I could picture her sitting with her back against about five pillows, smoking up a storm, while she tore Dad to pieces.

"What do you want to talk about?" I could tell she was sore at me for cutting her off.

"Anything you want." I looked outside. All the walkways were empty. Classes must have started ages ago. "I have to go, Gloria. I'm late." Suddenly I couldn't wait to hang up. "I better get off the phone."

"What's wrong, doll?"

"Write to me. Please write."

"I can't write letters," she protested.

"Even a word is okay," I insisted. "Say hello and sign your name."

"Tony."

"I have to go."

"I love you, doll."

"Don't say that."

"I love you," she repeated.

I didn't know what to make of Gloria. "I love you, too," I said.

"Call me."

"I will. Goodbye."

Father Murray, our math teacher, asked why I was late. I went to his desk and said, "I was sitting in chapel and lost track of time."

"Dear son," wrote Dad. "I think in days to come this letter may be of more interest to you than if we were to have spent a couple of hours talking today."

"Sunday" was written in the right-hand corner of the page. I checked the envelope. It was postmarked Tuesday. It had sure taken him long enough to get the damn thing in the mail.

"It may prove of interest to both of us, for future reference, because on some things I'll undoubtedly be wrong, and more amazingly, on some things I may be right. As we check in with each other from week to week we'll both have the chance to find out.

I don't want to rehash old grievances any more than the headmaster at school wishes to know of old problems. Fresh start all the way through, right? But here are a few reminders. Some will be interpreted by you as harsh criticism, but that is not the intention. The intention is, as always, to be of some help to you."

How do you like that? Mom and Dad were using the same lines. You would think if they were going to get together to make excuses for railroading me into another boarding school, they would at least be smart enough to say different things. Doing what's best for me. Ha!

"For instance, I have had the chance to watch some of your initial enthusiasm, both material and emotional. I have seen it riding very, very high into the stratosphere. Then the rapid landing or even parachute jump into a deep valley of self-criticism, complaint, or blame of others. No one was at fault, but the beginning expectations of yourself and of others were usually overboard or else the inevitable valley of despair and depression would not have been so deep. You are not competing with anyone, least of all me. That would be a foolish contest and a frustrating one, at least for a while. Now you have to teach yourself as fast or as slowly as necessary. It is to this kind of approach to things that I get slangy and say 'take it easy, but take it.' As always, Dad."

I crumpled the letter into a ball and squeezed it in my fist, then opened it and tore the page into four long strips. "I'll show him." Didn't he blame everyone for disappointing him? What makes Dad so special? Instead of showering and dressing for dinner, I put on my pajamas and climbed into bed. Roth came by on his way to the dining hall.

"What's wrong with you?" he asked.

"I'm sick."

He snickered like an old hen. He was enjoying every minute of it. I ignored him. The bugle sounded five minutes to dinner. Roth dumped his books and left. A few minutes later I got up and gathered together the pieces of Dad's letter. I slipped them back into the envelope, opened my trunk where I kept the rest of his letters, and placed it under the rubber band.

I went out before Reveille on Thursday morning and, big as life, got myself caught smoking again. I begged Waller not to turn me in, but all he did was shake his big head sadly. "You've antagonized ol' Billy. Now what did you go and do that for?" Captain

Patton, the student officer at my table, told me to report to Father
Chalmers' office after breakfast. I didn't eat another bite. I left the
dining hall and walked slowly, the long way around the parking lot,
to the administration building. The receptionist ushered me in to
see Father Chalmers. "Good morning, Tony," he greeted me cheerfully.

The phony bastard.

"Good morning, sir." I sounded real morose. Father Chalmers
motioned me to the chair I had used the day of the interview. I sat.

"Cigarette?" he asked. The smile vanished from his lips. His
eyes had never been smiling. "Oh," he said, "you don't smoke,
do you?" I had no answer. "If you do smoke," Father Chalmers
warned, "and continue to do so, we won't be able to have you stay
on here." He paused long enough to let the weight of his words
sink in. "Do you understand?"

"Yes, sir."

"Father Murray said you weren't in study hall last night."

"No, sir."

"He went there to give you a hand with your math assignment.
That was nice of him, wasn't it?"

"Yes."

"I suppose you'll be getting demerits for that," Father Chalmers sighed. He was really fed up with me.

"I wasn't feeling well, Father. I even told Roth when he came
by on his way to dinner." Father Chalmers shook his head while he
listened. Maybe it was more of a nod. I couldn't tell what he was
thinking for sure, but I would lay dollars to doughnuts it was his
way of saying, "Sure, kid." He rummaged through the papers on
his desk until he found what he was looking for. Then he adjusted
his glasses and read to himself. I waited.

"In your first week, you've been caught smoking twice, didn't
turn in an English assignment, were late for math class, and missed
a study hall. Is that correct?"

"Yes, sir." I squirmed. Boy, news sure got around fast.
I wondered if they even tapped the telephones. He had me on
everything. I felt like two cents.

"Not off to a very auspicious start, are you?" Father Chalmers
really smiled this time. I stared at my feet, praying it would be over
soon. "Are you still feeling sick today?"

"No, sir," I mumbled.

"In future, sick call is at 8.15 in the morning. Of course, if you're ill, you can go to the infirmary at any time. But you must tell your officer or teacher where you are going." I sat there like an idiot. The way he nodded all the time drove me nuts. "It's your first week here, Tony. I wouldn't want to put the mark of troublemaker on you."

"Thank you, sir."

"If anyone asks why you're not going home for the first two weekends, say your parents are away. Nobody will know any differently except you and me," Father Chalmers said.

He acted as though he were doing me a big favor.

"What'll I say at home?"

"I couldn't lie about it." He raised his eyebrows. "Could you?"

"No, sir," I answered, sincere as hell. "Of course not." I tell Dad that kind of thing every day. I did feel crumby, though. I had been acting pretty rank.

"Tony, you can thank Bill Waller for coming to me instead of the Senior Council. The seniors usually decide punishments." Father Chalmers got up. "You can go to class now."

I telephoned Gloria to ask her to cover for me with Dad by saying I felt at a terrible disadvantage having skipped a year and wanted to stick around school to get help catching up. Late Friday afternoon, after most of the kids had gone home for the weekend, I got a message to call Dad. "I talked to Father Chalmers yesterday," he said, "but he thought you'd want to explain." I told Dad the same things I had said to Gloria. He believed me. Father Chalmers made me feel like a heel for lying, but what was I supposed to be, a saint?

"I'm on the junior varsity football team," I announced.

"That's healthy competition," he said. "I'm very pleased."

"I tried out for end, but didn't make it. Maybe next year, if I'm still here."

"I hope you were able to benefit from some of the points I tried to make."

"I think so," I said.

"Good." One of Dad's famous silences followed. Then he said, "I'll get your allowance in the mail before I go on location next week. You won't need as much as I gave you during the summer."

"Thanks, Dad. Oh, I got a letter from Mom already."

"How's Jean?"

"Fine." I didn't tell him she had sent me five bucks. "I don't blame you for anything, the way your letter made out."

"You probably have legitimate reasons to be upset with me at times, but it's time to stop indulging yourself in disappointments."

"I don't anymore."

"Constructive action." I looked about the campus as he talked, wondering what I could do there to make me happier. Talking to Dad was like beating your head against a stone wall. "Life is difficult to cope with at times, particularly for people like us, who expect the best from ourselves and others."

"I don't expect you to be perfect," I jumped in.

"Let me finish," Dad cut me off. "I'm trying to tell you something. Don't lose sight of what's important, of what you really want to accomplish. How can I explain? There are times when you're doing very well in the eyes of others but your opinion of yourself might be one of failure. This is dangerous because in self-despair you might very well destroy all you have built rather than have it stand as only half of what you expected of yourself, or wanted to create. If the desires were unrealistic to start with, well…" Dad sighed, "…what you destroyed thinking you had failed might have been very good. But by negating it, you end up with nothing."

By that time in the conversation, which was very one-sided, I knew Dad was talking more about himself than me. After we said goodbye and I realized I wouldn't be seeing him for three months, I got this eerie sensation that there was something alike in us, something that had to do with finding out that men are really forever alone.

The End of the World

It made me damn angry to see Sumner's car parked next to Gloria's in the garage. He was supposed to be on location with Dad. I cursed as I slammed the gate behind me. Gloria said she couldn't pick me up at school because she had to take care of Tim. She could have brought Tim with her. So I hitchhiked and took buses all the way home.

It was 10.30 when I arrived. Three and a half hours to get home—and Sumner had to be there. An almost empty wine bottle and two half-filled glasses were on the coffee table in front of Gloria. Sumner sat on the couch. Gloria was on the floor with her back against his leg. They were both wearing bathing suits. Mingo jumped up and down against my leg trying to lick my hand. I pushed him down. "I'm glad you two are having such a good time," I said.

"We gave up on you," said Gloria. "It was getting so late, and I really wasn't sure you meant to come home alone."

"How are you?" Sumner asked, with his phony toothpaste smile.

"Fine," I answered. "Just ducky." I had wanted so much to enjoy this weekend alone with Gloria, like a soldier coming home from war. But with Sumner there I felt small and stupid in my uniform. I unbuttoned the olive jacket and took off my tie. With luck Sumner wouldn't make any corny cracks. He gave Gloria a funny look, as though he hadn't expected me to come home or something. How obvious can you be?

Mingo started chewing at my hands again. I wanted to kill him, literally kill him. The way Gloria fondled that damn dog all the time was nauseating. I had been so happy on the way home. Now I was morose as hell. "Where's Tim?"

"Mother took him so I gave Constance the whole weekend off. Go change," Gloria said. "The grunion are running tonight."

Sumner worked on his hair with a black comb that had been sticking out of his tight bathing suit. I could have sworn he was waiting for me to leave the room so he could make some lousy crack like shouldn't I be going to bed. You would have thought I was cramping his style. I couldn't stand there like an idiot all night. I turned on my heel and went to my room. I wasn't fooling anyone. I was still a kid. As far as Gloria was concerned, I could have been campused for life. I took off the uniform and put on my blue bathing suit and a T-shirt. "Have a sip of wine," Gloria said when I came back to the living room. I got myself a glass from the bar, half filled it, and drank it down.

"How long are you going to be here?" I asked Sumner.

"A couple of days. Nick sent me up to do some things."

"I bet." I said under my breath. Sumner looked like a Wildroot Cream Oil and Catalina swimsuit ad all rolled up into one. And don't forget the toothpaste grin. I sat next to him on the couch. "Did you stay here last night?" His teeth flashed as he laughed. Gloria shot one of her "are you out of your mind" looks at me. "No," Sumner said. "I was at my mother's house." He slipped his comb back into his bathing suit and got up to go to the bathroom. I emptied the wine bottle into my glass.

"My, you're getting possessive," Gloria kidded when Sumner was gone.

"What'd I do? I asked a simple question."

"Nothing," said Gloria, but I could tell she was bugged at me for thinking what I was thinking. "Don't drink a lot in front of Sumner, and try not to smoke. He's Nick's little boy." Gloria said she would fix me a sandwich, so I followed her into the kitchen. I couldn't have cared less about food.

"Did he stay here last night?"

"No," she turned away from me to open the refrigerator. "You have nothing to be jealous of. Nothing at all." I wrapped my arms around her neck and leaned my head against her back.

"Can I kiss you?"

Gloria's hands froze for a terrible waiting moment. I turned her around by the shoulders and gave her a peck on the cheek.

"You tease," she smiled. "Now go stay with Sumner."

Had there been a newspaper or a magazine around I would have read it. Anything to ignore Sumner. I stared at the ceiling like some kind of nut. "How's school?" he asked.

"Shitty."

"It's supposed to be a good school. Isn't it?"

"It's shitty. That's all." I shrugged my shoulders.

"Don't you like the other guys?"

"I don't care for most of them." I was absolutely exhausted with the subject already. "A kid got blackballed a couple of nights ago."

"Blackballed?" Sumner asked. He didn't even know what I was talking about.

"That's when the senior council gangs up on a kid and beats the hell out of him with garrison belts," I said. Sumner caught my eye appraising his reaction. "At least, that's what they do first."

"Hazing goes on anywhere."

"Then they heat black shoe polish until it melts. One of the seniors holds the poor bastard's mouth so he can't scream while the others dip his nuts in the melted polish." I could just picture Sumner listening, bug-eyed with his mouth wide open, but I didn't want to spoil it by looking at him. "They hold him there until it dries. It's almost impossible to get that stuff off without half killing yourself."

"Dinner's ready." Gloria poked her head through the door before Sumner could say anything. I went to the kitchen, still not looking at him. "What's wrong with Sumner? He looks shell-shocked."

"He's just a creep," I said. Gloria went to the living room and I ate my sandwich and drank my milk. Then I went back to the living room.

"It's high tide," Sumner announced. "Let's see what the grunion are doing."

We followed him to the door.

"What about a flashlight and a bucket?" I asked.

"They're in the yard," said Gloria. "We were out before. Bring another bottle of wine." She ran out the door after Sumner.

The dry red wine was easy to drink, and by the time I got to the beach, the bottle was a third gone. The sand felt good running through my toes. A cloud drifted across the high full moon. I focused my eyes on the tideline and took another swig of wine. While the bottle was still up to my mouth, I got a scary chill. I could have sworn I saw the exact spot on the sand where Dad had sat fishing without bait. At the same time, I felt him behind me. I spun around. Nothing. Nothing but black and the lights of the house. I looked back to the sea. It was cold and black, too. Everything gets pulled into the ocean. Everything dies. That's real.

Squeals, laughter and muffled shouts filled the dark gap. When the next wave broke, crashing against the sand, rocketing phosphorus beams shot into the sky like thousands of fireworks. I saw Gloria's shining hair and Sumner's hand around her waist. They were running farther and farther away toward the rocks at the other end of the cove. They romped in and out of the surf, trying not to be caught by the full force of the breakers, trying to catch grunion with the bucket in those few moments before the backwash returned them home to the safety of the sea. The flashlight in Gloria's hand threw crazy fleeting patterns against the water and sand. I ran to them as fast as I could.

Sumner and Gloria had collapsed, out of breath, on the sand near the tide line. I lay down beside Gloria. We watched the waves wash closer and closer to the bucket, which was between us and the ocean. A few minutes later the water turned it over and the flashlight rolled along the hard sand toward the water. For a split second the beam crossed our faces, then it was dark. Sumner ran to catch the flashlight. Gloria was shivering. I put my arm around her neck. Sumner's arm worked its way around her back like a snake.

"I'm still cold," Gloria said. Sumner crossed one of his legs over hers. I followed suit.

We sat there, all intertwined. But I didn't understand Gloria letting Sumner near her.

"What's going on?" I whispered in Gloria's ear.

"Fun," she said. "Just having fun."

"What have you two birds got up your sleeve?" Sumner butted in. "No secrets."

"We're planning the end of the world," I said.

"Let's get another bottle of wine," Gloria said. She raised her knees, throwing off our legs so she could get up.

"Let's race back to the house," Sumner suggested. He was the type that thought running your head off was the greatest thing you could do.

"You two go ahead," Gloria said. "I'll carry the bucket." Sumner counted to three and was off. I ran a few steps with him, then dropped back and took Gloria's hand.

"He's always showing off" I said. Gloria squeezed my hand.

"It's all he's got." We watched Sumner tearing up the beach. "Tony," Gloria said, "I have to go away soon."

"Where?"

"Florida. It's a marvelous part. All about…"

"How long will you be gone?"

"Oh, Tony."

"I don't want you to go."

"Baby." Gloria dropped the bucket and took my face in her hands. "Baby, baby."

"I love you."

"I know." She held me to her.

Sumner was waiting for us in the yard with one of his bright ideas, a freezing stream of hose water. "Don't get my hair wet," Gloria shrieked. She buried her head on my chest.

The sand washed away from our chests, backs, legs. Sumner finally stopped. He was so pleased with himself you could die. Gloria let me go and touched her sopping hair. It hung over her eyes and the back of her head like an upside-down mop. Sumner started laughing. Boy, what a morbid sense of humor. I tore the hose out of his hand. "Now it's your turn." I got between Sumner and the door to the house and turned the hose on him. Gloria blocked his way to the beach. No matter how many times Sumner shouted "enough," I didn't let up. In fact, I turned the nozzle tighter and tighter so the water came out hard as hell, so it stung. I aimed at his face. When he protected his head with his arms, I shot him in the gut. Sumner took a few seconds of that. Then he shouted "Goddamn it!" and ran through the stream of water to wrestle the hose away from me. I cocked my fist to slug him, but knew better. We left crooked lines of water in our wake as we went through the house to Gloria's bathroom to get dry. I wanted to tell Sumner to get lost so I could be alone with Gloria, but as she started to untie the top of her bikini, Gloria ushered us both out. Sumner and I went to my room to dress. I put on jeans and boots. Sumner was in the bathroom fixing his hair again, waving and patting it.

"Let's go!" Gloria shouted. She stormed through the living room. "Let's break out of this prison." She burst into the kitchen. When she saw me, she stopped and laughed.

"Have you gone crazy or something?" I said.

"Hi, dollface. How're you doing?"

I held up the bottle I had opened. "I'm fine," I said. Gloria threw her arms around my neck.

"You're beautiful," she said. "Really beautiful."

"Have a drink of wine before I call the men in the white suits."

"Defending me like that," Gloria giggled. "You would have killed him, wouldn't you?"

"Yes," I said. Gloria stopped laughing. There was something sad about the way she tilted her head and stared into my eyes. Sumner walked in. Boy, was he a nuisance. Gloria looked away, then picked up the car keys from the kitchen table.

"We're off."

Sumner drove. The top was down. Gloria found some modern jazz on the radio and I was custodian of the wine. Maybe it was because we didn't know where we were going that Sumner drove so slowly. It was sure bugging Gloria, though. "Oh, come on, Sumner," she finally said. "Stop playing chauffeur." She slammed her foot over his on the accelerator. "Drive! Drive!" I handed her the bottle. She took a long drink, then passed the bottle to Sumner. He took a less adventurous drink and passed it back to Gloria. She drank again, then gave me my turn.

"It's a woman's world!" Gloria threw her head back against the seat and closed her eyes. Her arms were stretched wide, one around each of us. A faintly mischievous smile crossed her lips. "Well, oh well, oh well," she breathed. "What am I going to do with two handsome men at the same time? Quite a problem." She wasn't really talking to us, but more to herself. "Everyone quiet while I picture it." Her lips were wet and parted. Her hair blew straight out behind her except for a few strands which played over her eyes and mouth. Gloria was a beautiful wild animal defying man to capture her, tormenting the hunters with insanely exciting invitations, then changing in the blink of an eye to an image of purity, of a little girl. Gloria spat some hair out of her mouth. She dropped her head on my shoulder and peered up at me. "Did you know that Sumner has been the closest kid in the world to your father? Did you know that?"

"Gloria…" Sumner said.

"Did you know," Gloria topped Sumner's objection, "that Nick treats him like a son? He encourages him, helps him, gives him jobs. He's also turned him into a lackey. Nick has a way of making servants of people." Gloria's tongue was heavy but her words were loaded with disgust and anger. "He only likes girls and boys much younger. Everybody's dumb. Nobody's smart but him. Everybody's a servant. Jesus, Nick's weak." Gloria closed her eyes. "Sumner thinks he's an actor. Don't you, Sumner? That's hysterical. You'll be a servant, too, won't you, Tony? Or an actor. Because you think Nick is God."

"Have a drink, Gloria." Sumner passed her the bottle. She held it in her lap and rolled it back and forth between the palms of her hands.

"I don't believe in God," I muttered.

"Sumner believes in the Sun God. He is a worshipper of the almighty tan. But Tony loves me. He does." Gloria stared up at me. "Don't you. Tony?" She gently touched my cheek. "Tony loves me as much as anybody in the whole wide world and I love him, too. Because he doesn't question. No questions, no obligations. You don't question, do you, Tony?" I said nothing. "Do you?" She insisted.

"No."

Gloria released me from her stare, which had felt like a heel in my face. Then she turned away. "Oh, shit. What am I saying? What am I doing here with you two bums?" Gloria raised the bottle to her lips and took a long drink. Then she focused on Sumner again. "Tell me, Sumner, I've done quite a lot of acting. What have you done?" Sumner didn't answer. He just drove. "C'mon, you big, strong lion tamer, tell me your proud conquests. Have you worked, trained, failed, tried again? An actor? Ha!" Gloria sat straight up and went in for the kill. She looked right at Sumner. "Don't be a fool. Go home to your mother, meet a respectable girl from Pasadena, and become a dentist."

A long time passed before anybody spoke. Sumner fiddled with the radio. Gloria stared at the sky. She was as still as someone who had died with their eyes open. She paused to search the stars for a clue. "No sleep with me, no take care of me, no love me. I love to cuddle! No, no, no, Nick Ray. You're a phony." She held the now empty wine bottle high in the air, fighting the force of the wind as if making a toast to the sky. "A great, great man. A great director. A great… why? I don't know why. Daddy wouldn't have left me if he loved me." Gloria poked her finger under my nose. "I'm not your little girl. I'm nobody's little girl. Men only want sex," she whispered in my ear. "That's why I can't let you have me. I don't want you to be like the others." Her voice became childlike. "Am

I evil? I don't want much. Really, I don't. I only want to be happy, happy, happy." I drew her close to me and she sobbed against my chest. Sumner drove past Topanga Canyon and I searched the night for the high plateau where Gloria and I had parked. "You have as much of me as I can give," she had said.

A few minutes later we stopped at the Sunset Boulevard exit for gas. I remembered the man with the signs strapped over his shoulders selling movie star maps and Gloria's laughter when I asked if her name was on the map, if she were a star. "What's a star?" she had answered. The wine bottle was thrown overboard. We drove off.

"Which one of you two gentlemen might kiss me?" Gloria asked with precise diction. She looked to Sumner who, without a word, before I could move, pulled her to him. He judged the hundred yards of road before him and dropped his foot off the accelerator. I didn't watch. The car slowing down turned my stomach like the elevator in the Empire State Building coming to a sudden halt after having fallen a hundred stories. I held my breath waiting for Sumner to hit the gas again. It would be over then. Every ounce of wine rushed to my head. I leaned into the wind outside the car window. Gloria pulled me back into the car and down onto her lap. Her hair tickled my cheeks, then smothered me as she bent over. I locked my arms around her neck. "I'll never let go," I swore, then kissed her. "Never."

Gloria and Sumner looked for an all-night movie on Hollywood Boulevard. My head felt as though a bullet had lodged an inch or so above the back of my neck. "Join the party," said Gloria. "Did you have a nice nap?" I focused on the rhinestone-studded sunglasses she had put on.

"Why don't you take those off?" I asked.

"What difference does it make to you if I wear them?" she taunted, picking up my tone of voice. We stopped at a light where a couple of creeps crossing the street slowed down to give Gloria the eye.

"Isn't it affected to wear sunglasses at night?" I asked. The rage was bursting out of me. I couldn't help it. As the light changed, Gloria slapped my face and slid over close to Sumner. She held one of his hands in her lap. When the car stopped again, I jumped out and ran like hell around the corner.

"Tony, Tony, come back!" they yelled, but I kept going. I ran all the way to Sunset Boulevard and ducked into the men's room of a drive-in restaurant. I leaned on the washbasin and saw my blood-shot eyes in the cracked mirror.

"I hope she thinks I'm going to kill myself," I thought. Then I threw up all over the place.

Being sure Gloria and Sumner were combing the streets trying to find me, I walked down Sunset a block, turned up a one-way street so the traffic came from behind me, and carefully made my way back to Hollywood Boulevard. I slipped into an almost deserted amusement hall, where I found a pin ball machine in a shadowy corner. If they came in there, I was going to make them think I was having one hell of a good time. "Who needs you?" I was planning to ask. But half an hour later they still hadn't come. I went back out onto the street. A huge clock shaped like a grinning clown with twelve different kinds of hamburgers for a face said it was ten after two in the morning. Spray from the street cleaner's truck washed popcorn boxes and candy wrappers to the curb. The neon movie house marquees were all dark except one, the all-night movie house, two blocks up. I didn't realize how hauntingly quiet the night was until I heard the roar of a bus starting. I hadn't noticed the sound of a bus since I left home in New York. Two in the morning California time, five in the morning New York time.

Mom always got up early to write. She was probably watering her geranium, or typing, or crying. She cried a lot. After deciding not to go to the all-night movie house, which was featuring a triple-feature horror show, there was nothing ahead but darkness. There was almost nobody on the streets. It was spooky. I stared down the boulevard trying to see the ocean, which I knew was miles away. Then I saw a policeman. I went up to him and asked how I could get back to Malibu. He told me what buses to take to get as far as Santa Monica, but was afraid the bus up the coast wasn't running this late. When I got to the beach I kept one foot on the curb, placed the other on the highway, and stuck out my thumb. *Jesus Christ*, I said to myself. *Here I am hitchhiking all over again.* I couldn't wait to get home.

Gloria was sitting cross-legged in the middle of the living room floor with a half-bottle of Dad's Scotch. Several photographs were strewn around her. She was facing the ocean, watching the beginning of a gray dawn. It was five o'clock in the morning. She hadn't heard me come in, so I tiptoed toward my room. I didn't want to talk about, or even think of, what had happened. Everything would be okay after sleep. It always is. I was halfway across the living room when Gloria reached out to pick up one of the pictures. I stopped short and held my breath. I could see one side of her face and the tip of her nose. It was a miracle she hadn't seen me. She gazed at the photograph as if seeing the grounds at the bottom of yesterday's cup of coffee, as though she wished the cup were still full. Tears rolled down her cheeks. I finally had to take a breath. I exhaled a tiny bit at a time then tried to breathe in slowly. Gloria spun around, startled. She lowered her arm to the floor and we looked into each other's eyes for a long time. Gloria extended her arms the slightest bit toward me and I rushed into them. Gloria held my face in her hands. "You must be frozen," she said.

"I'm sorry I ran away from you."

"I'm sorry I hit you."

"Who are these pictures of?" I asked.

"Oh, no one," she answered, starting to scoop them up into a pile. "My father and his new family. And these are some of my scrapbooks."

"Where's Sumner?"

"That bastard," she cursed. "I sent him away. He wanted me to go to a motel with him. Can you imagine the nerve?" Gloria kissed the end of my nose. "I told him I had to come home and wait for you."

"Did anything happen? Anything bad?" Gloria shook her head no, then turned and rested her head on my shoulder so we were both looking at the ocean.

"Gloria," I asked after a long time. "If I got older and anything happened between you and Dad, would you marry me?"

"Don't talk that way, Tony."

I fastened my eyes on a spot on the rug and sort of chewed on my lips. I wanted to cry. I knew it was stupid, but she could have pretended with me.

Gloria pulled my head in close to her, against her breast, and wrapped her arms around my back. "How could you ever support a family, anyway?" She tousled my hair and tried to make me laugh. "Those are a man's responsibilities."

A man's. *But I am a man*, I thought to myself. *I have to be.*

"I am a man," I told her.

14
Every Man for Himself

Dear Father Chalmers.

As both myself and Mrs. Ray will be out of the Los Angeles area for the next several weeks, with the exception of a few days at Christmas, would the school please board Tony on weekends until further notice? I will, of course, take care of any additional charges for this service. I am sure," Father Chalmers read on, "you will be able to explain the necessity of this action on my part to Tony. I am enclosing a check for $50 to be disbursed to Tony at the rate of $5 a week. Will your offices be kind enough to pass it along to him? Thank you for your cooperation.

Sincerely, Nick Ray.

"Sir," I said, "Gloria isn't leaving for ten days. Why do I have to stay before then?"

"I can only follow your father's instructions."

"Is that all, sir?"

"Yes, Tony. You're excused." I rose and turned toward the door. Father Chalmers stopped me with, "Tony, it's not like being campused. You'll be given passes to go to movies in Hollywood, or to museums, shopping, special events."

"Why didn't Dad write straight to me?" I asked. "Then I could have come to you like a man and said, 'Father Chalmers, Dad wants me to stick around for a while.' He doesn't let me do anything."

"Perhaps he didn't know how to tell you," Father Chalmers said. "It isn't easy for your father, either."

"Yeah, I know. He's always telling me. How come it isn't hard for Gloria?"

"What do you mean?"

"Nothing."

"Okay, son, you'd better be getting along to class."

Five dollars a week, plus I still had the other five from Mom. It was sure good to have money. I closed the telephone booth door and put a nickel in the slot. I called Gloria collect. So what if Dad found out I was calling Gloria? I could tell him the truth, that I wanted her to take me home.

"Hi, doll," Gloria said after accepting the charges.

"What are you doing?"

"Phonetics, voice work. Where are you?"

"At school, where do you think?"

"I don't know," Gloria sighed. "I wasn't thinking."

"Dad had me campused. The only way I can come home is if you take me."

"Guess where Sumner is?" Gloria asked, ignoring what I had said.

"I couldn't care less. As long as he isn't there," I said. "Don't change the subject."

"He's back on location with Nick. Don't you think he had a lot of nerve going back after what he tried with me?"

"I hate him," I said. "Will you pick me up on Friday?"

"Tony?"

"What?"

"If Sumner makes up stories about us, you'll be careful, won't you? After all, nothing has really ever happened."

"Yes, yes, yes. A thousand times yes." Boy, she was burning me up. "Will you take me home Friday?"

"I have a whole script to break down," Gloria said, "and if you came near me I'd scream."

"I miss you."

"You, too," she said. "Be a good boy." I hated her saying that. "Tony? Goodbye." I hung up without answering. She acted as though it would be an ordeal to have me around.

I met Joey, the school's maintenance man, late Saturday night. The old guy woke me up at three in the morning. He turned off the television set and told me to go to bed. I didn't want to make the trip down the hill from the recreation room to the empty cabin. What was the point? I was perfectly comfortable on the couch. When I curled up to go back to sleep, Joey shook my shoulders and invited me into the maintenance room next door. Gardening and cleaning equipment hung in neat rows along the walls. The edges of the room were lined with cans of paint, turpentine and brushes.

A gas heater burned in one corner. The *Form* and assorted tip sheets were spread out on a makeshift table made of two sawhorses and half an old door. I sat down. "I work nights," Joey said, "and go to the track in the daytime." He took two mugs off their nails above the hot plate and poured coffee for us. "Don't have family to worry about."

Joey and I became great friends. He taught me how to roll cigarettes and once in a while gave me a sip from his bottle of bourbon. I took great interest in learning how to figure the horses. He was a nice old guy who just wanted somebody to keep him company. After study hall one night I asked him if he liked any horses for the next day. He had picked two. I gave him $2 and asked to share a bet on each horse. Although I couldn't sit up with Joey on weeknights, I was able to keep my mind occupied a good part of each day studying the next day's races in the afternoon paper and waiting for Joey to come back with the race results. Who needed football? I had a chance to win a fortune. That was something to look forward to. The days passed quickly, blending into each other from newspaper to newspaper, bet to bet, the ecstasy of winning and the lows of losing. But no matter what happened, win or lose, tomorrow was always another day, another chance.

On my birthday, the 24th of November, a package came from Mom. Her presents always arrived right on the button. This time it was a pedometer. I strapped it around my ankle and wondered if, with all the demerits I had to work off, she was commenting on my behavior. At least it was more fun than the practical gifts of clothing she usually sent. Mom also sent the $5 I had asked for ages ago. That was the best part of her gift.

A few days later I got $10 from Dad. It came with a typewritten message, signed by his secretary that came with it. Sometimes I thought Dad was really dense. The next step would be to see how much I could get for the pedometer from one of the kids. Slowly but surely I was building my bankroll. "How could you take on the responsibilities of a family?" Gloria had asked. I hadn't heard one word from her since she went away. But I suppose, deep down inside, I didn't expect her to write to me. After all, she had told me she never wrote to anyone.

One Saturday, Father Chalmers gave me a pass to go anywhere I wanted for the day, on one condition: that I come to chapel Sunday mornings until I was allowed to go home again. I rushed down the hill to the cabin, put on my best pressed uniform, and set out for Hollywood.

I looked at the marquees and lobbycards of every movie on Hollywood Boulevard. No matter how good the shows looked, I couldn't see spending my whole day going from movie to movie. *Oh, yeah*, I said to myself as I went into the Roosevelt Hotel for a Coke. *This is where Joey catches the bus to the racetrack.* I felt a rush of excitement.

I asked the doorman where the bus stopped. He said right there at 11.20. I had fifteen minutes to kill. I crossed the street to the newspaper stand on Las Palmas and bought the *Form* and a newspaper. Tip sheets were hanging all over the place. I walked up and down the length of the stand trying to sneak a peek under the folded over, bright colored tip sheets when the newspaper man wasn't looking. But I never got a good chance. The expensive ones cost as much as $10 and guaranteed your money back if the horse lost. Not the money you bet, just the money you paid for the information. I had $13 in cash and my birthday checks. Boy, if I had only known Father Chalmers was going to let me out, I would have cashed my checks. I gave up the idea of buying a "guaranteed winner" and, armed with the *Form* and a newspaper, headed for the bus.

I found a seat in the back next to a fat woman wearing an old, beat-up black hat. She had a million papers in her lap and chewed gum. I scrunched down beside her. The driver's uniform, the smell of the seat cushions, two aisles of anxious people waiting to take off, all gave me the sensation of being on a plane. What would happen if I got caught or ran into one of Dad's friends at the track? He would flip. But why shouldn't I go to the races and do what I wanted with my own time and money?

The driver revved the engine and released the brake. We were on our way. Men and women chattered across the aisle about this horse and that track condition. This was going to be the most exciting trip ever. The fat woman stuck an elbow square in my ribs as she twisted her big ass around to get in position to open one of her papers. Every time she opened one, another fell from her lap to the floor. And each time she bent over with a groan to pick it up, she said a gasping, red faced, "Sorry."

"That's okay," I said about the tenth time it happened. "Who do you like today?"

"Wouldn't want you to knock down the odds," she guffawed in my face. Her breath stank from a combination of last night's onions and Juicy Fruit gum. She ripped the selections, graded handicaps and consensus opinions from each paper, then pushed the bulk of unread headlines and news to the floor. I went through the motions of glancing at each page of my newspaper, happened across the sport section, then, having satisfied myself and the world that I was up to date on the day's murders and robberies, I, too, tore out the racing news and dropped the rest to the floor. "Feels better, don't it?" the lady said.

"Yes."

"I'd pay twice the price not to have to carry all that garbage from the stand to the bus. It's hard enough earning a living without carrying the weight of the world around with you."

"Do you make a living at the races?" I asked.

"Try," she said.

We hit bumper to bumper traffic after an hour on the road. "Will we make the first?" one man shouted down the aisle to the driver. "C'mon, Mack," another complained. "This isn't a sight-seeing tour."

Red wooden signs with "Santa Anita Park" painted in white letters pointed the way to the track. The closer we got, the noisier the people on the bus became. They made last-minute selections and asked their neighbors what they liked in the daily double. Everyone's watch read within three or four minutes of the same time, but those three minutes made all the difference in the world before post time. It was as though getting there for the first race automatically made you a winner. Men wearing paper derbies with tip sheets stapled to them stood along the side of the road waving their arms, hustling their merchandise. We drove through the tall, steel gates of the bus entrance around a curving, beautifully landscaped drive and pulled up in front of the sprawling building. Steep mountains were the backdrop for the grandstand and track. Everyone crowded toward the front of the bus, filling the aisles before we even stopped. When the door opened, the people ran everywhere clutching dollar bills. You should have seen the fat lady go.

I bought my ticket and gave it to the man at the turnstile. At the foot of a wide flight of concrete stairs which led to the grandstand, men stood behind small counters yelling, "Programs! Programs!

Get your lucky pencil!" I bought a program and examined it on my way up the stairs. I passed through the smoky ground floor of the grandstand and went out to the track area. A bunch of horses walked toward the gate. The ever-changing tote board flashed hundreds of numbers made up of white lightbulbs. I scanned the program again. A horse named Shady Tony was running in the first race. How good a hunch could I ask for?

"Where do I place a bet on Shady Tony?" I asked the man beside me.

"Inside," he said, pointing over his shoulder without taking his eyes off the tote board. "Better hurry or you'll get shut out."

Several feet in front of the ticket sellers' windows was a line of posts with signs on them: "Minors not permitted to make or collect wagers." But that wasn't going to stop me. I asked a man near the front of the line to place my bet on Shady Tony. He took the $10 bill from me and a few moments later the transaction was finalized. He handed me my ticket and ran for the track area. A loud bell-like buzzer sounded, a metallic click turned off the mutual machines, and the public address system announced: "It is now post time." Hundreds of lines dissolved in a flash. "The flag is up." Another bell rang, from outside this time. "They're off!" I ran outside and stopped to peer through two men's shoulders. "Which one is Shady Tony?" I asked, but was ignored.

"C'mon, boy! C'mon!" one was yelling. "Thatta boy. You'll nail him!"

"No one's going to catch that horse," the other man said, disgusted.

"Now! NOW! Make your move," the first man urged his horse.

"Coming into the far turn," the address system called in a drawling monotone, "it's Freedom Bell by three, Green Gage Mama on the rail, and Miss Desirable. California Count moving up with a rush on the outside…"

The first man was jumping up and down, waving his tickets in the air. "Keep going!" he yelled. "Hang on, baby."

"Coming into the stretch it's Freedom Bell by one, Green Gage Mama and California Count." The crowd roared, drowning out the announcer's voice. The horses were all bunched up. They zoomed by the finish line.

"Phony favorites."

"Lousy jock."

People milled around. Some went inside. A few were still watching the tote board. I had no idea which horse won. I reached in my pocket for my ticket and money. "Oh, my God," I gasped. "Where's my change?" I held the yellow ticket and fifteen cents in my hand. Fifteen lousy cents. The man should have given me $8 change, but it had all happened so fast I hadn't noticed. I had just jammed the ticket in my pocket and run outside like everyone else. I searched for the guy who bought it for me for about five minutes, then gave up. What did I do this for? I felt about two inches high. Finally, I asked a man who was scurrying off to some obscure place in the maze of refreshment stands and bright lightbulb numbers if my ticket was worth anything at all. Numbers. Numbers. I wished I were a number, a dollar bill, a lightbulb.

"What number is it?" the man asked, coming to a halt.

"Number?"

"Number. What horse did you play?"

"I don't know," I said. "I asked for Shady Tony." I handed the man the ticket. "He cheated me out of $8. I can't even get back to school." I wanted to tell him not to laugh at me. If there was one thing I couldn't stand at that moment it would be being laughed at. The man compared my ticket with the numbers on the board. His lips curled in a smile the way Dad's might have at some rare moment.

"You have a big winner," he said.

"A winner?"

"I'll say."

"Who pays me?" My lungs filled and I grew ten feet. I won. I was the undisputed all-powerful victor. No one could change it or take it away from me. It was final.

"Go to the cashier's window," the man said as he took a step away from me. I caught his arm. He looked honest.

"Would you get the money for me?" I asked. "I can't. Would you, please?" Before he could answer I slapped the ticket in his hand. He shook his head and smiled. I followed him to the cashier's window. I didn't think he was going to cheat me, but I planned to watch him a lot closer than I had the man who bought it for me. I waited by the side of the window and kept my eyes on him at all times to be sure he didn't slip any of my money into his pocket. But it turned out I had nothing to worry about.

"You really hit," he said, turning a fistfull of bills and some change over to me. I began counting the money. Twenty, forty, sixty...

"How much is here?"

"$153.40."

"How did I get that much?" I kept counting. I had never had more than $20 or $25 at one time, let alone own it.

"Shady Tony was fourteen to one," the man explained, "and you had $10 to win on him. Breakage in the price gave you the extra three forty."

"Then the man didn't cheat me. He thought I wanted to bet the whole $10. My name is Tony," I said after pocketing the money. "I picked him because of that, and some other things, of course."

"I'm Mike." We shook hands.

"Would you collect my money? Please? I'm not allowed to."

Mike was the disc jockey for a radio station in Arcadia. He had Saturdays off so he came to the track. He caught a few races on other days when he could get away from the station. What a great life. Mike said I should go home while I was ahead, that I'd had beginner's luck. But I didn't see why I should do that. After all, I had only played one race. He shrugged his shoulders when he saw I had no intention of leaving and buried his head in the *Form*. I counted my money over and over again, then looked over the entries for the second race. Mike's face emerged from the *Form* about ten minutes later. He had been concentrating very hard and writing figures on the pages. When I saw he was through thinking, I asked what he was going to bet. But he wouldn't tell. He explained what touting was and why it wasn't a good policy, especially between friends, to tell another man what horse to play. "Never sway a man from his own judgement," Mike said, "because there's money at stake. I'd hate to feel responsible if you lost." I knew money was important. More important than anything, maybe. Dad was always talking about how he had to make money. Don't let anyone tell you what to do, and don't tell *them*. Your own responsibility. It was every man for himself. Whether I won or lost, succeeded or failed, it was on my own. I didn't need anyone.

A man in a bright red hunting outfit came onto the track and played a bugle. When he finished, the first of a line of horses stepped onto the track from the paddock. The public address system clicked on and the announcer said, "The horses are on the track for the second race." I consulted the handicapper in my newspaper and the consensus in the *Form*. It was hard figuring out what all the past performances meant and I gave up trying. I decided to put $10 on Blue Moon. I still couldn't follow my horse all the way around the track, but I could see the jockey's bright red and blue silks at the end alright. He was in front. Mike dropped a pile of tickets to the ground. I was jumping up and down with pleasure. "I'm sorry you lost," I said after I settled down. I never saw anyone so deadpan in my life. Losing didn't seem to bother Mike at all. It was almost as though he expected to lose. His expression was no different after the race than it had been before.

"Look!" Mike held his program under my nose. "I marked off Blue Moon." Then he showed me the *Form*. "He beat all these horses last year, right here," he said, pointing to a tiny row of printed numbers and signs which he had underlined. "I changed my mind because I thought the weight was too much for him. Why did you pick him?" Mike asked on our way to cash my ticket.

"Everyone liked him a lot."

"Hi, Mike," a man said as we passed. Mike didn't hear. Dad was that way sometimes, like he went into another world and didn't know what was going on right in front of him.

The afternoon raced by in a blur of important events. I told Mike I went to military school, as if he couldn't tell by the uniform, and that I was 15 years old. I wanted to tell him more about myself and ask what to do about Gloria. But I didn't. Before I knew it, I wasn't even thinking about things like Dad and Gloria anymore. I was completely involved with picking winners, in making money. Before the last race I had over $300. I decided to place $25 of it on the favorite. Favorites were the best bets. I had been lucky to win on Shady Tony, Mike had told me. It had been a photo finish. I talked Mike into telling me who he was playing. He was playing the favorite, too. We both had Yondetaga. It would be fun to root for the same horse.

Well, let me tell you, you should have seen Mike's face explode with pleasure when Yondetaga came flying down the stretch in front. He was jumping up and down, yelling and screaming like a kid, as the horses crossed the finish line. "It was a tap out bet," he said, shaking a handful of tickets up to my face. "All my rent and food money for the month was on him."

"Wow," I said. "What if he had lost?"

"He didn't," Mike said. We raced to the cashier's window. After getting our money, Mike said, "See you around, kid."

"I hope so." I followed him as he started to walk away. "Do you always stand where you were today?"

"Pole seventeen."

"I'll see you next Saturday," I said. "I hope I can find you."

"Okay." Mike waved over his shoulder at me. "Goodbye, now."

I watched him walking down the line of windows. He dropped his *Form* into a trash barrel, melted into the gray crowd that jammed the exit tunnels and disappeared. We hadn't shaken hands. I didn't know his last name. He didn't know mine. Make a friend, lose a friend. Here for a moment—then gone.

I looked out at the now empty grandstand area and the tote board that still showed the results of the last race. The money in my pocket felt real good. $370! I wrapped my hand around the roll of bills and worked my way toward the bus stop. The picnic cheer that had filled the bus on the way to the track had been left behind, deposited in the parimutuel machines. A cold gray drizzle began to fall. It was getting dark out. The windshield wipers clicked at the end of each stroke. Two men sitting a few rows in front of me were the only people talking. Most of the other people were either gazing blankly out the windows or sleeping. I thought of Mike showing me how he had selected Blue Moon but had changed his mind. The driver turned on the headlights. Two yellow beams seeking out the future. How dingy the people looked. Suddenly a great loneliness came over me.

Back at the Roosevelt, I bought the evening paper, the all-sports final edition, and locked myself in one of the stalls of the men's room. I spread the race results on my lap, dumped all my money on the paper, and reviewed the day bet by bet, dollar by dollar. When I was done, I counted the money one more time. Then I went from store to store exchanging my $20 bills for tens, the tens for fives, fives for singles. It felt like more money that way. I ended up with over three hundred dollar bills and a few tens. Every pocket was full of money. I felt invincible, and hungry as hell. But even though I hadn't eaten since breakfast, I decided to fight off the urge until I got back to school. Joey always had an extra half a sandwich. I wanted to save every dime for my next trip to the track. I would have to be careful not to get demerits at school. It would be a crying shame to have Father Chalmers take away Saturday passes. I was going to become the goody-goody of Harvard overnight. I had a new ambition: to have over $1,000, all in cash, all my own, in my pocket at all times. Nobody earned $375 in a day. Not even Gloria or Dad.

15
Eyes Front

Joey would have been proud of me, but his room was locked. Knowing, like a lost kid on the beach, that it was smarter to stay in one place and wait than to look, I settled on the couch in the television room. I turned on those phony wrestling matches. If Joey was around, he would find me sooner or later.

I fell asleep, but this time, instead of Joey shaking my shoulder, I was woken with a start by a nightmare. I hugged my knees to my chest trying to get warm, then peered around the dark room trying to get my bearings. Then I shut off the blank television set, turned on the overhead light, and sat down to recall as much of the dream as I could.

I was searching war-torn China for my father. I had to force my way through crowds of refugees flooding the road in the opposite direction. Each second was a battle. I kept getting knocked over, trampled by fleeing feet, run over by oxcarts. When I found Dad, he was shooting a movie there, in his new white house, where there was no sign of war. Flowers bloomed, filling the quiet air with a peaceful fragrance. The guards wouldn't let me through the gates, but eventually I convinced them I was there to help on the movie and they let me in. Dad told me to get out, so I ran and ran. Mortar and artillery shells blew up all around me. Camellia petals filled the air like chicken feathers during a pillow fight. A falling tree was about to hit me—when I woke up.

No sign of Joey. I felt my pockets. They were still full. A branch, swaying in the night wind, brushed the roof. I jumped. I didn't want to stay in that room anymore. But even if I got to my room safely, I pictured some lousy thief hitting me over the head with a lead pipe. I decided to run down the hill and go to the corner luncheonette. I sat at the empty counter. The jukebox blared too loudly for the small place, but it was a welcoming, comfortable sound. The waitress was at the far end, counting coins she had poured out onto the counter from a large glass. She looked up at me. "Coca-Cola, please, and a bacon, lettuce and tomato sandwich on white toast with mayonnaise," I said. She called the order over to the kitchen, brought my Coke, then went back to counting her tips. The jukebox stopped.

"You gonna play any music?" she asked.

"No," I said.

She took a coin off the counter, came around to the jukebox, and put her coin in the slot. "Saturday night is the loneliest night in the week…" Four motorcycles roared to a stop in front of the luncheonette. A group of guys about Sumner's age dismounted and came in.

"Hey, baby, let's have something sweet," a bearded guy said to the only girl. She wore wraparound sunglasses, a black sweater and tight-fitting jeans. Her blonde hair and bandana reminded me of Gloria. They all tried to squeeze into a booth but couldn't do it.

"The counter's faster anyway," another said. They got up and gathered behind me.

"Move over, soldier. We're five and you're in the four slot."

"Sure," I said and moved three stools to the very end. The waitress took their orders. I couldn't help looking at the girl. She was pretty. When she caught my eye, I pretended to be looking at the jukebox. She whispered in her boyfriend's ear.

You know the way you smile when you want to avoid a fight? Well, that's what I did. When the waitress passed by, I asked for my bill. I got up, turned my back on the gang, and uncurled a dollar bill from my wad without taking more out of my pocket. I had the urge to walk up to the cash register, lay the whole roll on the counter, and choose a $10 bill. "Keep the change," I would have said to the waitress. Then the girl would have been sorry it wasn't me she was with. I bought a pack of Pall Malls at the gas station on the corner and walked back to school.

It was awfully far away, but on Sundays there was racing at a track called Caliente in Tijuana. I could never get a pass early enough to get there because I had promised to go to chapel on Sunday mornings, and it would have been impossible to get back by Sunday's four o'clock roll call. I would have to wait until next Saturday to get back to work building my fortune. I slept in the television room the rest of the night.

"Onward, Christian soldiers…" we sang in the almost empty chapel. There were only two other boys, Father Murray, and four resident teachers. Father Chalmers led the service. I was tired and couldn't wait until it was over so I could go back to sleep in my own bed. I slept until noon, then wrote a letter to Gloria about the kind of life I wanted. I didn't even have an address to send it to. I tore it up. Then I propped myself up with both Roth's and my pillows and started reading Jules Verne's *Mysterious Island*. Roth arrived at five, a full hour after check-in time.

"I'm late," he said. "Polish this up for me." Roth threw his belt across my stomach. I ignored him. "Hey! Didn't you hear me?"

"Go to hell."

"What?"

"You're not going to order me around anymore. Just because you've been here longer doesn't give you the right."

"Please, Tony," he said.

"Screw off, Seymour."

"I'll get you," Roth spat. He was the most ridiculous specimen I had ever seen. I picked up his belt, opened the window, and threw it outside.

"How are you going to get me, Seymour?"

"You wait," he hissed. "Why'd you throw my belt out?"

"Because I felt like it."

"You'll be sorry." Roth turned on his heel and went out to retrieve his belt. I was ready for him when he came back.

"Roth," I said as I carefully marked my place in *Mysterious Island*, "if you do anything—ANYTHING—to make trouble for me, I swear to God I'll hire some motorcycle gang to smear your face all over the sidewalk." Roth was wide-eyed. "Do you understand?"

"How are you going to manage that on your stupid allowance?" I jumped up, closed the door, and started pulling money out of my pockets. I threw it all over my bed. It was very impressive. Then I twisted Roth's tie in my fist. "Roth," I said, "from now on, if anyone gets in my way, I'll get rid of them." I let him go.

Billy Waller blew dinner assembly. I waited for Roth to go, then stashed my money in a dirty sock and hid it in my laundry bag. I walked up the hill with Lieutenant Larson.

"Keeping your nose clean?" Larson asked.

"Clean as a whistle."

"Ray, you didn't French my bed, did you?"

"No, sir, Lieutenant Larson. I swear I did not French your bed."

"How come you're so cheerful? I thought you hated it here." We passed the senior smoke shack, the television room, and Joey's room. It was still padlocked. I couldn't figure out what had happened to him. "Ray?"

"Oh. I'm sorry, sir. I had a very nice weekend, that's all. Father Chalmers let me go into town yesterday."

A few nights later, I had to write something about *Julius Caesar* for old man Sherman's English class. White-haired Sherman was the oldest teacher at Harvard, and this was his final year of teaching. What happens then, I wondered? Do old people just go away and die like elephants? What was the point of living?

"Cadet Ray," Captain Griswald's voice snapped from the officer's platform in front of study hall.

"Yes, sir." I jumped to attention beside my desk.

"Come up here," Griswald ordered. I walked to the foot of the platform. It was like standing before a judge's bench. "Ray, report to the men's room in this building."

"What for?"

"Now!" Griswald's hard face and cold blue eyes told me nothing. I saluted, did an about-face, and walked slowly up the aisle. What the hell could I have done? It wasn't good, that was for sure. I stalled at my desk to close my books.

"Roth," Griswald's voice called again, "report to the duty officer's desk."

I couldn't hang around any longer. I left study hall and waited for Roth in the corridor. He stopped short and almost ran in the other direction when he saw me.

"What's going on?" I asked him.

"I don't know."

"Why were you scared to run into me?" I asked. "I'm not going to hurt you."

We had walked around the corridor and were in front of the john. I pushed through the door ahead of Roth. The bulk of the senior boarding class was there. They stopped chattering the moment we walked in and stood around looking grim, as though we had crucified Father Chalmers or something. Griswald came in right after us. "Gentlemen," he said to his classmates. Then he turned to me. "Report."

"Cadet Ray reporting to the men's bathroom as ordered, sir," I rattled off.

Griswald returned my salute. I remained at attention. Billy Waller sat in one of the stalls shaking his head in dismay. What was he doing there? He wasn't a senior.

"Eyes front," Griswald ordered. I stared straight ahead again. "Welcome to your first, and I hope your last, session with the senior class disciplinary council." Griswald beckoned to Roth. "Come here." Roth stopped in front of Griswald. He stood so rigid, I swear I could hear his knees knocking. Griswald turned Roth around so he was facing me and put his arm across his shoulders. "Roth says you go out before Reveille every morning to have a smoke. Is that true, Ray?" Griswald's icy eyes were riveted right into mine. That sweltering turd, Roth... He was sure having his day. I wanted to rush him, dunk his head in the toilet, then flush it.

"No, sir," I answered finally. "It's not true. Roth is taking out a personal grudge."

"My, my, Ray." Griswald smiled disapproval at his comrades, who had formed a half circle around me. "I should think, having had time to weigh your answer, you would have decided to make a clean breast of it. Billy." Griswald snapped his fingers like a prosecutor calling his first witness. "Billy, come out here." Waller waddled out of the stall and stopped behind Griswald. "Billy," Griswald asked, "is it true you see Ray on the football field taking a stroll, as you put it, every morning before Reveille?"

"Yes, suh," Billy answered, "but I never saw him with a cigarette or other smokin' equipment."

"That's all," Griswald dismissed Billy. He saluted and left the bathroom. "I only wanted to substantiate the whereabouts of Ray during the early morning hours as reported by this conscientious cadet here, Roth." He patted Roth on the shoulder as if he were a shaking lap dog. I half-expected Roth to start licking Griswald's boots.

"May I leave now, too, sir?" Roth asked in a thin, weak voice.

"Seymour. I know you hate being called Seymour," Griswald said. "You will watch. As a lesson on the importance of discipline and to give you a constant reminder of the good work you've done. Stay at attention, Seymour, and keep your eyes open. If I catch you looking away, I'll hang you by the back of the neck on a coat hook and tan your hide." Griswald took off his hat and put it on one of the wash basins. "Alright, gentlemen, we shall commence."

"I'll watch the door," Davis volunteered. Griswald took two packs of Camels from his breast pockets and tore them open.

"You're going to smoke a lot," he said. The circle of seniors tightened around Roth, Griswald and me as they watched to see what he had planned. Griswald took out five cigarettes and lit them all. "Notice how they burn by themselves. Deadly chemicals are used to make cigarettes and paper. Cigars won't burn that way. Now take a drag." I reached out for one of the cigarettes, but Griswald stepped forward and shoved all five in my mouth. I took a short puff and blew the smoke out. "No, no, that won't do at all, will it, Seymour?"

"No, sir," Roth jumped. That chicken-livered son of a bitch.

"Larson, Patterson, help me do the honors." They stepped forward out of the group. "Patterson, you hold his nose. Larson, take his arms. Now, Ray," Griswald started to explain, "you want smoke, not air. Take a drag and inhale. Inhale deeply." I sucked in as little smoke as possible. But there was no little about it. One has to breathe and with your nose being held the only way is through your mouth. "Hold it in, Ray." When I couldn't anymore, I spat out the cigarettes and got some air. Griswald picked them up and patiently placed them between my lips. He told Patterson to let my nose go just long enough to exhale, but not to inhale. They made me do that until the cigarettes were burnt to butts. At first I thought I was going to choke, but after the fourth or fifth drag I got dizzy. Very dizzy. Griswald and Roth spun around me in wild circles. The whole room spun. As I sank to all fours, panting for air, I heard Griswald ask, "That was better, wasn't it, Seymour?"

"Yes, sir." I tried to lunge at Roth but Griswald caught me by the arm and stopped me. I was sick to my stomach. Griswald filled a glass with water. He was about to hand it to me when he saw that Roth had turned away. He stopped in the middle of his motion to me and threw the water over Roth's head. Roth yelped.

"Watch, creep," said Griswald. He refilled the glass and handed it to me. "Clear, cool water. Drink up." I drank, then ran for the wash basin, where I vomited right in Griswald's hat. Griswald wasn't upset. He looked at the hat calmly. "I'm sorry," I said. "My own fault, Ray," he replied. We went through the same procedure until the first pack was gone. Griswald took the second pack and put them back in his pocket. "I'll save these," he said, then announced to the group, "We will now play torpedo." I was told to strip down to my undershorts. When I had, Patterson dumped a glass of water over my rear.

"Hurts more that way," Patterson said. The seniors lined up, six or more on each side, to form a gauntlet. Some held garrison belts, some paddles, others plain leather belts.

"Come to me," Griswald ordered from the far end of the gauntlet, "at a duck walk." He seemed a thousand miles away. There's no such thing as a really fast duck walk. Every time a solid blow got to me, I toppled over. In the time it took to get upright again, five or six more lashes landed. There's a point in pain, after you realize the inevitability of it, when you cease to feel it so sharply and almost accept it. I fell down at Griswald's feet. The lightbulb swayed back and forth from the ceiling, or was it Griswald's head? I reached back and touched the welts. "I don't feel them," I mumbled. I lifted myself to a crawling position. The hardest part was getting up from there. Griswald took my arm but I shook it away. My gaze was focused on Roth, who had turned away again. It pulled me up like a magnet. "Look, you bastard." Roth didn't turn around. Griswald took Roth by the hair and lifted him almost clear off the floor. He pushed his face right in front of mine. "I'm going to kill you," I said to him. They made me go through the cigarette routine once more. I felt bad. Real bad. "Enough," I said to Griswald.

"Get dressed, Ray." Griswald nodded his head at me. For some reason I thought he liked me. God knows why. Two guys brought my pants and held me under the arms while I got into them. I was weaker than I thought, almost shaking. "Davis will walk you to your room," Griswald said. "Don't talk to anyone for a while. If you're asked why you're not in study hall, you didn't feel well and I excused you. Understood?"

"Yes."

"Can I go back to study hall now, sir?" Roth asked.

"Can you go?" Griswald laughed. He slapped Roth hard across the back. "Roth, I want to thank you. We all want to thank you. Let me shake your hand. C'mon, shake." Davis and I were at the door but the tone of Griswald's voice forced us both to turn around and see what was happening. "Shake everybody's hand. That's it." Roth was going from senior to senior shaking their hands.

"Why, Seymour," Griswald said, "we wouldn't think of making you go back to study hall after your good deed. Would we, gentlemen?"

"No," they all chimed in.

"Thank you, sir."

"You're next," Griswald snapped.

"Why me?"

"You're a rat, Roth."

As Davis and I started to push out the door again, Roth shrieked. We spun around to see that Griswald had placed his vomit-filled hat on Roth's head. "Officer material." Griswald said to us, "Goodnight."

A peculiar glow burning inside me said, "You're part of them now. They like you so much, one of them is making sure you get to your room alright." It was as though I had been at school for a hundred years, that I belonged there and was as much a family member as Father Chalmers, old man Sherman, or any of the seniors. Davis asked if I could make it alone from the cabin door, but I had him stay with me until I reached my bed, although I needed him like a hole in the head.

"Thank you, sir," I said as I sank down on my stomach. "It was fun in a way." Davis looked at me as though I had gone stark raving mad and left. Maybe you did have to be crazy to find pleasure in a beating, but they were my buddies now. After Davis was gone for a few minutes, I got up and took my money-filled sock out of the laundry bag and put it inside my pillowcase. Mom would have been proud of me for not complaining. I went to sleep.

If Roth had come back to the cabin, I would have pounded whatever sense he had left smack out of his head. But he didn't come back that night or, for that matter, ever again. He was gone. My tail was getting sorer instead of better. But in a way that was fine with me. The seniors left me alone and didn't make me work off demerits. I quit football. That gave me two free hours every afternoon to spend picking the horses on paper as practice for Saturday.

16
You Can't Win

The last football game of the season was in progress when the loud-speaker ordered me from the bleachers to my room. Dad paced back and forth like a caged lion. I was surprised to see him and wanted to say how happy I was that he had come, but I could tell he wasn't in a good mood. He sat on Roth's stripped bed, got up, tapped his fingers on my bureau, glanced out the window at the game, then sat down again. I waited in the doorway for him to speak. He paced again. "What's wrong?" I asked. No answer, only a dirty look. What was he upset about? I straddled the desk chair, crossed my arms over the back, and waited. You had to wait for Dad. Everything troubled him, so there was no way of telling what was on his mind. "When did you get home from location?" I ventured. Right then I craved a drink from Joey's bottle of bourbon.

"How to get through to you…?" Dad sighed. He lit a cigarette and scanned the room for an ashtray.

"There aren't any." I took the burned-out match, excused myself, and went to flush it down the toilet. "If I'd thrown it out the window," I explained when I came back, "someone would have found it and accused me of smoking." No comment from Dad.

A mass shout rose from the bleachers, crossed the football field, and reached us as a distant "YEAH!" The school band played.

"We must have scored a touchdown."

"You're not playing anymore?" he asked from the window.

"That's a varsity game. But I did quit. I needed more time for schoolwork." I got Dad the top of a shoe polish can to use as an ashtray. He turned the lid over in his hand.

"Sy Roth's son was your roommate, wasn't he?"

"I didn't know you knew Roth's father. He told me his dad sold plumbing supplies."

"He's the cameraman on my picture."

Dad turned from the window to face me.

"Seymour took quite a beating, didn't he?"

"I wasn't there," I said. That was the truth. I mean, all I actually knew was that Roth hadn't come back to the room after study hall. "Did you finish the movie?" I asked.

"You were first," Dad drove on, "weren't you, son?" I fiddled with a pencil, tapping it against the desk a few times before nodding my head yes. "You got the same, didn't you?"

"It wasn't too bad." Was Dad sorry for me, or mad, or only trying to get information? His face didn't show which.

"What did you do to deserve it?"

"Nothing," I said quickly. "Roth was taking out a grudge, that's all."

"A grudge?"

"He can't bear being called Seymour. All the kids called him that when he got out of line. So he made trouble. Roth wasn't very well liked."

"But why did they beat him up?"

"Ratting." I broke the pencil in half. "He went to the senior council and said I was smoking."

"To get even with you for calling him Seymour?"

"Yes."

"Were you smoking?"

"No," I answered too fast. My cheeks flushed hot. "Roth deserved whatever he got." Dad nodded knowingly. About what, I didn't have the vaguest idea. I wiped the palms of my clammy hands on my pants. "Let's not talk about that anymore, please. Don't let Roth ruin our visit."

"Alright."

Dad knew I was lying. I could tell. I tried to be cheerful. "It'll be good to come home this weekend. Should I get ready now?"

"Gloria's back from Florida," Dad said. "We were going to ask if you'd mind our having the next couple of weekends to ourselves." I couldn't believe it. Why wouldn't Gloria want me home? Why hadn't she called me since coming home?

"I don't care. Do whatever you want."

"You'll be home for Christmas vacation…"

"Sure." I couldn't stop grinding my teeth and a damn tick started in one eye, forcing me to wink every few seconds like an idiot. I had to move, so I walked to the window and pretended to be watching the football game. "I thought you came to pick me up. But thanks for coming by to visit. I'd rather see you for a little while than not see you at all."

Jesus... I had been on campus since September. There I went, feeling sorry for myself again. To see me would have made Mom sick, but I couldn't help it. Dad came up behind me. I stalked away before he could speak. It was the first time I had seen him since being cooped up in school and all he could talk about was Roth. I punched the door as hard as I could. I closed my eyes. My knuckles hurt. What a stupid thing to do. Living slides flashed across the screen of my mind—fragments, incidents. Dad, drunk, rolling down the hard sand into the ocean. A ringing telephone cutting me off every time I asked an important question. The everything-will-be-alright smile which always left me wanting more, but with no answers. Gloria's hair blowing in the wind. The sun shining. The car stopping at a light and her saying, "If we can trust each other, we can have a lot of fun." Smoke from her mouth filling my lungs. Candy. Dancing. I tried to reach up and tear her out of my mind. Loving her was wrong. When at last Gloria dissolved, I fought to think about things like Dad and me at a football game or Mom taking me uptown to the theater district to visit him. But, instead, I thought of tearing off Gloria's bikini, of Sumner watching, laughing, of Gloria telling me to leave the room.

That wasn't how it happened. I rubbed my face. How *did* it happen? What was going on? A kaleidoscope of vague memories came one upon the other, going backward in time like the rewind of an old movie. Snow covered the fire escape outside my bedroom. Then nothing. A peaceful blank, as if I had awoken from a dream. I felt fresh and clean. The cold air was full of autumn smells. Dad was dozing in the chair. The red light of sundown filled the room. The ash from Dad's cigarette broke and fell over his wrist. His eyes flashed open. "Hello," I said.

"You threatened Seymour, didn't you?"

"Let's talk about something pleasant."

"Don't be coy, Tony. No more evasions."

"Why can't we start over again?"

"You threw a great deal of money around and told him you would use it to have him taken care of if he made trouble for you."

"Oh. That."

"Aren't those the words you used?"

"Roth couldn't have taken me seriously. None of that is important."

"He tried to have you expelled from school." That I had shaken Roth up so much pleased me. It was damn funny he had tried to get me bounced. "Wipe off the smirk, Tony."

"I'm sorry. It's only that…"

"How much money do you have?" He was closing in again. I started to panic about my money. I couldn't understand why he was so anxious to find fault in me. I wished I could have willed my bureau through the wall and buried it ten paces from some distant tree. The sock in which I had crammed my winnings suddenly seemed the most obvious hiding place in the world.

"Answer."

"Only a few dollars," I said. "All singles." Dad gave me no choice. I had to lie. He always made it sound as though the truth would seal a fate of doom for me in his eyes.

"Give it to me." Dad extended his hand. I emptied my pants pockets into his outstretched palm. I had only $3 and change on me. Dad frowned. "Where's the rest of it? Sy said it must have been hundreds." Dad snapped his fingers impatiently. I was tongue-tied. "Which is your bed?"

"There," I pointed to the only one that was made up. Dad looked under my pillow and into the pillowcase. Then he felt around the blankets. "There's nothing there," I pleaded. He lifted the mattress. The *Form* and newspapers were there for him to see. Dad froze for a moment, then dropped the mattress back into place. I should have stopped him from looking, should have given him the money and told him I had been saving for years. Too late. Everything happens too late. Dad turned on me.

"Gambling," he whispered. Every nerve in his face, the opening and closing of his hands, every flicker in his eyes, read disgust. "Where's the rest of the money?" I went to the bureau and got the sock for him. A strange calm fell over me as he pulled out the roll of bills. I wanted to burst out and say how thrilling it had been to win, that I understood why he liked to gamble. "Gambling," he uttered again. "Charming."

"What's wrong with that? You do it."

"Don't compete with me," he said. "You can't win."

"I was only having fun, and I did win."

"You can't win," he repeated. Dad took a threatening step toward me. I backed off. "Do you understand?" I looked away. "You can't win. Do you understand that?" When I still didn't answer he turned his back on me.

"Hit me," I said. "Go ahead and hit me."

"It's too late for that."

"No, it's not. We can go back."

"Too late. In the garage, the first time I caught you smoking, do you remember how Gloria stopped me from punishing you? Now do you think she did you a favor that morning?"

"I don't know anymore."

"Was she bringing us closer together or driving us apart? Answer that one."

"Help us get close," I said. "Give me that whipping now."

"I've made other arrangements," Dad sighed. "You have an appointment with Dr. Myrtle Allenstein. Talk to her. Cooperate. She's a good doctor. Maybe you can examine your relationship with Gloria, too." Dad emptied the shoe polish lid into the wastebasket, brushed off his pants where ashes had fallen, and walked to the door. He was ready to leave. "You need help, son. Have faith for a change. There's nothing to be ashamed or embarrassed about."

"But I don't need a psychiatrist."

"I'm going to great expense for you." He waited for that to sink in, then continued. "A car will pick you up at 3.30 on Tuesday afternoon. Make use of the time. Right?"

"Right," I repeated, but there was a hollow ring in my voice. Dad smiled. I looked for the assurance that always filled his eyes along with that smile, but it wasn't there. I didn't see what I used to see in his eyes. His face had turned to stone, into a statue reflecting a lost dream. It made me sad and alone. "May I have $30 of my money back?" Dad raised his eyebrows. "I have to buy Christmas presents. And that much was birthday money and allowances I saved."

"I'll give you thirty." Dad took two bills from his pocket and handed them to me.

"That's from me to you. The other money is still yours. I'll hold it until you're old enough to handle it. You needn't gamble, steal or connive to get what you need. Do you understand?" I didn't answer. There was an awkward moment during which neither of us

knew what to do or say. We were like two boats drifting farther and
farther away on a lake. Finally we nodded to each other and he left.

Through the window, I watched him cross the football field.
The game was over. Dad disappeared into the tree-lined walk up
the hill. A few minutes later his car wound down the slope and
away. Friday night. I was alone again. I scooped the racing pages
from under my mattress and threw them in the wastebasket. I had
put together over $500 in a few weeks and he had taken it away.
There was something about flashing a lot of money that made me
feel confident, superior, good about myself.

"The world stinks."

In the morning, I got a pass from Father Chalmers to go Christmas
shopping. I took the thirty bucks and caught the bus to the racetrack. If I could make $375 on ten, then build it up to five hundred,
there was no telling how much I could make starting with thirty.

I didn't want to see Mike. How could I explain the tremendous cut in my capital? He would be sure I had lost it. I had no
trouble finding people to make bets for me. And as far as cashing
them goes, well, I never made it to the cashier's window. I lost $10
on a nag named Thanatopsis right off the bat. He looked great,
I swear to God. He was miles in front all the way to the end, at
least almost to the end—then he ran out of gas and died like a dog.
I was dead broke after the fourth race. I didn't even have bus fare
back to school. I was so sure that last horse would win. I wandered
around the grandstand wondering what to do. I should have gone
shopping. Now I had no money for Christmas. Jesus, what was I
going to do? I wanted to kill myself for being so stupid. How could
I have bet $10 on the first race?

Sure, I had bet ten on Shady Tony my first time at the track
and won a lot of money, but that had been an accident. Thanatopsis
was a favorite. Almost a sure thing. If I had only bet just $2 a race,
I would still have $22. Losing was damn depressing. I watched the
fifth. There was an objection after the race, and hundreds of people
bent over to scoop up tickets which had been thrown to the ground.
They hoped some idiot had thrown away tickets on the winner.
In less than a minute, every ticket on the ground must have been
picked over. I even checked the ones that were near me, turning
over those that were face down with my toe. An old man with
yellow teeth and beat-up shoes sorted through a handful of tickets

he had gathered from a green trash barrel. An employee I had never noticed before, a man who spent the afternoon plucking discarded tickets from the ground with a pointed stick like a park attendant gathering ice cream cups and candy wrappers, made an impersonal path through the masses. Unnoticed by the listless players in their wishful trances, passing through the zigzagging paths of their fantasy meanderings like death in disguise collecting once-known corpses, he dumped each stick-load of worthless tickets into the trash can. Eventually they were all gone, one by one, tickets and lives.

New dreams take the place of old, old hopes are rescued in new forms for fleeting moments, but eventually we die. I hated the outsider, the woman I heard say the people looked shabby. What did she know about horses in her new blue coat? Sucker. She only had a newspaper, and she was carrying around the whole thing, news and all. Any idiot knows you need the *Form*. Even though I had only been to the track a few times, I knew I was a regular. Sure, I felt different. I was meant to be a winner. I was smarter than the others, apart from them. I would never pick through garbage cans. My shoes were scuffed, my pants dusty, my hands black from newsprint. But I was me. The track and all who dwelled within were part of my world, not I of theirs.

The crowd released a roar of approval when the official sign lit up, disallowing the losing jockey's objection. The favorite had won. I felt sick to my stomach. *You can't win*, I thought, as I watched the winners streaming past me on their way to cash in. Only thirty percent of the favorites win, Mike had said. The sun lifted the stale odors of beer, spit and cigarette smoke from the concrete to my nostrils. When the pay-off lit up the tote board, oohs and ahs from winners buzzed through the air. Three to one was good odds for a favorite. "I had it," I said to the old man at the trash barrel. It felt good to say, even if it wasn't true.

"How could you miss it?" the old man asked. "I wanted to put a hundred on that filly myself, but I got shut out."

"Good luck," I said. "I'm going to cash in." I forced my way through the crowd toward one of the exit tunnels. The passageway was jammed with men studying their forms. The big business of the *Form*. Executives working at their portable desks with their portable invulnerable importance, building castles on the sandy shores of their childlike imaginations. I turned to take a last look. The people, fluttering like cast-off tickets in the wind, swaying to and fro, jumping, scattering, running, shouting, buying, dying, clutching at their groundless self-manufactured faith in their own ability to capture the world and hold it, like an ice cream cone, in their hands. "The horses are on the track for the sixth race." A paper cup on the ground, crushed, a cigarette butt rolling down the inclined pavement toward the track, gasping for a last breath, people rushing to get in, trudging with heads bowed to get out. They race into the track at the beginning of the day on the wings of desperate confidence. To miss a race is to miss a chance. A chance? A chance? As long as there's a chance, everything is fine. No matter how much you lose, what you lose, no matter how unhappy you are, all's well if there's another chance.

People hurried past me to the sellers' windows. Baggy pants, a loose jaw, union badge, faded grays, washed-out blues—all kings of the same kingdom, all seeing the world through a strange, magical lens.

"If he lays off the pace, he'll win," I heard behind me. I turned toward the exit again, toward the group of men studying their forms. It was Mike who had spoken. I rushed up to the group.

"I had a hundred on the last winner," I told Mike.

"Hi, kid."

"Did you hear that? I had him big."

"That's great," Mike tried to say enthusiastically. It wasn't hard to tell he was having a bad day. "Quit while you're ahead."

"I was just leaving," I said. "Goodbye."

"Bye."

The men cleared a path for my exit. I passed through it as if I were royalty, the victor supreme. On the other side of the tunnel the gaping emptiness of twilight slapped me across the face. I wished I had $2 to bet. I was sure I would win, and if I didn't, it would only be $2. The toothless confidence of the cigar-smoking misbegotten was mine.

"I lost, Dad," I said to a wind-blown newspaper as I crossed the parking lot on my way to the tall black gates. "Are you happy now?" I pulled up my collar, lit a cigarette, and put my hands in my pockets. How much I loved Gloria. How much I wanted her. How much I wished at times that we were both dead. The hollow, empty night fell frighteningly fast, lending no warning of what it held. No answers, no guarantees, no excuses. If I only had another chance.

17

Prisoner of War

The sleek black studio car pulled up in front of a fancy apartment house. Eddie, the driver, handed me a white slip of paper with the address and apartment number written on it. I rang the bell of 113. A slight, tailored lady wearing baby-blue framed glasses opened the door. Her short brown hair cut in a straight line below her ears made her look like an ancient beagle hound pretending to be a little girl. "How do you do?" She couldn't have sounded casual no matter how hard she tried. "I'm Dr. Allenstein."

"Tony Ray," I saluted. "Rifle number A3-03-6593428." Dr. Allenstein was taken aback, but there was a laughing flicker in her eyes. "According to the rules of war, the only information I can give is my name and serial number. Of course, being only a lousy military school student, my rifle number will have to do."

"Oh," she laughed. "Well, come in, prisoner of war." I followed her through the door. I hadn't shaken up that dog any. Dr. Allenstein took my hat and set it on a chair. It was an ordinary apartment, like any other. No big, brown desk in a room lined with medical books that made you feel like a case.

"Are you sure you're Dr. Allenstein, ma'am? The one and only Myrtle Allenstein? Or could Dad have made a mistake?"

"No," she said. "You're in the right place." We passed through the living room and I then followed her down a short hall. "Let's go in here." She pushed through a door into the den. A worktable with a telephone and typewriter on it and a one-drawer filing cabinet underneath filled one corner of the room. But it still wasn't a real office.

Dr. Allenstein sat in a comfortable-looking easy chair. That left me a choice of a straight chair or the brown leather couch.

"Ah," I said. "There's the couch." I pointed at it as though it were as natural a tool to her as a dentist's chair to a dentist. "Everything's kosher, I see."

"You've seen a psychiatrist before?"

"A3-03-6593428," I rattled off. "I suppose my father didn't tell you."

"He said less than you probably think." She curled her legs under her in that little girl way. There was silence. Then, to break the silence, she asked, "Would you like a cup of coffee or a glass of milk?"

"Sure, why not? Coffee." When Dr. Allenstein left, I got up and sat in her easy chair. Let her sit on the couch if she wanted to. It was nice of her to make coffee, though.

A watercolor of a girl on a swing hung on one wall. The girl's dress was yellow, the sky blue. The walls were all soft gray except the one behind the couch which was cocoa brown. The typewriter amused me. How could she be so stupid? I could just picture her typing long reports to unsuspecting kids' parents. Of course, she would include the bill.

Dr. Allenstein came back with the two coffee cups. "How old are you?" I asked. It was funny to think I would ask something like that.

"Why?"

"I don't know," I shrugged. "Just curious. I wondered how long you've been out of school." I didn't get up to take the coffee from her because I was sure as hell she would slip back into her own chair. She searched for a place to set the cups and ended up placing them on the seat of the straight chair. Dr. Allenstein knew damn well I had taken her chair on purpose, but as she left to get the cream and sugar, I could have sworn she smiled. She wouldn't have been bad-looking if her face wasn't sort of messed up. It had pock marks all over it. If I really wanted to be mean, I could call her craterface. But her body was nice. *What am I doing thinking about sex*, I asked myself. *Wow, that school must be really goofing me up.* Allenstein returned with a silver tray, which she held in front of me.

"I brought some cookies," she said.

I took cream and sugar, then helped myself to a fistful of cookies. "Thanks," I said. "You'd make a fabulous waitress." Dr. A. put the tray on the worktable, brought over her coffee cup, helped herself to everything, and sat down on the edge of the couch.

"Well..." It felt like she was examining me as if I were a piece of bacteria under a microscope. "I'm not going to bite you, you know."

"How do I know that? Because you say so?" That she was stupid enough to think I would trust her really aggravated me. "I don't know why my father sent me here."

"I think you do know, Tony." Her tone of voice became businesslike. Maybe I was beginning to get to her. That would be great, if she fired me for being uncooperative. "This is your time. Not mine."

"That line gets me every time. Where have I heard it before?" If she said anything stupid, I was ready to throw the coffee right across the room, right at her precious girl on the swing.

"Where *have* you heard it before?"

"I've been to two psychiatrists before," I said. "They said the same thing all the time, over and over. 'This is your time, son,' or, 'It's a shame you don't know how valuable a doctor's help can be'—stuff like that." The motors were beginning to churn inside. My voice was getting loud and hard to hold in. "And things like, 'This is costing your father a lot of money.' This isn't my idea, so don't tell me how much it's costing my father. If I break my leg, I'll go see a damn doctor. And if my father stops taking away my money, I'll even pay for it myself. How's that?"

"See," Doctor Allenstein said, pleased with herself. "I already know something I didn't know before."

"I'll tell you more," I shot out. "I'll tell you. I'll tell you exactly… I don't give a flying fuck for money. When are you people going to shut up? Take your goddamned money and shove it."

"Tony."

"You wait!" I shouted. "I don't care about movies. I don't care about taxes. I don't care about custody or support." I counted the items on my fingers. "I don't care about school. I wish my father was starving to death. Broke. What do you think of that?" I ran out of things to say, ran out of breath, and sat there biting my thumbnail. Allenstein said nothing. I listened to the ticking of a clock. "Alright, I'm sorry, but if you want to play that game, I'll work with you the same as the others. Stay out of my life. I might shock you."

"I doubt that, Tony."

"Don't bait me."

"What did you do with the other doctors?"

"The one I went to in New York while I was in public school let me make guesses at how much he made. Do you make a lot of money?"

"Some. But that's not your business, is it?" She sipped her coffee.

"And what I think about isn't yours," I said. "I mean, don't you see how much this gets in my way? Look at what I have to go through at school to come here. The kids are going to think I'm nuts if they find out. Look," I went on, "I'm going to tell you something. This isn't my idea. There's nothing wrong with me. I'm not a psycho. But if this keeps up, I'm going to go bats. I'll go crazy and hurt somebody because I'm getting mad." I gave that a second to sink in, then said, "My father's got the whole world going to doctors. Even Gloria. There's nothing wrong with her, either. She's great. She's the greatest thing I've ever seen."

"Your father goes to an analyst, Tony."

"How do you know?" I asked. "You're just telling me that, that's all."

"I don't think he'd mind my telling you. There's nothing to be ashamed of. Mr. Ray told me he sees a doctor."

"Well, that's his problem, not mine." I thought it over for a second. "Maybe he's got a case of doctoritis or something."

"You were caught smoking, weren't you?" Allenstein tried to change the subject.

"Doctors…" I muttered. "You'd think they were a fabulous new fad." I shook my head. This whole thing was disgusting. "Did Dad tell you they caught me?"

"Yes," she answered. "It's true, isn't it?"

"No, it's not! Roth told a lie. Hey, what is this, a remake of the Spanish Inquisition?" Doctor Allenstein didn't answer. She adjusted her glasses and tried to smile. "Myrtle," I said. "What a name!"

"How about some candy?"

I nodded. She went to the kitchen.

Myrtle wasn't so bad. Just trying to do her job. Trying to earn her money. Boy, money got under my skin. I'd be damned if I was going to tell her anything about me. How to get money for Christmas presents was the real problem. If I keep thinking about that, she wouldn't get me. Myrtle bounced back into the room with a dish of chocolates. "Here we are," she said, holding the candy under my nose. I chose the two pieces that were most likely to have cherries inside.

Allenstein sat on the edge of the couch again. I could tell she wasn't used to sitting there by the way she had to look for places to put things. It was funny, the doctor on the couch. She had the coffee cup, a creamer, a sugar bowl, a tray, a bowl of cookies and a dish of candy spread on the floor in front of her. She couldn't even put her feet down flat. There was barely room for her pointy-toed shoes between the coffee cup bribe and the cookie bowl bribe.

"Tony, anything we talk about is secret." Allenstein tried softening me up again. "You must know that part of our code as doctors is not divulging confidences." I concentrated on Christmas, on what to buy Gloria, on how to get money. "Do you know what the doctors' oath is called?"

That's it. I decided to call Dad and tell him I'd bought a present for Mom that cost $17 or $18, plus mailing. Could he give me enough of my money or advance me enough from my allowance to get the rest of my presents? If he told me I had spent too much on Mom, I'd tell him I had to buy her a nice present because she missed me so much. On the way back to school I'd have the driver stop at a store for a few minutes. I'd find something that costs that much money, like a traveling clock or something. If I could get $30 more from Dad, I'd be even for what I had lost at the track. Then I could go win enough for my presents, or, if I only broke even, I could wait and send Mom's present later. I could say it was delayed in the Christmas mail, or even lost. I was pleased with my plan.

"And about this gambling business?" asked Allenstein. To hell with her and Dad, I thought. I didn't answer. "Tony," she said, "truly—I have no arrangement to report on our meetings to your father."

"That's a nice typewriter. It must have cost a pretty penny."

"You're impossible," Allenstein laughed.

"Did you paint that?" I asked, looking at the watercolor of the girl on the swing.

"Uh-huh," she smiled. "Do you like it?"

"Yes," I said. It was fresh and airy. Free.

"Painting is my hobby. Do you have any hobbies?"

"Horseback riding. I'm good. And I used to collect stamps."

"Gambling?" She tried to sneak that in.

"Oh, gee," I put my hands over my ears. "Do you have to keep driving at that? I was just beginning to like you. I tried something, that's all. And I won. That's more than Dad can say. So what?"

"Never mind." She closed the subject. "Tony?"

"I think Dad's jealous because I won."

"Tony?"

"Yes, ma'am."

"A minute ago I was talking and you didn't respond at all. It was as though you had gone into another world and didn't hear me. What is that?" she asked. "A family trait? Do you daydream a lot?"

"No. I don't think so."

"Well," Dr. Allenstein rose from the couch. "Time's up."

"Already?"

"It's 4.20," she said. We walked through the hall and into the front room. At the door she handed me my hat. "I'll see you Saturday at the same time."

"Saturday?" I couldn't come then. Jesus, what was I going to tell her? "Look, does it have to be Saturday? That's really my only day off from school and all. It's the only chance I have to catch up on my studies. And Christmas shopping. How about another weekday instead?"

"You can shop before and after you see me, can't you?"

"Yes," I admitted.

"Those are the only times I'm free to see you, and you can come then."

"Yes, ma'am." That killed the track for me. I opened the door to leave. Dad must really be wise to me, I thought. "You're 33 or 34." I guessed at Myrtle's age. "Right?"

"Pretty darn close," she said. "Maybe even right."

"Goodbye."

"Goodbye." I started down the flagstone path. I would have to figure out something. Her door closed behind me. I should have said 73 or 74. The bitch. Well, at least she wasn't getting anything out of me. That was one consolation.

I called Dad at the studio to tell him I had sent Mom an expensive traveling clock for Christmas. He thought I'd gone overboard, but when I explained what a good idea it had been, that now there would be no chance of her missing her plane if she ever came to visit me, he agreed to have Eddie, the driver, bring me $20 more shopping money. That was all well and good, but it didn't solve the problem of my having to go to Dr. Allenstein's on Saturday.

I would have to find some way other than playing the horses to get the rest of my money back.

A week later, when Eddie picked me up, he handed me an envelope with my name on it. Two $10 bills were enclosed between the folds of a blank piece of white paper with "Dad" scrawled at the bottom.

"That's some allowance," Eddie said.

"Are you kidding?" I sneered. "Dad's returning part of some money I lent him." I asked Eddie to roll up the divider window, telling him I had something important to think about.

We wound around the curves of Coldwater Canyon, then sped down Wilshire Boulevard to Dr. Allenstein's office. She was standing in the den window, waiting, and waved. I pretended not to see her. Instead of going right up to her door, I started to walk around the block. "It's right there, kid," Eddie called after me.

"Leave me alone!" I shot over my shoulder. *People can't stand minding their own business*, I thought. When I came back about five minutes later, hound dog Myrtle stood in her open doorway — erect as a pointer that had just spotted its prey. Eddie was standing next to the car. "What's the matter?" I asked him under my breath. "Have the Russians landed?"

"Hi," Dr. Allenstein said when I was halfway up the flagstone walk. "Come in."

She was as phony as a $3 bill, trying to act cheerful. I dropped my hat on the chair and followed her into the den, only this time I lagged behind with my head bowed and feet dragging. She had moved a wooden table in front of the couch on which sat some coffee, with a saucer balanced over the cup to keep it hot, cookies and a napkin. "You're a few minutes late," she said as she plunked down in the easy chair. Smart, I thought. I sat on the couch. But even though I was dying to, I didn't touch the goodies. She had to think I was too upset to eat and drink.

"I went around the corner for some aspirin," I said, to account for being late. I stretched out on the couch. "You people act like I planted a bomb in the drugstore," I mumbled.

"Don't you feel well?"

"Just great," I said. My back was to her. I stared at the brown wall. Don't you feel well? What a stupid question.

"Then why so glum, chum?" she asked cheerfully. You would think she was the great Messiah, walking around with a bundle of happiness miracles. I ignored her.

"Have your coffee and cookies," she tried. "It'll make you feel better."

"I don't want any."

"Problems at school?"

"No." I turned onto my stomach and wrapped my arms around my head. "Everything's peaches and cream, can't you tell?" I lay there for what felt like hours, but couldn't have been more than two or three minutes. The phone rang. Allenstein told whoever it was to call back in an hour, that she was in a session. *Maybe I should get up some tears*, I thought. The headache wasn't working. Not like I was going to break down or do anything hysterical. I remembered a movie I had seen with Richard Widmark. I pictured Mom strapping herself to a wheelchair and pushing herself down the stairs at home.

Suicide.

Tears started to form in my eyes. I sat up.

"Decide to have a cookie, after all?"

"Uh-huh," I grunted.

"Want it warmed up?"

"No," I shook my head. "But thanks, anyway." I took a sip. My eyes were downcast, on the floor. I hated dainty cups. I liked mugs like Dad had in his office. I wrapped my hand around the whole cup and took a sip, then I took a bite of cookie. *Jesus...* I asked myself. *How long is it going to take her to pry it out of me?* Mom was mangled. Her hair, gray from working too hard and worrying about me, was all torn right out of the top of her head. It was my fault because I hadn't written in so long or sent her a Christmas present.

I would never see Mom again. And Dad. "Oh, God." Gloria and I were together on the bed.

He walked in the door. "It's not me!" I screamed, "it's Sumner. Beat him up! Kill him!"

"Please tell me about it," Dr. Allenstein said. "I'm your friend. I want to make things easier for you."

"I know."

Dad and Gloria together at the beach, how she hadn't called or written on my birthday. Sumner. I'm sure she made it with him.

"What am I going to do?"

"What is it?" she urged.

"Promise not to tell my father?"

"I won't say anything you don't want me to. I promise."

"If you do," I warned, "I'll run away and never come back. I mean that."

"You have nothing to worry about," she said. "None of us want you to run away. Now…"

"I'm in trouble," I said. Allenstein waited for me to go on. I lay down again.

"What kind of trouble?"

"Dad came and took that money. You know—the money I won at the racetrack?"

"Yes."

"I was too scared to tell him I owed the bookmaker $155," I poured out. "Now the bookie's making all kinds of threats."

"I see," Allenstein said gravely. "You have no way of paying this man."

"No. But if you tell Dad, I'll absolutely go. I swear it."

"How did you ever meet a bookmaker?" she asked.

"There was this guy," I started. I hadn't expected her to ask me that in a million years. "Joey! The maintenance man at school. He worked nights. In the daytime he was a bookie. See, he worked so he could show income for taxes. Now he's not there anymore. He got fired and he hangs around the parking lot with these two tough guys trying to get the money out of me."

"Don't you suppose that if you told your father that the money he took wasn't yours, he'd understand?"

"No, I don't." I said flatly, "or I would have gone to him already."

"Why not?"

"I don't know." I twisted on the couch trying to figure out what to say. "He just wouldn't. I couldn't face him about something like that. It's hard enough getting him to like me." The truth was, I knew Dad would see through me like a plate glass window.

Boy, I prayed Allenstein would forget about Joey. All I needed was for Dad to sic the police on him. What a mess that would be.

"What if I spoke to your father myself?" Dr. Allenstein finally asked. I wrapped the pillow around my head. One way or another this was going to work. I could feel it. "I could simply say, 'Look,

Mr. Ray, Tony's in a jam with someone he owes money to and he can't pay it back.'"

"Someone at school I owe money to," I inserted.

"I'll explain that part of the money he confiscated wasn't yours," she went on. "I'm sure your father would understand that." She made it seem so logical.

"And you'd ask him for me?" I sat up and looked her square in the eye. "You'd do that for me?" Allenstein nodded. I knew she thought she was getting somewhere with me. I couldn't help smiling inside.

"Yes," she said. "You certainly can't go on owing money to shady people like that."

"No, ma'am," I said seriously, as though I were ashamed of having been such a fool. "I sure can't."

"Okay, then," she said, slapping her hand against the arm of her chair, "it's settled. When do you need the money?" I bit my lip.

"I'll be safe for a few days." I took my time to think it over. "Ask whenever you feel best."

"Fine," Dr. Allenstein said. "Now, how about a glass of milk and a cookie before you go?"

"Thank you."

18
Save the Box

Christmas vacation finally came. I waited for Dad by the gate at the bottom of the hill. Most of the kids had left between four and five, a few stragglers around six. After that the campus was still, the parking lot empty. The sun had long since fallen behind the ridge and it was getting dark. Cold air swept over the grounds. Old man Sherman and his wife walked arm in arm past the gym. He waved his cane at me. That meant Merry Christmas, I suppose. Had he tried to call out, his thin voice wouldn't have reached me. I waved back. I felt lousy for not trying hard in his class, but I was still doing fine. There he was, so old and everything, and all he did his whole life was to try and bat some knowledge into dense skulls like mine.

I got tired of kicking stones and unfolded the top of my bag of presents. There was a bottle of perfume for Gloria. Dad was getting a great book on movies. His name and a list of his movies were in it. He would get a kick out of that. Tim was going to have to settle for a box of different colored clays, and for Constance, a box of chocolates. I wished I had bought something for Judy Archer, but she would understand. The lights of Dad's car swung into the driveway. I closed up the bag, picked up my suitcase, and got in. "How's school?" he asked right away. "No more trouble?"

"Everything is cool, calm and collected," I said.

Dad smelled of liquor. He rambled on about how his war picture was a classic, how he had pulled exciting performances out of mediocre actors, and how, in spite of interference from everybody, he finished only a few days behind schedule.

"I have to go back on location the day after Christmas to shoot some damn airplanes and clouds. I'll be back for New Year's Eve."

"Can I go with you?"

"Not yet," he said. "When you're older." We stopped at The Point, a beachside bar not far away from home. Dad told me about his creepy underhanded producers and how, when I grew up, I should never be self-satisfied. "Self-satisfaction is death," he said. "Self-satisfaction leads to mediocrity. Damn clouds," he cursed as he paid the check. "That's second unit work."

Tim was screaming bloody murder when we arrived. Constance was feeding him creamed something or other. Dad tousled Tim's hair, felt his bottom, and pushed through the door to the living room. Gloria was working at the table, reciting Shakespeare into a tape recorder. "Change the baby," Dad said to her and went to his room.

"Hi," I said. She waved her book at me to signify hello. Gloria looked pale. Maybe it was because her lipstick was pale. She switched the recorder to playback. Her voice had an English accent and I couldn't make sense out of the lines. Then Dad came back. Gloria turned off the machine. Why couldn't she have stopped working twenty seconds earlier? Didn't she want to talk to me? Dad lifted Gloria by the hands and kissed her. Not a long kiss, but a kiss. It made me sick.

"You taste like toothpaste," Gloria said. Dad led Gloria over to me and put his arm around my shoulder.

"Tony's doing better in school," he said. "As soon as he learns to keep in step with everybody else, he'll be in good shape. Right, son?"

"Right," I said half-heartedly. I didn't like him talking that way in front of Gloria. "He'll be coming home weekends pretty soon," Dad announced. I was delighted. I watched Gloria's face to see if that made her happy, too, if things were the same for us. But she showed no expression at all.

"I'm glad to be home."

"Let's get dressed." Dad chucked Gloria under the chin. "It's getting late."

"Where are you going?" I asked.

"To a party," he said. "We'll be home late." Dad started back to his bedroom. "Fix me a drink, Tony," he said on his way. I felt like Sumner. "And Gloria, change the baby." Gloria stretched her arms over her head like a cat, then let them fall free with a sigh.

"Nick's always saving the baby," she said. We looked at each other. I tried to take her hand, but she pulled it away and placed her palm on my chest to hold me off.

"Don't," she said. "Are you crazy?" We listened until the shower water was running. Then Gloria led me to a corner of the room. We kissed. "Happy now?"

"I guess so." But something impatient in Gloria's voice made me feel like she kissed me because I thought she had to, not because she wanted to. "You and Dad are getting along better, aren't you?"

"For the moment."

"I can't go to the party, can I?"

"No," Gloria laughed. "It'll be almost morning when we get home. Nick would have a fit if we even asked."

"I bet you wish I had stayed at school over the holidays."

"Oh, Tony. Stop it."

"Are you and Dad really that much closer than before?"

"You'd better get that drink made," Gloria said. The shower had stopped. She started off to the kitchen to have Constance change Tim.

"Where's Sumner?" I asked. Gloria turned around to face me.

"He was drafted," she said. "Why do you ask?" I knew I was being mean, but I couldn't help it.

"Oh," I went on. "I was just curious if you were seeing a lot of him."

"No, I haven't seen or heard from Sumner since he went away. Nor do I expect to." Gloria's face flushed with anger. "Gee, you're ugly," she said, storming off to the kitchen.

"I'm sorry," I said under my breath. I was beginning to wish Dad had left me at school over the holidays. Forever, in fact.

Dad was going to be too busy at the studio to think of "entertaining" me, he said, and he had some Christmas shopping to do at lunchtime. He gave me enough money for lunch, a movie and bus fare to Dr. Allenstein's, then dropped me on Hollywood Boulevard. He said he would pick me up at Allenstein's at 4.30. It was nearly 6pm when he screeched to a stop. "Sorry," Dad said with a half-smile. There wasn't a present in the car, unless he had hidden it in the trunk.

Dad gunned the engine and in a few seconds we were in traffic. When we got to the beach highway, the traffic thinned out. Dad smiled as though he had conquered the world.

"What time is it?" he asked.

"About 6.30," I said holding up my wrist. "No watch." That's what I wanted for Christmas.

No more sessions to bluff through until after Christmas. Then I would get the money. I had asked Dr. Allenstein not to speak to Dad until after Christmas Day on Thursday, but warned her he was leaving for location on Monday. He gave no sign of knowing anything. I began to believe Myrtle was actually being true to me. Wouldn't that be a gas, if she were really someone I could talk to?

Dad squinted at the road ahead. "What are you thinking about?" I asked. He shook his head. "Past, present or future?" He sort of smiled but still said nothing. He never told anyone about himself. What made Dad think he had to be better than everyone else?

What was he thinking right now? There is no present, I decided, only needlepoints of time seen through the peephole of that ever-changing kaleidoscope, and by that time the present was past. "You know something," I said. "If you asked me right here and now anything about my life, I'd have a hard time remembering how it really happened." I wasn't sure if Dad was listening. "Maybe all people are like that, making their memories come out the way they want, the way they wish they had happened."

"Uh-huh," grunted Dad. That was it. I thumbed through the script lying on the seat between us. The printed speeches on several pages had handwritten figures next to them.

"That's private," Dad said. I closed the binder and put it back on the seat.

Private? I said to myself. *It's only a script.* Everything about him was private, as secret as my life was becoming. The one thing Dad wouldn't be private about was buying presents. He would be proud of that.

"How did shopping go?"

"Terrible crowds," he said, "but fine." There was nothing to say after that. How could I tell him I knew "fine" was a lie? But maybe he had won. He was in a good mood.

I had loved Dad more when I knew him less well because the more I learned about him now, the more I realized there was no hope of ever knowing him. He drove me nuts.

"Dad?" I asked, "Do two people ever get really close?"

"Your voice is changing."

"You noticed! I'm growing a beard, too."

"One way or another," he said, "you're growing up."

Opening presents is a drag when people hate each other. I'm talking about Gloria and Dad. They had a fight on Christmas Eve. Something about her being disgusted with his character and Dad being disgusted because she wasn't a woman—whatever that meant.

Gloria sat on one end of the couch, Dad sat on the other. One cushion of the three-cushion couch separated them. But that distance seemed as wide as a lifetime. They looked like strangers on a bench waiting for a bus. One thing was certain: Dad and Gloria weren't hitting it off the way they had been when vacation began. I was sitting, waiting, under the Christmas tree. "Go ahead," said Dad when Constance brought Tim. I took a package from Dad and tore off the wrappings with as much courteous control as I could muster. The box revealed a gleaming Colt .22 target pistol. I beamed thanks.

"Of course, it's only to be used under proper supervision."

"Wouldn't you prefer a wristwatch?" Gloria asked. "You could use it all the time." I could have shot her.

"No," I said. "I wanted a gun more than anything in the world. I can use it at the Archers', can't I, Dad?" He smiled a yes. "Let's find one for you," I said to him.

"No, no," Dad waved. "Tim first."

I skimmed over my gift to Tim because I wasn't sure he was old enough to use it. Instead, I gave him a huge box wrapped in bright red paper. It was almost as big as he was. I helped him unwrap what turned out to be a mountain of multicolored alphabet blocks. Then I quickly handed Dad my gift. Before he had a chance to be disappointed in getting a lousy book, I showed him where his name and all his movies were listed. He was really pleased. Gloria bounced down beside me and chose another gift for Tim, then she gave me mine from her. It was a watch! I hugged her and she hugged back. Gloria gave Dad a beautiful alligator billfold with his initials on it in gold. "Subtle," Dad said wryly.

"I think it's beautiful," I told her. She was disappointed in Dad's reaction. He told me to fetch a small square box in silver paper and give it to Gloria. She gasped when she saw the ruby and diamond ring. She slipped it on her finger and held the hand far in front of her. But then a peculiar look, like a cloud passing in front of the sun, came over her face. Something was wrong. She didn't like it. I realized Gloria never wore jewelry.

"I can exchange it for something else."

"No, Nick," Gloria said. "It must have cost you a fortune."

"But if you don't like it…"

"I do," she insisted. After the rest of the gifts were opened, Dad and Gloria had a private talk in the bedroom. I was toying with the new gun when Dad lumbered through the living room and into the kitchen.

"Don't throw the box away," he said as he passed. "We'll use it for storage." Gloria settled next to me on the couch. I was aiming the gun at a Christmas ornament. "Don't get too fond of it," Gloria said. "I have a strange feeling it's going back."

"You must be kidding."

"I'm to wear this heap of rocks until after the guests leave this afternoon. I was told to save the box, too. Nick is insisting on getting me something else."

19

A People Party

Cars were parked on either side of the street in front of one of the new houses. The place was in a Pacific Palisades tract built high on the cliffs overlooking the ocean. It was eerie. Most of the homes were still unoccupied. No lights or cars, just windows with no curtains and the florescent light of newly installed street lamps falling on bare, lifeless earth.

Gloria's heels clicked against the pavement. Rain had stopped and the full moon came out from behind the clouds. The world was taking a strange turn. Halloween at Christmas. "It's like we're being watched," I whispered. A "FOR SALE" sign with a larger "SOLD" sign attached to it was stuck in the earth in front of her friend Julie's house. Gloria struck the tall narrow door with the gold knocker.

"It's just a housewarming party. A people party. Relax," she said.

"I'd be more relaxed in a graveyard."

Julie opened the door. Her eyes were covered by large harlequin sunglasses. "Baby!" she shrieked and threw her arms around Gloria. "I didn't think you'd ever make it." When they got through kissing each other like a couple of nuts, Julie held my shoulders at arms' length. "Hi, sweetie," she said, then turned back to Gloria. "What did you do with El Señor?"

"He's on location."

"Ah, to be married and the husband on location!"

In the foyer, a milk glass Venetian lamp spilled dim light into the living room. Seven or eight small groups of people sat on the floor around their own candles in glasses, ashtrays and wine glasses. A jazz record played from a console in a corner. It was the only furniture in the room. The floor-level glow cast creepy shadows on their faces. "The house is adorable, Julie. I want to see the rest of it."

Gloria let Julie take her coat. She was wearing a shiny white blouse and dark velvet pants.

"Find a patch of floor, children. I'll get you a drink."

A young man looked at Gloria and raised his eyebrows in greeting. His shirt was open to the navel. Gloria smiled, then looked away. "Who's that?" I asked.

"We were good friends once."

"Gloria!" A pale-faced young man reached down for her hand. "How are you?"

"Married," she scowled.

"God is love."

"Tony, meet Bill Barnes, the best singer in Hollywood these days."

"Any day," Bill Barnes corrected. I had never heard of him. "What's your name, boy?"

"Tony Ray, sir." Gloria and I moved on. Gloria stopped a few steps away and whispered in my ear.

"Forget the 'sir' stuff, dollface. This isn't school. You're free. I'm free. And these are friends."

"Who was that guy?"

"Bill?"

"He was queer as a $3 bill."

"So what?" Gloria was sore at me for saying that. "He's a marvelous fortune teller."

"You said he was a singer."

"Oh, come on." Gloria dragged me off with a jerk. We weaved through a few more couples when Gloria spotted someone else she knew. She crept up behind a black guy and wrapped her arms around his head and eyes. "Guess who?" The man made no attempt to get loose. "George Freeman!" exclaimed Gloria. He turned around when she let go.

"Gloria, you old whore. God, it's good to see you."

"George, this is Tony. He's my date tonight." She turned to me. "George will be a star someday."

"Who ever heard of a Negro movie star?" I asked. I knew right away it was wrong of me to say that.

"Tony's really my son," Gloria announced. George held his candle up to my face.

"You're jiving me, baby," said George. "This man's at least 40. Look at the hate in his eyes."

"I don't hate anyone."

"I'm only putting you on. And there aren't any black movie stars. Yet. How old are you, Tony?"

"I don't know tonight. Gloria, how old am I?"

"Are you an actor?" George asked.

"Sure, why not?"

We were back to our seats when Julie appeared with our drinks and candle. She set them down, then ran her hand through Gloria's hair.

"See you later?"

"Yes," Gloria answered fondly, as if making a date. Julie disappeared into the crowd.

Two girls danced. People were talking very softly and almost no one was moving around. Then I spotted a fat, elderly woman in an elaborate red gown. She talked with a lot of flamboyant gestures, stabbing the air with an empty cigarette holder to make her points. Seeing Gloria, she immediately excused herself and came over to us.

"Gloria. Love. How are you?"

"I finished the play."

"Darling. I heard. I love your shirt. Where is the great man?"

"Location."

She turned to me smiling. She wore heavy red lipstick and rouge and what I could have sworn was a wig. Then it hit me. She was a man.

"This is Heathcliff," said Gloria, introducing me.

"Darling, how wonderful. You're so pale, love," he said, turning back to Gloria. "Didn't they have sunlamps where you were?"

"They wanted me pale."

"Oh, how we suffer for our art."

Gloria got up, saying she wanted to check in with a few friends and have a chat with Julie.

"I'm Samson," the man said. He looked at me, holding a smile a second too long. Getting no response, he said, "Do you know Gloria well?"

"Since this summer," I said. I was relieved Gloria hadn't called me her stepson. But why did she introduce me by that funny name, Heathcliff? This strange person seemed to believe I was Gloria's date. I tried to look as adult as possible. How long would we have to stay at the party? I wanted to be at home, alone with Gloria.

"She never told me. She never even hinted." He beamed at me. "Heathcliff. Before he ran away. Early Heathcliff. I adore that film."

I had no idea what the creature was talking about and simply said, "I didn't see it."

"Oh, darling, it's divine. Oberon and Olivier running across the moors. Those marvelous faces. How old are you, Heathcliff?"

Hoping the dim light was on my side, I said. "Seventeen."

"Oh, how naughty of Gloria. Please don't tell her I said that. She can't bear to be called naughty. In her heart she is always daddy's good little girl. It's part of her charm. And attraction."

I sipped my wine. It had a slightly bitter taste. Noting the look on my face, Samson remarked, "I do think Julie could have been more generous in her choice of wine. She's done so well for herself. I must speak to her about a business manager. It's difficult for a woman in her position."

"I guess it is," I agreed. If I went along with Samson's conversation, I might understand some of it. "This is a nice house."

"Oh, yes, my dear. Such a bargain, too, at forty thousand. Five thousand down and a little payment every month. It's half what companionship would have cost him ordinarily. And, of course, if he wearies of her, he merely stops making the payments. But Julie's a canny bitch. It's in her name. I absolutely insisted on it. When she spoke to me about it, I told her, 'Get him to put it in your name. You never know what the future holds.' The property values in this area can only soar, so if she hangs on to it for five years, it will put her in a very nice position. Oh dear, Heathcliff. I swore I wouldn't talk about real estate tonight. It's so uncreative. What's your sign, Heathcliff?"

"Sagittarius."

"How perfect for Gloria. Stanley was a Taurus, you know. When she told me, I simply threw up my hands. I felt more hopeful about the director. He's a Leo—so fiery, so arrogant. But a drunk," Samson said regretfully. "A gambler and a drunk. How déclassé." Samson fitted a cigarette into his long holder. "Gloria can't bring herself to leave him, even though I tell her, 'Darling, you must. He is simply destroying you.' He's the daddy who ran away, and she can't believe he doesn't love her. Creative men are so often beasts to their children."

Samson saw someone coming in the door and began to move away. He took my hand in both of his. "We must talk again soon." And he was gone.

A woman jumped to her feet and shouted, "What the hell do you know about acting?" She was so drunk she could hardly stand. "Don't give me any of that Method crap." She squared off, standing flat-footed on both feet with her legs spread for balance. Everyone in the room watched. I was beginning to feel like we were at a circus where everyone in the audience contributed their own little sideshow. The woman leaned forward precariously. "You don't have to prepare before a scene. Prepare? Prepare what?" Her finger stabbed the air in front of the nose of the man she was chastising. Hushed giggles rippled through the room. "You're telling me about acting. Ha!"

"You're drunk," the guy said. He reached up to calm her down, but she slapped his hand away with a mighty sweep of her arm. When it was clear that nothing more was going to happen, she stormed out of the room, weaving miraculously through the obstacle course of people without stepping on a single one. A moment later she reappeared with a bottle of wine and her coat thrown over her shoulder. She spotted the guy she had been attacking and maneuvered through the guests again. "Excuse me, excuse me," she said in a pseudo stage voice. She stopped behind her friend and, before anyone could give warning, casually tipped the bottle of wine over his head. Everybody laughed. He did, too. "Take me home, sweetie," she said, bending over to give him a kiss on the head.

"Your home or my home. Any home. It doesn't matter." They left.

Julie brought over another bottle of wine and set it between us. "For special guests, in case you run out." She disappeared as fast as she had come. I don't know why, but something told me I didn't like her as much as before. Gloria moved around close to me and started pointing out people.

"That's Frank Chatham," she said. "He's gay, but you wouldn't want a more wonderful friend. Like the mother of all lost souls. Girls adore him because he has big ears." Chatham had long black hair that curled behind his neck and thick lips which remained perpetually pursed as though they had been shot with Novocaine. A long college-type scarf was thrown carelessly around his neck. He sat like a yogi and the string ends of his scarf lay draped on the floor beside him. He was a handsome man.

"What does he do?" I asked.

"Throws parties."

"I mean for a living," I persisted.

"Nothing," Gloria said.

"Nothing? How does he live?"

"Jesus, Tony." Gloria looked at Chatham, then took a sip of wine. I glanced at him again. He caught me. It happened real fast but I could have sworn two things, that he winked at me and that he had the longest damn eyelashes in the world. "His mother sends him the rent," Gloria said. "He's very close to his mother and he earns a few dollars here and there."

"How?" I asked.

"Why do you have to be so nosy? He makes his money going out with women for money. Satisfied?"

"Oh." I tried to slough it off. "Why didn't you say so before?"

Gloria stared at me. But this time it was like she was trying to pull out every wire and coil of my brain for inspection. She broke it off with a piercing "Ha!" that I knew saw through my lousy veneer of understanding. I was as confused by her and the surroundings she had brought me into as a steer being herded through the slaughter pens.

"How did you meet these people?" I asked calmly.

"When I was married to Stanley," she said. "That's Bette Van." She pointed to a real cute blonde girl whose head was on another girl's lap. "You'll hear a lot about her soon. She's a good actress. And over there, see, the girl with her hair in a bun, that's Frieda Stern. She's a stripper—has two beautiful kids—hooks on the side."

"Gloria?"

"What, doll?"

"What does hook mean?"

"She's a call girl. A whore."

"What's a john, I heard that, too?"

"A john is a man who pays a girl for sex, or sometimes just for companionship."

"Whew," I said. "I'd never hire a girl. I wouldn't know how."

"Everyone gets their kicks differently." Gloria was deadly serious. "Maybe you're lucky. Maybe you'll turn out normal."

"How do you get yours?" I asked.

Gloria thought it over for a few seconds. She answered seriously. "I know I like sex." I kissed her hard on the mouth, then she pushed me away.

"Normal," I said.

Gloria spotted someone she had been looking for. She got up, went over to him, and whispered in his ear. "Oh man, for you two." With a deft movement he took a thin cigarette from his shirt pocket and handed it to Gloria.

"One for Julie."

"Share it with her. It'll blow your heads off."

Gloria nodded across the room to Julie, who nodded back, and the two of them disappeared up the hall. It struck me that Julie liked Gloria more than she liked anyone else at the party, and that together they behaved like little girls in grade school, the kind of girls who sat on stoops and made fun of the boys.

The noise of the party had become a low roar, with everyone talking at once. Now and then a high-pitched laugh or a shout punctuated the hum. The black man who had called Gloria an old whore looked at me without interest. Samson was at the door greeting newcomers. "Madame is preoccupied. So nice you could come." I heard someone complain there was no food.

"Julie never thinks of things like that."

"Where is she?"

"She's with Gloria."

"Julie has a crush on Gloria."

Gloria and Julie came back. Gloria was talking to the black guy again, and now he got to his feet and he and Gloria were dancing. They moved in and out of my line of vision. Julie was watching them. The man danced easily, smoothly, in a way I knew I could never do. Gloria dropped her head on his shoulder. When her eyes met mine, it was though she hadn't seen me. Julie walked away from them and came over to me. "Are you doing alright? Don't be lonely. Everything's alright." Julie went back to Gloria and the black man. I went to the bathroom and waited a long time, until two girls came out giggling hysterically. Coming back, I didn't see Gloria. But then I saw her at the other side of the room. The black man's hands had moved to Gloria's buttocks, and their pelvic areas were pressed close together. How could I stop them? I couldn't. I was powerless. Everything's alright, Julie had said. Julie joined them and the three of them, their arms around each other, swayed together. George said something that made Julie laugh. They were at the hall that led to the back of the house, the bathroom and the bedrooms, and they danced down the hall until they were out of sight.

I didn't understand at all. I wanted to hide. They had left me alone. But there was nothing to hide behind, only the clumps of people. My spot on the floor. I wandered into the kitchen. The counter was strewn with empty wine bottles and half-full glasses. How long would she be in there? What were they doing? Had she forgotten him? Two young men came in and looked in the refrigerator. "Swiss cheese," one said.

"Oh, darling, I loathe it."

"I'll be ill if I don't eat."

"Perhaps we should leave?"

With half a dozen people, they left, saying goodbye to Samson, who attended the door.

"Tell Julie it was divine."

"Thank you, child, I will."

I hate her. But with determination and ultimate belief, I waited for her.

"Heathcliff. Poor darling, you've been deserted." It was Samson, who stood beside me and put his arm over my shoulder. I could think of nothing to say. Samson smiled and shook his head sadly. "Not a nice thing to do to you. Are you alright? Would you like another drink? There is a ton of marijuana around. Shall I get you some?"

"No, thanks."

"Poor dear." His hand began to knead the muscles in my neck. Samson smiled persistently, as if making some kind of offer. I yanked free.

"Please take your hands off me." I shook my shoulders. "And my name isn't Heathcliff, it's Tony."

The eyes blinked, then Samson said, "Of course," and went away.

Drag queen. Drag queen.

Gloria was still in that room with Julie and the man. Were they both fucking him? Or were Gloria and Julie part lesbian? Was there such a thing as a part lesbian? Were they taking money from him? Gloria was always sexy to me. My confusion was becoming unbearable. All I knew was we had to get out of there. I had to be with Gloria by myself. Maybe they were just talking. Maybe my imagination was running away with me. I couldn't stand it. Why didn't Gloria take me into the room?

Beside the sink I saw a large wastebasket stuffed with crumpled newspapers. I struck a match and carefully set one edge of the papers on fire. The flame wavered, then caught on. It was burning high, toward the window. I ran out the kitchen door. I waited in the car. It seemed so impersonal, as though I hadn't set it at all. I was just waiting for Gloria. Fog was rolling over the hill, softening the harsh light of the florescent streetlamps. The noise of the party was muffled. For some strange reason I felt okay, peaceful. A few minutes later I heard the first squeal, followed by shouting, rushing around, and at last, from a long distance, the piercing wail of the fire engines. People came running out of the house, got in their cars, and drove away. I lay down on the seat so no one could see me and connect me to the fire. My heart was pounding with fear for Gloria's safety, until I heard her footsteps approach and she opened the car door. I straightened up.

"What a relief." she said, "I wondered how I'd get out of there."

"What's happening?" I asked in a false sleepy voice.

"Fire. Julie threw everybody out. God, I hope they save her house."

A fire engine hurtled past, siren blaring, then stopped with a last moan. The men shouted at one another, and over all that noise I heard Julie screaming, "It's in the kitchen!" A second truck was heard whining toward them. Gloria started the car. "I guess there's nothing I can do."

There was fog on the highway. Gloria drove with her eyes fixed to the road. I sneaked a look at her. In the dashboard light her face was almost white.

"Was George disappointed? Or Julie?"

"What?"

"George and Julie, who you went to the bedroom with?"

"Tony, don't let that worry your little head. That was like acting. Nothing more. Do you understand? Acting."

"I don't know about things like that."

"Why didn't you dance with me?" Gloria asked. I couldn't answer. She drove in silence all the way home. Gloria stopped the car at our house and sat hunched over the wheel.

"May I kiss you," I asked.

"No."

"Please."

"I have to brush my teeth. I have to take a bath."

"I love you, Gloria. I love you so much."

"That's too bad."

"Why?"

"All so dirty. Good girls don't do things like that."

"It's okay. Would you teach me?"

"You mustn't love me, Tony. Please don't." She got out of the car and took a deep breath. "God, the air is good."

"It's just you and me now, Gloria. We can be alone. We can hold each other."

"Come, Tony." We walked toward the house. "I love you, you know. I truly do. Just the way you are. No acting. But be a boy, Tony, nothing else." She held her breath for a moment. "I'm very attracted to you as a boy."

I reached into my pants pocket and withdrew the roll of bills Dr. Allenstein had given me. I held them out to Gloria. "Do you want this? Could you act for me? Could I be your john?"

Gloria ran away from me and into the house.

20
A Lousy Dream

The bus roared up the ramp onto the freeway. The noonday sun burned through the roof. Waves of heat pressed me deep into the seat. Holiday crowds on their way to Santa Anita. Bus windows don't open. No air. Sealed coffin shut. Two to five. Royal Town Miss. Safety Zone. Confusion. Nine. Fourteen. Holiday, nineteen fifty. One plus nine plus five plus zero equals fifteen. Numbers are safe. Numbers don't know. The bus stopped.

Swept into the excitement of the day. Running to the grandstand. To be first even though the first race was an hour away. First. Number one. No stalling. No hedging. No excuses. No lying. It would be run. The hour of waiting would be filled with contemplating that glorious daydream. Hope of being the victor. Hope of being right. Hope for anything. It doesn't matter. Lose. There was the second, third, fourth… tomorrow, next year, a lifetime to be run. A lifetime of beautiful sparkling numbers.

On the way home, I bought Gloria a glass stallion and a book of poetry. It cost most of the money I had left. But it was worth it. I wanted to write "I love you" on the first page but didn't. What if Dad saw? I felt better even though I had lost. It had been a relief, like going to the bathroom or waking from a long sleep. Sure, I felt bad about the money. But what was $150, anyway? I could always get it again somehow. Next time I would probably win, so what was the difference? I felt clean and cheerful. Besides, if I hadn't gone to the track I never would have bought the presents for Gloria. So the day hadn't been a total loss after all.

I asked Constance to put my dinner in the oven with Gloria's. I placed the book of poems on her plate, sat at the table set for two, and waited. Night had already closed in on my mother in New York. She was probably at her desk in the smoke-filled study, writing. At least she had her roommate, Amy. Amy and my mother slept in the living room. The two beds were made up to look like couches in the daytime. The bedroom was Mom's study. Mom had written that they were tearing down our building soon and that she would have to find another place to live, a smaller place now that I was gone.

When it was pitch dark, I turned on all the lights and the record player. I was always afraid of the dark, of being alone at night. It was two in the morning when I fell asleep on the couch. Gloria hadn't come home. I woke with a start. The needle clicked back and forth across the record. I stretched into the new day and turned off the record player. It was Constance's day off. She always took Tim with her or to Gloria's mother's house when there was no one home to watch him. Good. I could have the house, the day, my thoughts, to myself. Sunlight poured through the windows into the living room. I whistled the tune of an old folk song, the words to which I had long since forgotten, and put water on for coffee. There was no need to creep around quietly or tiptoe up to Gloria's door to see if she had ever come home. I knew she hadn't. But to kill any doubt, I checked. The room was empty. The pillows were puffed, untouched. The smooth tucked blankets were covered by the clean white spread. The absence of stale smoke, perfume, a piece of clothing thrown over a chair, an empty glass, a full ashtray—it all made the room seem unused, never the container of lives, loves, hate, passion or even sleep.

There were no Glorias. No women, no mothers, no daughters, no lovers. No father. There never had been. So why was I kidding myself. It was all a lousy dream. And here I was alone, a stranger to this place.

I opened Dad's closet. The rows of shoes could have been those of a dead man. I took one of the suits off the rack. It had a musty, unworn smell. The kind of smell that comes back with the cleaners. There was no emotion attached to it. I carried the suit to Gloria's closet, swung the door open, and took down a blue dress with a small diamond pin still clipped to it like a star sparkling against the sky of some forgotten night. I held the two together, the suit and the dress, in front of the full-length mirror on the back of the closet door. They were empty. But had they been full of flesh, of people, of *yak-yak* and eyeballs, they would have been no more alive. It was as though these people didn't exist.

I unclipped the diamond pin and put it in my pocket, then returned the dress to its place. Dad's suit rewarded me with a crumpled $5 bill, some small change, and a yellow $50 win ticket that was almost two years old. I smelled coffee, which meant one thing: I had let it boil over. I went to the kitchen, turned off the flame, poured the black, burned liquid down the sink, and started over. It was 8.30 by the clock over the stove. I checked my watch, the one Gloria had given me, and the time was the same.

Sitting at the kitchen table was strangely comfortable, peaceful. Mother, your petticoat smells like bacon. I smiled. It was as though she had gone to work and I had a summer day to plan—to go to the beach with my friend David Ratner, who lived down the street, or play ball in Central Park. California wasn't my country, my home. There weren't any candy stores, alleys, cement parks, clotheslines stretched from fire escape to fire escape. I even missed the tough kids standing on the corner having a smoke, the buses rumbling over the cobblestones, the subways rattling the windows like earthquakes. I placed a person-to-person call to Mom. The phone rang and rang. I felt I was being carried on a magic carpet through the cables into the apartment. I could see the phone ringing, but I couldn't see anything clearly or remember exactly where everything was. "No answer," the operator said. Nobody anywhere, not here, not in New York. I was getting morose.

I spread a sheet on the sand in front of the house, brought out the portable radio, a stack of comic books, the sun tan oil, a quart of beer, a bag of lemon drops, two apples, an orange, the sports section, a green covered paperback of Henry Miller's *Sexus*, a pencil, stationery, because I really needed to write to Mom, and a submarine sandwich for later.

The phone rang once during the day. I ran to catch it because I thought it might be Gloria, but it was only Constance calling to remind Gloria she was dropping Tim off at Gloria's mother's house for the New Year's weekend.

At four o'clock, a fishing boat churned toward the Malibu Pier. I had forgotten all about my appointment with Dr. Allenstein. But she would understand how far I would have to come by bus. It would take two hours each way. I gathered up all my stuff, tied it in the sheet, and dumped the bundle in the house. Then I filled the barbecue with charcoal. I dressed and strolled down the highway toward the grocery store. The table was still set from the night before. The book of poetry was still on Gloria's plate. I smiled. There was even a bottle of red wine on the table. The few bucks I had left from the track and the five I had found in Dad's pocket would be enough to buy two fine steaks, salad stuff, and two candles.

The third full load of charcoal was red hot and covered with white ash when Gloria came home. It was after eight. I quickly lit the candles before she reached the living room. But Gloria stormed through without noticing the preparations. She closed the bedroom door behind her. "Get washed," I called in to her. "Dinner's coming up."

"I'm not hungry," she said. I got the steaks from the kitchen, went outside, rolled the barbecue right under her open window, and threw the meat on. "Did you make salad?" she asked a few moments later.

"It's in the icebox keeping fresh. I even made dressing."

Gloria moved out of her room to the living room. She came to the back door and opened it. "Oh, Tony," she was holding the book of poetry. "You shouldn't have." I turned the meat casually.

"I wanted to. It doesn't mean anything."

"Yes, it does. Thank you."

We ate a quiet dinner. Gloria apologized for not calling to say where she was. I wanted to ask if she had been staying with Julie, but didn't dare. For some strange reason I wasn't even angry. I was more relaxed and at peace with myself than I could ever remember having been before. It was as though I were seeing Gloria from a distance for the first time. I felt I had lost her, and wanted to cry. While Gloria cleared the table, I built a fire. Then we sat before the fire and I brushed her hair and she read aloud: "O waste of lost, in the hot mazes, lost, among bright stars on this most weary, unbright cinder, lost! Remembering speechlessly we seek the great forgotten language, the lost lane—end into heaven, a stone, a leaf, an unfound door. Where? When?"

Gloria closed the book. She leaned back and rested her head on my lap. "I'm tired," she said.

"I wrenched my back or something," I said. "It aches."

"Oh."

"Would you rub it for me?"

"Sure. Go lie down in my room, I'll get the oil."

I went to the bedroom, took off my shirt and shoes, and lay down. Gloria sat on the edge of the bed and poured oil on her hands. She started to massage. For an instant I wished it could be the beginning of something else. It felt so good.

"Nick will be home tomorrow."

"I'll have to go back to school soon." There was an ocean-filled silence. I wanted desperately for her to tell me everything she had done the last two days, but I knew she wouldn't. The world was trying to rush in, a torrent of fragments, nothing complete.

Nothing is ever erased. Every moment we live travels with us forever. "I'll never forget you, or stop loving you."

"You'll change," she said. I shook my head. "Wait and see. You'll outgrow me. No one ever stays together. There aren't any great loves, except in the movies." I wanted to tell her she was wrong. "We're both younger than I ever thought. At least I am, or this never would have happened. But now it's over." Over. I refused to believe what I was hearing. Nothing is ever finished, only begun. Gloria helped me under the covers, tucked me in, and went to bed in my room.

21
Everything's Fine

It was late Friday night. Dad stuck his head in my door to say hello, then lumbered down the hall to bed. Shortly before dawn I was awakened again by shuffling and low conversation. "What are you doing, Nick?"

"Going to town."

"Come back before dinner, please. I have a surprise."

Dad's car sputtered, revved a few hundred times to get warm, and took off. I turned over and went back to sleep. At breakfast Gloria said nothing about Dad leaving in the middle of the night. She couldn't have been less interested, or she didn't let me know. It was New Year's Eve and Gloria was concentrating on making herself beautiful again.

She had an appointment to spend five hours at the Elizabeth Arden beauty parlor for a complete makeover. It wasn't like me to turn down going anywhere with her, but that seemed just a little too boring. I decided to spend the afternoon at the Archers'.

"Rhapsody in Blue" was playing at the height of the hi-fi's volume when I came home later. The kitchen reeked of Scotch. A pile of empty Old Rarity bottles filled the sink. Under that odor was one of food burning. Smoke drifted toward the ceiling from the oven. It smelled like burned oranges. I turned off the oven and went into the living room. Gloria was sitting on the floor facing the ocean. She froze, as though my presence had turned her into a block of ice. "Leave me alone," she murmured. She spun around on her haunches and leaned forward, supporting herself with one hand. She picked up a pale blue bandana and waved it up and down as though shooing me away. "Oh, it's you," she glowered. "Where's Nick?"

"I've been riding all day."

"Where the hell is Nick? Where are you, you bum?"

"Were you cooking?" I asked. Gloria thought it over, then shook her head.

"What a dumb question." She took a swig from the bottle next to her. Her mouth, eyes and the flesh of her cheeks bunched in around her nose to make a terrible face. "Yes, I was cooking. What the hell do you think was going on in there? A bar mitzvah?"

"I turned off the oven," I said.

"I didn't tell you to do that." She threw her crumpled bandana at me as hard as she could. It unraveled in mid-air and floated gently down to her feet. That infuriated her. "What right did you have to turn off my oven?"

"Something was burning." Her level unwavering stare of drunkenness bored holes in me.

"That was Nick," she said factually. "A duck I burned. A Nick damned duck. Put him in that damned oven and burned him." Gloria bolted unsteadily to her feet. "Do you hear me, Tony?" She ran helter-skelter, slamming her way through the swinging doors, into the kitchen. She was striking a wooden match against the wall when I came face to face with her. "Happy New Year! I'm lighting that oven again. I am. I am. Do you hear me, Tony?"

"Don't, Gloria." I reached for her wrist. She belted me across the side of my head with the back of her hand.

"Damned match went out," she mumbled. "Don't do that again." I leaned against the sink, away from her, and closed my eyes. It had been a solid blow. I was sick to my stomach, the way you get sick when the doctor punches your arm with a needle and pushes that aching fluid in. But it was over as fast as it had come, like a wave of nausea.

"Are you okay, baby?" Her arms were around my neck. She pulled me close to her, burying my head against her breasts. "I emptied all his precious Scotch. Aren't you glad?"

I opened my eyes. The bottles sparkled before me. Everything was clear, the porcelain of the sink was gleaming white, the drops of water falling from the faucet made giant crystal splashes, the gold-amber remainders in the bottles were blazingly bright. It was none of my business that Dad drank. It wasn't my problem. Gloria drank, too, and so did I. It was as though I had been walking around with a net over my eyes and then, suddenly, through some shock of recognition, my vision cleared.

"Do you hear me, Tony? I emptied all his precious Scotch down that damned sink." It was her voice, her being, that seemed so far away. Who was she? Where did she come from? How did she get into my life? She sounded like a stranger talking through an echo chamber. I tilted my head toward the open window above the sink and filled my lungs with air. It was clear and salty. "Except one little ol' bottle I kept for myself. Now that's gone, too," she droned on, "and he won't have any and I've had plenty and I can't find more." I raised myself erect and became aware of the airiness, the lightness, of my body. This was all a dream. "I'll show him. You wait and see." She opened the oven door. A cloud of smoke poured from the black hole into the room. "Oh, man, I'm going to light you up again and let you burn until you're a cinder in hell." She turned on the gas and lit a match. Supporting herself against the stove, she leaned over and touched the fire to the gas. The blue flame started over again with a sudden whoosh that also ignited a pan of fat. "God, damn it!" she shrieked and slammed the oven door shut. "Oh, I could die. I'm so mad." She was standing absolutely straight, almost on tiptoe, as though reaching for the ceiling with the top of her head. She held the flesh of her lower arm. "I burned myself, you bastard." Then she turned on me. "And it's all your fault."

"My fault?"

"Where's Nick?"

"Have you tried to call him?"

"Two hospitals, The Point, studio, morgue," she checked off on her fingers. "That's one hand." She ran the fingers of one hand across those of the other. Her arm followed the hand, her head the arm, and she rested her head on the table.

"What time was he supposed to get home?"

"How the hell should I know? It's New Year's Eve!" she shouted with renewed strength. "He walked out of here in the middle of the night. Cooking for him. What a laugh. That's the last time I make a fool of myself."

"Can I turn off the oven now?" She didn't answer. I turned off the gas and opened the window over the sink as far as it would go. The room was full of smoke.

"I never want to see you again. You're a son of a bitch." Gloria spoke, muffled, into the sleeve of her sweater. "You're no good, never have been, never will be good." Then she was quiet. I went behind her chair to calm her down. When I put my hands on her shoulders, she bolted away to the sink, screaming, "I hate you! I hate you! I hate you!" She picked up two bottles, one in each hand, and started swinging wildly at me. I moved behind the table, out of the way.

"You'll fall," I warned.

"Get the hell out of here." She swung again. I backed around the table to the door. "Get out."

"I live here."

"I pay the rent!" Gloria cocked her arm and threw one of the bottles as I opened the door. It bounced across the lawn, then stopped. I kept walking, expecting any second to be hit in the head. "That's right," she screamed after me. "Walk out!"

The highway stretched before me, infinitely dark, forever, into nothingness. The narrow white line was ridiculous. What was the point of drawing a line that started nowhere and had nowhere to go? So people on either side wouldn't crash. That was logical. I crossed halfway and stopped on the line. Cars zipped by, blowing their horns, on both sides. What if someone had to live in the middle of the road? How terrifying.

I had no place to go.

I crossed the other half of the highway and walked toward the Archers' house. I had no real intention of getting there. It was only a direction to take in the meantime, while I was making up my mind. I couldn't just stand around like an idiot. When it's important for a person to get where he's going, his arms swing, his head is high, his eyes count the steps brightly. It doesn't matter where he's headed. Maybe it doesn't even matter if he gets there. I kicked stones ahead of me, followed their jagged paths. When I came to the mouth of the Archers' road, I didn't even consider turning up it. Being confused is no fun. If I were drunk, I would wander back to the beach and watch the men fishing with their long poles. They build fires at night and occasionally they stop, leaving their poles stuck upright in the sand, for a cup of coffee and a wax paper-wrapped sandwich from home.

There weren't too many fishermen on the beach this time of year, perhaps only three or four strung out along the cove, not wanting to be too near each other, maybe not even caring if they caught fish. Men need time to think. My last stone guide landed at the foot of the porch steps of the Malibu Inn. I decided to go

into the weather-beaten old building. If you could call it a decision.

Gloria didn't say she had called the Inn. If Dad was inside,
I wouldn't ask him about not coming home. I would just sit at
the counter next to him and wait until he finished eating. Then
we would have a long talk. About anything—even God. Do you
believe in God?

Dad wasn't there.

I ordered coffee. I was the only customer in the once summer-
filled place. The waitress sat at the end of the counter, reading,
after serving me. I added cream and sugar to the coffee and stirred
endlessly. The wall behind the counter was decorated with tier
upon tier of once glossy photographs of movie stars who had come
and gone from Malibu. Pictures of silent stars now dead or living
in mansions, their memories protected by stone walls and barking
dogs, or working as extras and living alone with their memories in
furnished rooms above Hollywood Boulevard. Faces that couldn't
be recognized today by the pictures on the walls. Not now. Not
anymore. Forgotten, changed faces, lost to time, to death. Jesus
Christ, why do we have to die?

If Dad had been there, we wouldn't have talked about movie
stars, movies or the pictures on the wall. I don't know what we would
have said to each other, but silence can be beautiful, too. Gloria's face
hung above a giant steel coffee maker. I tried to imagine what the
picture would look like in fifty years. The glass would be thick with
dust and grease. The white of the picture would turn yellow, the
black to a dull, decaying gray. What would Gloria look like in fifty
years? Maybe the Inn would be torn down by then and replaced by
a modern hotel. I didn't know. Nobody did. It didn't matter that
Dad's picture wasn't hanging on the wall. He wasn't a movie star. All
people cared about were the movie stars. That Dad be happy while
he lives is important, not what he wants people to remember of him
when he's dead, not how many suits, cars, dollars, or shoes he had,
not even how many pictures he made. If he did one thing that made
him happy and no one else in the whole world liked it, that would be
okay. You have to be a fool to live for other people.

I gave up thinking like that. It was depressing. I finished my
coffee, bought the morning paper, and left the Inn. I walked briskly
toward the beach. I had made up my mind to stay out all night and
go into town to pawn Gloria's pin in the morning. That is, if Dad

still hadn't come home. Maybe I could make friends with one of the fishermen. When I got too sleepy to stay awake, I would bury myself in the sand, push together a pile for my head, and use the newspaper as a pillow case.

Morning sun poured into the gaping black holes left by the fishermen's fires. The men were gone. The poles were gone. The fish were gone. Charred bits of driftwood, an empty Coke bottle stuck upside down in the sand, a child's small pile of hard found seashells, remained. The sky, the ocean, the beach, the houses were all still and crystal clear. It was a beautiful morning. Tiny particles of sand ground into the crevices of my body as I walked. A seagull was lying still and cold, caked with night death, near the water. Hordes of sand flies picked and stabbed at the dead bird's body.

I had to get clean. I undressed. Once beyond the surf, I backstroked. Seeing the cove before me, the houses like toys, I remembered Dad swimming next to me the first day I came to Malibu. Are houses, parents, shells, all meant to be left behind? Neither Dad's face nor my fight with Gloria seemed real to me. It was all so far in the past. *Now* was important. The now of being alive, of the New Year, of being naked. I swam toward the beach. "Taxi," I shouted and caught a breaking wave to shore. I dried myself with my shirt, shook out my jeans, and got dressed. I had to go home sooner or later. And it was so early in the morning that if everyone was sleeping, I could just go to my room and climb into bed. If Dad had come home during the night, I would simply say I slept on the beach, that I wanted to be alone. He would understand.

Approaching the house, I saw a bunch of stuff thrown out on the beach. It was Dad's suits, jackets, shirts, records, books, a hairbrush. As I gathered them up, I saw that some of the lapels on Dad's jackets had been cut off, and there were slices cut in some of the pants. It looked like Gloria had gone crazy with a razor blade. I put everything in a pile over the fence in our own backyard. Before going in, I checked the garage. Gloria's car was still there, but Dad had not come home. The back seat of Gloria's car was stacked with clothes on hangers and suitcases. She had really had a fit.

The kitchen door was locked. I went around to the beach side. That door was locked, too, but the metal hook holding it was easy enough to break and fix later. I forced my way in. The pile of glass was still in the kitchen sink. I drank a glass of orange juice, put coffee on, refilled the juice glass and took it to Gloria's door. I knocked. No answer. I knocked again. Still no answer. I guess it was pretty early. I put the glass by the door and went back to the kitchen to watch the coffee. The next time I passed Gloria's door, on my way to change clothes, the glass of juice was gone.

"Gloria?"

"What do you want?"

"To see your smiling face. It's a beautiful day." I waited for her to say something. "Are you up?"

"I'm awake, thanks to you."

"Happy New Year," I said, as though that alone should have been enough to wipe away her bad mood. "Can I come in?"

"No!" she yelled. "I told you to go away." A shoe or something banged against her side of the door.

"Why are you hiding? I know what curlers look like. They're ugly."

"Ha, ha."

The door was held closed by another of those eye hooks. I gave three fast pushes and it fell to the floor. The room was a disaster. Things were thrown everywhere. Gloria sat in the middle of the bed with her feet tucked under her. She held the blankets up to her chin.

"Out!" She pointed a rigid finger at the door. Her raised eyebrows made it even more amusing.

"How can you get me out with that finger? Where's Dad?"

"He called in the middle of the night, as though that were enough, but he didn't say anything about where he was. I can just guess."

"Boy, are you morose." I sat on the edge of the bed. She kicked furiously.

"I want to be alone. Get off my bed."

"Why?"

"Because I want you to," she said, level as death. "Because you broke in here." She turned over, away from me, and pulled the covers over her head.

"That's stupid." And then, still trying to cheer her up, I said, "Who would I have to talk to if I left? Anyway, I still love you."

"Love!" Gloria laughed into the pillow. "Tony loves Gloria. Ha. Ha. Ha." She said each separately, each one meant to be more biting than the one before. "That's funny. What right do you have to love me?"

"What right?"

"Yes, with what right? What do you know about love?"

"I just do. I thought…"

"That I was Camille and you were my favorite lover." Gloria whipped around and sat up facing me. "You think love is like in the movies, happy endings. Well, there are no happy endings. There isn't any love in the whole damn world."

"You don't believe that. I know you don't."

"Get out, Tony."

"You're not the same. You're turning into a hysterical witch."

"Go away," she screamed.

"Why? Why? Why?" I screamed back. "Because you're telling me to?"

"Because your darling father might walk in. How would he like to find his son in bed with his wife?"

"Now you're ugly. And I'm not in bed with you."

"Well!" She gasped as though I had really insulted her.

"Suddenly you're worried about Dad. Why, Gloria? Who do you think you are, his wife?"

"Stop it."

"Do you?"

"Please stop."

"No. Tell me why he should be angry. Why should he be the least bit upset?"

"I'll kill you."

"You haven't told him anything, have you, Gloria?"

"I hate you," she turned away again.

I took a handful of blankets and sheets and tore them off the bed. "Pay attention," I shouted.

From under the pillow, quick as a whip, Gloria drew the gun Dad had given me for Christmas. She held it in both shaking hands, pointing it straight at my face.

"Don't talk to me that way," Gloria stammered. "I'm fine. I'm a good girl. And you don't own me."

"I know that."

"I should have known not to trust you."

"Where did you find the gun?" I tried to calm her down. "I was looking for it."

"He took my ring back to the store. I told you he would."

"Give it to me." I extended my arm. Gloria pulled her knees under her again. She seemed to be pressed by a great force against the headboard.

"I'm warning you," she said.

"The gun isn't loaded. I could take it away from you." I reached harder for the gun. She pulled the trigger. The hollow click rang as loud as a gunshot. Gloria's eyes filled with tears. Before mine passed every breath of time I had spent with her. Click, canceled. The harmless sound of metal striking metal echoed like a death rattle. I ran to the kitchen in search of the largest knife I could find. The phone rang. Dad must never know. Nothing mattered anymore. When I was back at her door I yelled, "I'll show you how scared I am of you!"

"Goodbye." Gloria dropped the receiver on the hook and picked it right up again.

"Who called?"

"None of your business." She dialed the operator.

"Who are you calling?"

"The police," she said matter-of-factly. "I'm going to say you broke in here and tried something."

"Go ahead," I dared. "How can you prove it?"

"There's the lock. Hello, give me the police."

"Put the phone down," I said. "Gloria—don't."

"This is Gloria Grahame at 14 Malibu Colony. My stepson tried to rape me. Get here fast." She hung up. "That should take care of you and Nick."

I threw the knife. It bounced harmlessly off the headboard and onto the bed. She was no more amazed than I that I had even thrown it. "They're coming, Tony."

"You didn't really call," I pleaded. "You faked it."

"I'm going to leave that knife right where it is for them to see." She was pleased with herself. She began fixing her hair as though everything were settled and I was dismissed.

A siren screamed down the road, then softened, and stopped in front of our house.

"Satisfied?" I asked. Gloria was startled. The hard lines of fighting dissolved and her face became that of a girl again. Another police car whined along the road.

"Oh, Tony," she gasped "I'm sorry."

I tore out of the beach door before the police were even in the house. They wouldn't get me. They weren't going to take me away. I raced toward the rocky end of the cove.

"Stop! Stop, Tony!" I heard behind me. I glanced over my shoulder. Three officers had filed onto the sand. Mike and Louis, the Malibu Patrol men, were coming out of the house. I could beat them. But how far did I have to run? Over the edge of the Earth? Lift your knees, take deep breaths, use your arms like pistons. That's what the coach said. Where was the finish line? The goalposts? They were forty or fifty yards behind me. Windows and doors opened. Curtains parted. Gawking heads craned for a look. It was impossible to scale the rocks around the point to the next beach. I started climbing. If I could only make it to the highway. The rocks were slippery near the water. As I climbed higher the footing got better. I looked up to the highway. A squad car was parked there. Two tacklers waiting for me. Couldn't I ever win? Instead of going on, I climbed into a small cave. I sat there. I was satisfied that I couldn't be seen from the beach, the house, by Gloria. Losers shouldn't be seen. I waited for the cops to come after me. "I don't care. I don't care," kept pouring out of my mouth. "It doesn't matter. Nothing matters." I tried to make my mouth stay shut, but it was as useless as trying not to shiver on a freezing day. The police got to the base of the rocks. It was all ending so fast. Dad. They pointed to the cave. One of the two Malibu patrolmen started climbing. The others were state troopers. They waited at the bottom. I toyed with Gloria's pin. The stones glittered in my hand. There was enough room in the cave for me to sit in a black corner. The sun poured onto my feet but left my head and body in darkness. It was Louis who squatted at the mouth of the cave. He fanned his face with his cap.

"Whew," Louis sighed. "That was some workout you gave us." I stared at the pin cupped in my hands.

"It was all a terrible mistake," I said.

"Tony?"

"Yes, sir."

"Mrs. Ray said it wasn't true. Was it, son?"

"No, sir. We were fighting. She made it up."

"Do you want to come outside now?"

"No, sir."

"Why not?"

"All those people." My body was shaking. "I feel like a fox in a tree."

"I'll tell the state boys to go if you'll promise to come with Mike and me." Louis was a nice guy. He and Mike patrolled our beach and the houses. "Deal?" he asked.

"Okay," I said. Louis got up and waved to the men below. "Mike," he yelled to his partner, "bring the truck up to the highway. Tell the other boys we'll meet them at the station house." The troopers started walking back to the house. The police car up above pulled away. Louis crouched at the mouth of the cave again. "We have to stop by the station house on the way to town," Louis explained, "to be sure Mrs. Ray withdrew her complaint."

"On the way to town?" I asked.

"Didn't you know? I called your house about half an hour ago. I told Mrs. Ray we were coming to take you to your father. She hung up on us. Then, when Mike and I were on our way to get you, the state cars pulled up behind me and said they were called on some crazy charge. See, we're just a private patrol."

"Nothing like that happened."

"She already told me. You shouldn't have anything to worry about." A horn honked from above. Mike was waiting with their truck. "Gloria was hysterical," Louis said as we climbed to the road. "What did happen?"

"We had a fight and she got all excited and called the police. That's all."

"How did the knife get on the bed?" he asked.

"What knife?"

"You don't want to talk about it, do you, son?"

"No, sir."

"Well," Louis said a few seconds later, "she was probably upset over Mr. Ray's leaving. Maybe she thought she could hold onto you. Women are funny."

"Yes, sir." I held the pin out to Louis. "Would you give this to Gloria for me?"

The officers at the police station were very nice. They gave me a couple of magazines to read and asked if I wanted to wait in the empty courtroom. I sat in the back row. It was like a small empty theater. The hammer and gavel, the flags, the air in the room was so still. If a fly hadn't been buzzing around the motionless propeller fan that hung from the ceiling, I would have thought there were moments when the very world stood still.

"C'mon, Tony," Louis said from the double doors behind me. "I'll take you to your father now." I didn't want to leave. I wanted to become attached to the bench I was sitting on and become a piece of the furniture, a stone. "He's staying at The Garden of Allah in Hollywood. Nice place. What's wrong, kid? Everything is fine." I just shook my head.

I didn't want to see Dad.

"Hey, we better get going."

"Sure, Louis."

I think I asked Louis why Dad was staying in Hollywood, but I'm not sure. Louis already told me he had left Gloria. But why did he ask the patrol to bring me to him? What happened between Gloria and Dad that he couldn't come get me himself? I knew Dad didn't like scenes. I couldn't think about it.

I had the sure feeling I was never going to see Gloria again. I realized how little I had actually slept on the beach the night before. It was so long ago. I wondered if Gloria had found the glass stallion I left under her pillow. My eyes stung and closed. *Sure*, I said to myself. *Everything's fine. Happy New Year.*

22
The Finish Line

Louis took me to the desk, made sure I had a key, and someone to take me to the room. Dad had left instructions for me to spend the day swimming at the hotel. He would pick me up for dinner around six. Maybe that was just as well. I wasn't in a hurry to see him. I charged a bathing suit to Dad's room at the hotel store.

Occasionally a waiter scurried past the vacant pool area with a tray balanced between palm and shoulder. The hotel was pretty fancy. There was a main building where I checked in and stucco bungalows with tile roofs surrounding the pool. There were lots of tropical plants and palm trees. A dark-haired girl with a towel draped over her shoulders came through one of the street entrances and sat on the other side of the pool. She oiled herself. I swam the length of the pool underwater and pulled myself up on the edge. "Much warmer than the ocean," I said without looking at her.

"You're new here, aren't you?" she asked.

"Yes. I'm Tony."

"I'm Beverly." I sat down on a lounge chair next to her. It was a great relief to have someone to talk to, even if only about stupid things. Beverly was 14 and went to Hollywood High School. She was in the ninth grade too. She lived down the street, on Fairfax Avenue, but had permission to use the pool whenever she wanted. "I made friends with one of the cooks. He told the manager I was good decoration."

As morning gave way to noon time, small clusters of fat, bald-headed men sat at tables around the pool under umbrellas. They wore baggy bathing suits, socks and flip flops, and played gin rummy in silence. Some of them smoked cigars like big shots. I was glad to be the only young guy out there. If I were a girl, I thought, I wouldn't have much to do with men if that's the way they were. I told Beverly I was from New York and had come out to live with my father, that my stepmother was a movie star, and my father a movie director. She wanted to know why I was at the hotel. I explained that my father's marriage wasn't working out.

"Catch me!" Beverly jumped up and dove into the pool. I grabbed her ankle mid-way across. She twisted around and kissed me. It was fun under water. We got out and went back to our chairs holding hands. "Can we go to your bungalow?" she asked.

"Sure."

We necked for a while, then Beverly wanted me to order lunch. "What about the waiter?" I asked.

"Don't worry," she said. While I was on the phone Beverly got out of her wet bathing suit and wrapped a towel around herself. Then she brought me a towel and watched me change. I was getting all jumpy inside and I was embarrassed to undress in front of her, but I didn't say anything.

When the waiter knocked on the door, Beverly disappeared into the bathroom. "Save some for me," she called after I got rid of him. "I'm always so hungry afterward." We went to bed. How simple.

The maître d' led the way to the only unoccupied table in the Italian restaurant. There were only eight or nine tables in the whole place. Ours had a reserved sign on it, which the maître d' picked up. There was a four-stool bar near the door but nobody sat there. It was used mostly for the cash register and telephone. The kitchen was through a regular house door in back. Soft classical music filled the room. The walls were papered with deep red velvet. A painting by Modigliani hung near our table in the converted living room. Candles supplied the only light. "Old Rarity, Mr. Ray?" the maître d' asked after seating us. Dad smiled a yes and ordered a screwdriver for me. I was surprised but said nothing. The painting of the brooding girl with sad, almond-shaped eyes peered down at me.

"It's a very fancy restaurant, Dad. You didn't tell me to bring clothes."

"I'll have all your things picked up tomorrow." The maître d' placed two menus on the corner of the fine white tablecloth. I started to pick one up.

"We have plenty of time," Dad said. He placed his hand over mine. "Let's not rush our drinks.'

"Won't they get in trouble giving me drinks?"

"They know me very well here. It could just be orange juice."

"I can hardly taste the liquor," I said of the screwdriver. "It tastes good."

Dad looked as though he were adding a long column of high numbers in his head. His brows were furrowed, his lips moved every so often, but he said nothing. As soon as he finished his drink, the waiter miraculously appeared with another one. "For the young gentleman?"

"Yes." Dad dismissed the waiter and looked at me. "I wanted very much to get into the army during the war, but they wouldn't take me. Heart murmur."

"Gee, Dad. I didn't know."

"I tried the other services. Same story."

"Why were you in such a hurry to go to war? I mean, if you were sick."

"I had a chance to go to England during the Blitz with an Office of War Information unit, but it didn't work out." Dad fell silent, drank his drink. I sipped on mine. He wasn't in as good a mood as I had thought. "Responsibility! That's why. Sounds stupid to you, doesn't it?"

"No."

"Yes, it does." He overrode me. "Stupid is one of your favorite words. It must be stupid to you. You couldn't smell responsibility if it were made of shit and put on your dinner plate." He waited for me to say something, to defend myself, to argue. I didn't know what. It was all happening so fast. "Yes," Dad said when he was satisfied I had nothing to say. "Responsibility is one of the virtues you still have to learn about." He shook his great head and held the bridge of his nose. Then he looked straight at me and lowered his voice. "Gloria wasn't the one you were responsible to."

"You never talked to me. You never had time."

"Let's order," Dad said. He signaled the waiter.

"What'll it be tonight, sir?"

"One large antipasto and two scaloppine marsala. Sound good to you, Tony?"

"Sure."

"A wine?"

"Choose a Chianti for us, Alberto."

"Of course." The waiter took the menus and went to the kitchen.

"You think I deserted you and Jean, don't you?"

"No."

"Then why do you hate me so much?"

"I don't. You think everybody's against you. All I wanted was to be close to you."

"I doubt that," he snapped. "By your behavior I'd judge that if you came to California with a mission, it was an underlying desire to destroy me and my marriage." Dad waited for an answer. I had nothing to say. It all sounded so ridiculous to me. "Be honest for a change."

"It's not true," I said.

"Don't argue! I know what I'm talking about."

"Dad, you think I need a psychiatrist because I borrowed a pair of your shoes. I just needed a pair of shoes." Dad hated for anyone to disagree with him. I should have remembered that and remained quiet, but I couldn't, not anymore. He motioned broadly with his glass held high. The waiter nodded. Dad pointed to my glass, too. The liquor was already going to my head. "No more for me, Dad."

"You're supposed to be a grown man," he mocked. "Drink with me."

"You drink too much," I said. The truth was simple, so easy. I didn't mean to insult him. It was just the truth. Dad couldn't believe his ears. I thought he was going to reach across the table and hit me.

"What did you say?"

"Nothing. I didn't say anything, mean anything."

"You've got a hell of a lot of nerve telling me how much to drink considering you're 13 years old and well on your way to being a drunk."

"I said I didn't want any more."

"How's the gambling going, son? You going to get a shoeshine box soon?"

"Shoeshine box?"

"That's all you'll have if you keep it up. All you'll ever have." There was a welcome silence, then he started again on a quieter, more controlled level. "You think I've never done anything for you. Stop feeling sorry for yourself. I've supported you all your life." Dad blew a fine line of smoke up toward the painting of the girl. He looked at it. I wondered why Mom and I never had any money, why she had to work so hard, if he was telling the truth. I thought of him borrowing money from Gloria. I studied the painting. The girl's brown hair was drawn back tight against her head. Her eyes were remembering something sad, but at the same time reaching out, hoping, trying to catch something.

"She looks like a picture I saw of Mom when she was young," I said. Dad's gaze returned to his drink. "I never really knew you. I still don't." He said nothing. "I wish you could have mailed a postcard or telephoned more often. But it's not important anymore. I'm older now." I smiled at him because I meant what I was saying. "I know this is going to sound corny, but I guess I wanted apple pie and Main Street, like the Archers. I wanted you. My father."

"You're feeling sorry for yourself again, being unrealistic."

The waiter brought our food and wine. If it had been possible, I would have invited the waiter to join us. Anything to stop Dad from tearing me apart. "I told you not to compete with me." I decided not to say anything. I just shook my head and started eating. Dad gave me a look which suggested he planned to prove his point when the time came. It left me feeling very uncomfortable. We ate in silence.

Gloria? Was that it? I couldn't pretend to understand about her, not even to myself. A lot of it had to do with sex. I knew that now that I had met Beverly. Something of Gloria had faded in my mind since this afternoon. Part of the mystery of her was gone. But Gloria and I were so alike. That's what made her different from Beverly. And I loved Gloria. I didn't even care about Beverly. Or was I kidding myself? Was it only because I wanted to go to bed with Gloria that I loved her? No, it was so much more than that.

All the time we had spent getting to know each other, and really liking each other. Dad couldn't be thinking of Gloria when he accused me of competing with him. He didn't know. I stole a glance at him over a piece of bread. He was busy eating. They couldn't have loved each other. They weren't alike at all. Their marriage was going to break up anyway. I tried to convince myself I shouldn't get upset, that there was nothing to worry about. When I looked at Dad again, he was watching me, seeking me out. "May I have another glass of wine?" I asked. Dad poured without saying anything, without ever taking his gaze from my face except to pick up and put down the bottle. Maybe he was thinking of a movie he wanted to make in five years. He could do that and be looking at you at the same time. I didn't ask. I sopped up the last bit of wine and mushroom sauce with a piece of bread, then watched dad wiping his mouth with a napkin. At first I saw a double image of him. I was almost drunk.

"What happened between you and Gloria this morning?"

"Everybody fights," I said.

"Must have been quite a row," a smile cracked on his lips, "for her to tell the police you tried to rape her." Blood rushed to my head. "Tell me about it."

"Dinner," I whispered.

"I heard there was quite a bit more to it." he said. I looked at the table.

"Who told you?" I asked. I wanted to know if it had been Gloria or Louis. She had told Louis it wasn't true. She even told the police.

"Let's hear your version."

I told dad how I had come home from riding at the Archers' house and found Gloria was burning a duck in the oven, and that all his Scotch bottles had been emptied into the sink. I told him that Gloria had been drinking a lot and that she got mad when I turned the oven off and threw me out of the house and told me not to come back. I could tell Dad wasn't satisfied, that he was waiting for more. "She was sore because you didn't show up for New Year's Eve dinner. That's all there was to it." Dad beckoned the waiter, told him to clear the table, and ordered zabaglione for two.

"What's that?"

"Dessert," he said. I tried to look cheerful, as though I was enjoying being treated to this wonderful restaurant, hoping he believed me. But I was wringing my hands under the table.

"It's nice wallpaper," I said.

"But you did go back to the house, didn't you?" Dad forced my unwilling attention. I watched the waiter cross the room with his full tray of dirty dishes. He pushed through to the kitchen and was gone. What else could I look at? "Didn't you?"

"Not until morning," I said. But I could tell by the way dad chewed on his cigarette and set his jaw that he thought I was lying. "I slept on the beach. It's true. I wanted to be alone. And in the morning, I saw all your clothes on the beach."

"So you went back to the house in the morning. Gloria asked you to leave again and you refused. You broke into her room and she called the police with that story. Is that right?"

"Yes." I wiped my face with the napkin.

Dad was still smiling faintly. It was almost sickening. He seemed pleased with himself. Dad stopped our waiter. "Alberto, bring us each a double Courvoisier."

"Dad," I protested, "I've really had…"

"Have it."

"But…"

"We're celebrating after a fashion. Having our first good talk. I insist." He smiled fully and reached across the table to pat my shoulder.

"Dad?"

"Yes, son?"

"Why are you staying at the hotel?"

"I've left Gloria, or hadn't you guessed?"

"I'm sorry," I said. But in a way I was relieved. Dad lit another cigarette. He squashed out his old cigarette with his thumb. "Why didn't you pick me up at the beach?"

"I hate scenes." The frothy zabaglione was piled high and white in champagne glasses. It melted into smooth, glowing nothingness on its way down my throat. "Like it?"

"Very much," I said. I watched the way dad picked up his brandy glass, at the top of the stem with two fingers, and did the same. The liquor shot tears to my eyes.

"Youth is a funny animal," sighed Dad. "The moments are so long and tortuous, the years so short." He put his glass down and twisted it round and round. Watching it made me dizzy. "Hard to think of myself as nearly 40." Dad followed each bite of dessert with a sip of brandy. "I thought I understood adolescent rebellion." He twisted his glass again. "But this was a deliberate diabolic scheme to hurt me."

"I haven't tried to hurt you," I protested. "I wasn't scared when I came to live here. But things kept getting worse and worse, more and more confusing, and now I am scared of you." I wanted him to say everything was past, that Gloria was gone, that we would have a new start. Just he and I. "Can you understand what I'm saying?" But Dad wasn't even paying attention. He was still turning that goddamned glass, still sure he was always right, that I was out to get him. He was so sure and it made me so mad that I wondered if I did hate him. I took the last swallow of brandy in my glass and said, "I think I've had too much to drink."

"Don't be dramatic!" He scolded. "Just tell me how long you've been fucking my wife." He swung that line like a giant sledgehammer, from the pit of his stomach, with all his strength. It hit me full force as though I had been pushed before the flaming mouth of a blast furnace. I tried to breathe but the air was too hot. Dad had erased every hope, every attempt I had made at convincing him I wasn't out to get him, to let what was over die its own death. Or was this part of the death, these false accusations? Again, convinced he was right. "Now, about you and my dear wife?"

"That's not true."

"Waiter! What else, Tony? Did you go to parties together?" The waiter came. "Two more brandies."

Parties. Yes, I'd have another brandy. More. More. More. I was trapped. What he was saying wasn't true, but even the truth would ruin any chance I might have with Dad. Lousy tears were welling up in my eyes. "Did you go to parties?"

"Yes." My Adam's apple scraped my throat like a dry piston hitting a gravel-filled cylinder. I drank the brandy like water.

"Marriage. What a farce."

"Dad, did you love Gloria?" The moon is gray behind walls of rain. Rain, stop stinging my eyes. Music, stop playing. Damn painting! Stop staring at me. "Damn, damn! Stop it now. I can't stand it."

"Tony, pull yourself together."

"I want to die." Babble, father, babble through mountains of memories. See if you can get through clean. I can hide, too. You can hide. I can hide.

"I need to talk to you."

"Talk. Ask me." I defy you. "I wanted everybody to be happy. Someday! Someday, Mom always said, and then it happened and now it's all my fault. Someday is over. Everything's no good." Break down the walls of hungry vacant stares. Tear up those stupid paintings. Unlit trains going home. Yes, I know trains go both ways. There's always an end of the line. End of the line, U.S.A. I'm going to lose my hours, Gloria. The people think they're indestructible, that they'll never die. They live like robots: labor, money, labor, money. Neon signs bring business. Business money to build golden sandpiles to buy immortality.

"You're not going back to Harvard." We all have to die. I wiped my eyes and braced open the lids with the will to face him head on. His image was fragmented by the two sheets of water through which I looked. "You'll be going to Sebago, a home for boys, in St. Louis." My head spun. I was being sucked into the whirlpool of liquor. What wonderful refuge. The table turned. A myriad of refracted colors, red velvet, yellow paint, skin, heads, glasses, raced about like my high-speed kaleidoscope, a priceless time machine that tore me back thread by thread, hand and foot, memory by memory. But look at all the dreams I could see. What beautiful dreams. Oh, Mom. What do I do? What have I done? What can I do now? I'll go to another school. Fanny the pony, the kid screaming and jumping out the window, the housemother tumbling down the stairs. I didn't burn down the barn.

"I want to run."

"Did you hear me, Tony? You have to tell me the whole story because I want a divorce. I need your help, your honesty and loyalty to me. Do you understand?"

"You want my help?" I gripped the ashtray tight, as though it could hold me and that one sentence of his there forever. "I wanted to give you all those things. Now I'm so ashamed. But we were never that way. I swear to God, not like you mean." Dad's eyes changed from those of appealing kindness. His eyes opened wide and glared at me in wonderment, asking how I could possibly deny it. He withdrew a neatly folded piece of Kleenex from his pocket and handed it to me. "Thank you." I started to wipe my eyes.

"Don't thank me, son. Open it."

I turned back the folds of tissue with the care given a precious gift. But in place of the anticipation of a wonderful trinket there was the expectation of finding something horrible. When I finished unwrapping, I held a button cupped in the palm of my hand. It was as gold and shiny, brassy and fresh as new. A button from my olive drab uniform. "I did lose this. Where did you find it?"

"It tickled my ass when I climbed into bed one night," Dad said. I couldn't answer. What is real? What never was? What should have been? Is this why self-satisfaction is a deadly virus? Because being passive and stagnant is an unnatural state? What is real?

The horses run to the finish line. Men run—in search of what?—to their death. Is change the only truth? Is the search for truth the only truth? Is it that in the vast spectrum of the universe nothing stays exactly as it was a moment ago? Was Dad right? Is it man's nature to excite conflict? Truth is reality, and reality is always changing. Might it just as well have been true? There was the button. It was real. And on its surface the faces of a thousand truths were reflected, the relationship with Dad that had never been, the bond with Gloria I never expected to happen. And now the dissolving, like flesh falling to pieces in acid, of a hope for a unity, a oneness with my father. The button, a clasp as cold as the metal it was wrought from, challenged me to deny its ownership, to hand it back to Dad, to say it isn't my truth. We are forever alone in search of ourselves. But this conflict is as close as we have ever been, Dad. I said nothing.

"I want you to make recordings about this, Tony." Dusty, graying, dying hope was being pumped from my veins. I drank brandy to fill the gap. He must have ordered more. I was glad. My hands were clammy. I was exhausted. War was tiring. But there was relief, peace, in frozen, numb exhaustion, the twilight before blacking out and giving oneself over to synthetic dreams which no matter how terrifying are always washed to sea with each new awakening. New light, new life, change was comforting. "The recordings will save me thousands of dollars in divorce court. I hate having to ask you to do it, but you must. No. No check yet. Bring us one more brandy." I don't want another drink. I don't want the bottom of the sink filled with bottles. I don't want to hear trucks shifting gears, speeding through the fog on gray, timeless highways. Blue, gray, nothingness is what I want. To sleep is what I want.

No, air. No air at all. Tony, please don't heave. Don't let out the green swarming swim of nausea. No wonder you're sweating, holding your breath that way. Do you want to die, Tony? Is that it? Are you choking yourself because you don't want to go on? You have to go on or die, You can't win. "Answer me, son. Will you do it?" Cry out for a return. I want a return bout. Gloria, I can't. I can't hold out any longer. I can't reach you now, can I? I can't save us. I'm alone. There is no return. Is that how to save myself? A home-made confessional? Father Chalmers, do you approve? I won't lie. I'll tell the truth, what there is to tell. He's right about loyalty, isn't he? Responsibility? But that's all I ever wanted. Now I have my chance. "You'll make them tomorrow at the hotel. I'll show you how to operate the machine so you can be alone. I promise they'll be destroyed when this is over. In a few days you'll go to St. Louis. There are three counselors for the nine boys in the home. You'll have a new start." God, my ribs ache. I better get fresh air.

"Excuse me," I pushed myself away from the table.

"Where are you going?"

"Outside. I need air." How long had we been there? I sat on a bus stop bench. For some reason I was smiling inside.

I was drifting. It was cold outside. A pot of fudge, real thick, was making slow bubbles on the kitchen stove at home. And my thoughts were bubbling like the fudge, slower and slower. Outside the poor snowflakes came down freezing. They tried and tried to keep themselves cold but couldn't because they always melted. Then there was a great emergency. Hunters came along and shot down all the fields, and all the skies and forests got burned up. Mommy, your petticoat makes a nice noise, like bacon. In the country we had nice flowers, nice grass, nice trees, lots of mosquitoes. And it was always nice when Mom came to visit me at school. We swam in the Hudson...

The chick ran from his mother. The trees and branches pinched at the wind, and the wind died with them. Poor wind. Poor chick. He got into trouble. Then he found a scrap of paper. On it was written: "Little chick, come back! We have found a nice King. He will give you a nice lunch, a nice supper, and a glass of milk."

Postscript

It is now 2002, 52 years after my first encounter with Gloria and 44 years since I wrote this manuscript in 1958. As fate would have it, my life experience with Gloria was to be rekindled.

My father, who I had seen only a few times since 1950, called me early in 1960 to ask if I would meet him at the airport in New York for a drink. He was on his way to Hollywood from Spain and had an hour or so stopover. He looked recovered from his alcoholic bout. His face was chiseled, his hair turning gray was full and wild, and he wore a patch over one eye (why I would never find out). He asked me if I would like to come work for him on *King of Kings* later in the year as his assistant. I pictured myself making drinks and taking notes, as Sumner had done. It wasn't for me.

I explained that I was busy with my own career as an actor and that I went to California in the summers to seek work in film and television. I declined his offer. I was now 22 and experiencing some minor successes. Three years on the television soap *Search for Tomorrow*, leads in two minor films, two Broadway plays, including *The Dark at the Top of the Stairs* by William Inge, directed by Elia Kazan, a good deal of television and Off-Broadway theater, and a role in John Cassavetes' *Shadows*.

My father finished his two scotch and sodas, reached into his briefcase, and took out his address book. He took a small pad from his jacket pocket and wrote a number on it. He pushed it across the bar to me and said, "Why don't you look up Gloria?" I was dumbfounded, actually at a loss for words. I remember putting the phone number in my pocket and saying nothing. It wasn't mentioned again for the rest of the visit. He did ask if I had seen *Rebel Without a Cause* and some of his other films. I said that I had. The visit was awkward and I remember excusing myself.

I had been deeply affected by his suggestion. I had had no contact with Gloria since I was 13, but had pined for her throughout my teens. I had kept track of her through her movies. She had won the Academy Award for *The Bad and The Beautiful*, and had won critics' praise for several other films. When I got to California, I called her. She wanted to see me immediately. I wanted to see her immediately.

We agreed to meet at the corner of Laurel Canyon and Ventura Boulevard. She would be driving—as she had so many years before—a black Cadillac convertible. When she pulled up, I jumped in and we hugged each other for a long time. I saw that in the back seat there was a suitcase and a box of groceries. We drove to the modest guest house I was renting and unpacked Gloria's things. She had not come for an hour-long visit. She had come to stay.

Gloria and I were married on May 13, 1960. It was as though there had been no nine-year gap. We just picked up where we left off. I inherited the role of stepfather to my half-brother Tim, then 11, and Paulette, Gloria's daughter by Cy Howard. I quit acting and became an assistant director, then production manager. Later in my career I co-produced *An Unmarried Woman*, *The Rose* and several other films. In 1965, Gloria made an attempt on her life and had a serious nervous breakdown. She became unbearably jealous, refused to take part in any social activities, and was drinking very heavily. I was drinking and acting on my compulsions to gamble.

Gloria bore us two sons—Tony in 1963 and Jimmy in 1965. What is important is that Gloria became so ill that she remained in bed for days at a time, not caring for me or her children. I became more dependent on alcohol and gambling, and in 1973 was introduced to cocaine. We parted in 1976. I was granted custody of the boys. The judge said I was the lesser of two evils. But Gloria and I saw each other often even after we separated. We still loved each other very much. Gloria found the divorce proceedings and the divorce comical. As far as she was concerned, we were still together, and those events were just part of the fabric of our relationship.

My father continued to work through the mid-'60s, but his addictions, which now included drugs, led to the complete collapse of his career. He died of cancer in New York in 1979, at the age of 69. Gloria died of cancer at the age of 58 in 1981.

I have been living with my wife, Eve, since 1981. We have a lovely 12-year-old daughter, Kelsey. We live modestly in Maine. By the grace of God and a lot of support, I have been clear of acting out my addictions for many years.

One thing has come to disturb me, though. I have been in treatment for manic depression since the mid-'80s. During one episode of deep depression, I related my story of Gloria and me to the therapist. He responded by saying, "You were molested." When my half-brother, Tim, was in his thirties, we had lunch one day. He told me then that he believed his mother had molested him when he was 11 or 12. At the time, I dismissed his claim. After re-reading this manuscript I need to ask: is it possible that an adolescent experience could so traumatize a young person that it affected most of his adult life? Or was it truly a romance?

I chose to believe it was romance.

www.ingramcontent.com/pod-product-compliance
Lightning Source LLC
Chambersburg PA
CBHW061725120626
46550CB00005B/1707